SUCCESS

Role Models of Winners

Emerson Klees

Emerson Klees

Cameo Press, Rochester, New York

Cameo Press
P. O. Box 18131
Rochester, New York 14618

Library of Congress Control Number 2016912172

ISBN 978-1-891046-26-1

Printed in the United States of America
9 8 7 6 5 4 3 2 1

DEDICATION

This book is dedicated to Mary Lash, my editor / proofreader for nearly twenty years. My manuscripts are significantly improved by her advice, including the elimination of extraneous words and phrases, which makes for a tighter text.

OTHER BOOKS BY EMERSON KLEES

Role Models of Human Values Series
One Plus One Equals Three—Pairing Man / Woman Strengths:
   Role Models of Teamwork
Entrepreneurs In History—Success vs. Failure: Entrepreneurial
   Role Models
Staying With It: Role Models of Perseverance
The Drive to Succeed: Role Models of Motivation
The Will to Stay With It: Role Models of Determination
Emotional Intelligence: People Smart Role Models
Emotional Intelligence: People Smart Role Models II
Emotional Intelligence: People Smart Role Models III
Rebounding from Setbacks: Role Models of Resilience
The Creators: Role Models of Creativity

The Moral Navigator: Stories From Around the World
Inspiring Legends and Tales With a Moral I
Inspiring Legends and Tales With a Moral II
Inspiring Legends and Tales With a Moral III

Books About New York State and the Finger Lakes Region
People of the Finger Lakes Region
Legends and Stories of the Finger Lakes Region
The Erie Canal in the Finger Lakes Region
Underground Railroad Tales With Routes Through the Finger Lakes
   Region
More Legends and Stories of the Finger Lakes Region
The Women's Rights Movement and the Finger Lakes Region
Persons, Places, and Things In the Finger Lakes Region [6 lakes]
The Crucible of Ferment: New York's "Psychic Highway"
The Iroquois Confederacy: History and Legends
Rochester Lives
Wineries of the Finger Lakes Region—100 Wineries
Persons, Places, and Things Of the Finger Lakes Region [11 lakes]
Paul Garrett: Dean of American Winemakers
A Song of the Vine: A Reflection on Life
Finger Lakes Wineries: A Pictorial History

THE ROLE MODELS OF HUMAN VALUES SERIES

"Example teaches better than precept. It is the best modeler of the character of men and women. To set a lofty example is the richest bequest a man [or woman] can leave behind."

Samuel Smiles

The Role Models of Human Values Series provides examples of role models and of lives worthy of emulation. The human values depicted in this series include perseverance, motivation, determination, resilience, and creativity. Role models are presented in biographical sketches of historical figures that describe the environment within which they strived and delineate their personal characteristics.

These profiles illustrate how specific human values helped achievers reach their goals in life. We can learn from these examples in strengthening the human values that are so important to our success and happiness. The Introduction in each book highlights the factors that contributed to these achievers' success.

PREFACE

"Most of the important things in the world have been accomplished by people who have kept on trying when there seemed to be no hope at all."

Dale Carnegie

This book provides role models of success through profiles of thirty individuals who were successful at one phase of their lives or throughout their lifetimes. The thirty biographical sketches represent six areas of endeavor:

Creators / Founders

Couples / Teams

Reformers / Activists

Songwriters / Composers

Late Or Unrecognized Success

Overcoming Obstacles To Success

The subject of this book is success. These individuals displayed other strong personal characteristics, including perseverance, motivation, determination, resilience, and creativity as discussed in other books in the Human Values Series. It was not obvious to many of these individuals early in their lives that they would ultimately be successful. Some of them considered changing to other careers. Some were unrecognized in their lifetimes or late in their lives and others overcame serious obstacles to continue in their line of work. They provide us with role models. We can learn from them.

TABLE OF CONTENTS

Page No.

Page No.

INTRODUCTION

"To laugh often and much; to win the respect of intelligent people and affection of children; to earn the appreciation of honest critics and endure the betrayal of false friends; to appreciate beauty; to find the best in others; to leave the world a bit better, whether by a healthy child, a garden patch, or a redeemed social condition; to know even one life has breathed easier because you have lived. This is to have succeeded."

Ralph Waldo Emerson

Many definitions of success exist. To some, being happy is being a success. To others it is the accomplishment of their career goals or achieving financial success or the respect of others.

Senator John McCain has commented on success:

> Although success can easily be defined as the achievement of goals, there's a difference between temporary and lasting success. I don't think you achieve lasting success unless you add another ingredient to the mixture, and that is to serve a cause that is greater than yourself. That's what lasting success is all about.

> I can't tell you the number of people I have met who have been successful in the pursuit of wealth, but late in the day began to sense that they didn't really succeed. And yet, I have known people from all degrees of financial wealth who have dedicated themselves to causes greater than themselves and their own self-interests who have led a very satisfying life.

In order to evaluate success, we must consider some of its components such as goal setting and overcoming obstacles. Also, we must consider the fundamental principles that underlie successful efforts that lead to achieving our potential. In *If Success Is a Game, These Are the Rules*, Cherie Carter-Scott considered these truths in providing ten rules for success:

Rule One: Each person has his or her own definition of success. There is no universal definition. Everyone has their own individual vision of what it takes to be fulfilled.

Rule Two: Wanting success is the first step toward attaining it. When you experience the initial spark of desire, you set the game of success in motion.

Rule Three: Self-trust is essential. To be fulfilled, you must know yourself and honor your truth.

Rule Four: Goals are stepping stones on your path. Your journey to fulfillment is propelled forward by the goals you set along the way.

Rule Five: Your actions affect your outcomes. The quality and quantity of energy you put forth directly impact the results you achieve.

Rule Six: Opportunities will be presented. There will be moments in life when you will be presented new options. What you choose in those moments is up to you.

Rule Seven: Each setback provides valuable lessons. There will be disappointment and perceived failures along the way. Learning from these experiences offers you precious insights that lead to future successes.

Rule Eight: Managing your resources maximizes your efforts. Your time, energy, relationships, and finances are your most valuable assets. Handling them wisely enhances your ability to succeed.

Rule Nine: Every level of success brings new challenges. Each accomplishment alters your reality, either slightly or dramatically. Your task is to maintain your balance when your game board shifts.

Rule Ten: Success is a process that never ends. Each plateau has a new ascent. Once you reach the top, there is a new peak to embrace.

The establishment of attainable goals is critical to the success of any endeavor; however, its importance is not universally understood, perhaps because we have an inherent fear of failure to reach our goals or because we do not know how to establish reasonable goals. Some people think that the more that they want something, the greater the disappointment if they do not get it. They are afraid to risk failure and the accompanying anguish.

Another fear in setting goals is fear of success. Lack of self-confidence and self-esteem are usually factors in this case. Individuals may feel, subconsciously, that they do not deserve the success for which their conscious self is striving. These individuals tend to magnify the difficulty of attaining a particular goal and may become discouraged from setting a goal.

Also, some people subscribe to the philosophy of "whatever will be, will be." These individuals think that everything is preordained. The viewpoint that fate dictates the outcome of everything that they do is a demotivating influence in setting goals. Their fatalistic outlook prevents them from extending themselves in establishing goals and from expending effort in reaching those goals. Setting an attainable goal is the first step in achieving success. The goal may be a "reach" goal or a "stretch" goal, but it must be attainable.

We may have a fear of failure, but the important thing is how we deal with the setback. Some individuals are motivated just to give in. We can learn from the adversity, however, and actually become stronger individuals because of it. Some individuals who experienced trauma note that they now enjoy life more and have better relationships with their friends and family than they had before the adversity threatened to break them.

A young entrepreneur traveled to Silicon Valley to apply to a venture capitalist for financing to begin his start-up. The venture capitalist told him that he would rather invest in an entrepreneur who had failed four times than one on his first attempt. The venture capitalist believed that the one who had failed four times knew what not to do.

Overcoming difficulties can make us stronger individuals than we would have been if we had not encountered adversity. For example, Nelson Mandela thought that the twenty-seven years he spent in prison helped to develop hidden strengths and to forge personal capabilities that served him in leading South Africa out of apartheid and in becoming the leader of the country.

Franklin Delano Roosevelt went through an extremely debilitating illness, polio, when he was thirty-nine. It appeared that his time in public life was over. He continued to be optimistic and to do everything he could do to utilize the physical strength that remained. His wife, Eleanor, and many historians believe that FDR was a better President because he had suffered and overcome polio than he would have been if he not had that experience.

We are more likely to achieve success if we are working in the area in which we choose to be working and are good at working. Author Mark Sullivan has observed:

> To find a career [or endeavor] to which you are adapted by nature, and then to work hard at it, is about as near to a formula for success and happiness as the world provides. One of the fortunate aspects of this formula is that, granted that the right career has been found, the hard work takes care of itself. Then hard work is not hard at all.

Also, we have to be sure that when we arrive at forks in the road, we analyze all of the factors involved at the time in deciding which branch to take. We don't want to waste time later wondering if we made the right choice. Unfortunately, we can't take Yogi Berra's advice: "When you reach the fork in the road, take it." (Both branches led to his house).

The best advice is to do your best. "Do your best" is part of the Cub Scout motto. You could not receive better advice. If, in fact, you have done your best and have not achieved the success that you were seeking, you cannot fault yourself. After all, you could not h have done better than your best.

Success has many facets. Many human values are required to achieve it, including perseverance, motivation, determination, resilience, and creativity.

CHAPTER 1

Creators / Founders

"The line between failure and success is so fine that we scarcely know when we pass it; so fine that we are often on the line but don't know it. How many a man has thrown up his hands at a time when a little more effort, a little more patience, would have achieved success. As the tide goes out, so it comes in. In business sometimes, prospects may seem darkest when they are really on the turn. A little more persistence, a little more effort, and what seemed hopeless failure may turn into glorious success. There is no failure except in no longer trying. There is no defeat except from within, no really insurmountable barrier save our own inherent weakness of purpose."

Elbert Hubbard

STEVE JOBS (1955-2011) *Founder of Apple, Inc.*

"His tenacity is what makes him great. Several years after leaving Steve's employ, Susan Barnes conducted a study about family run businesses. She found that the key to success was 'pure staying power, persistence, continually believing in something, doggedness to get things done, and continual optimism.' That was a good description of Steve Jobs. Steve was beaten down many times but 'he kept getting off the mat,' she says."

Alan Deutschman, *The Second Coming of Steve Jobs*

Steve Jobs was one of the first to envision that people would buy a computer for their home because they wanted to do some business tasks or to run educational applications for themselves or their children. Furthermore, he foresaw the need to link the home with a "nationwide communications network," the Internet.

Jobs became interested in electronics at the age of 10. Many Hewlett-Packard engineers lived in his neighborhood in Mountain View, California, and he was intrigued with many electronics projects assembled in neighborhood garages. One neighbor instructed Jobs in electronics and enrolled him in the Hewlett-Packard Explorer Club, where he learned about calculators, diodes, holograms, and lasers.

Jobs's first project for the Explorer Club was building a frequency counter. He needed parts and obtained them with the assertiveness for which he became known. He looked up Bill Hewlett in the Palo Alto phone book. Hewlett answered the phone and talked with Jobs for 20 minutes. He not only gave Jobs the parts he needed but also gave him a summer job at Hewlett-Packard assembling frequency counters. When Jobs needed another part, he called the Burroughs Corporation in Detroit, collect, and asked them to donate it.

Jobs's future partner, Steve Wozniak, was only 19 when he met Jobs, but his knowledge of electronics was advanced for his age. He had won prizes in local electronics fairs against tough competition.

Wozniak dropped out of Berkeley during his junior year and accepted a position as an engineer in Hewlett-Packard's calculator

15

division. He became a regular attendee at meetings of the Homebrew Computer Club, a gathering place for computer hobbyists, engineers, programmers, and suppliers. Attendance at club meetings increased exponentially after the January 1975 issue of *Popular Electronics* was circulated. It included an article about the Altair 8800 computer kit produced by MITS in Albuquerque, New Mexico. The Altair central processing unit used an Intel 8080 microprocessor. The Altair was a collection of parts with meager documentation and little input / output capability. Orders from hobbyists for this first mail-order computer overwhelmed MITS. BASIC programming language for the Intel 8080 was developed by Bill Gates and Paul Allen, who later founded Microsoft Corporation.

Wozniak designed his own computer. He took his computer to meetings of the Homebrew Computer Club, but they were not interested in it because it was not based on the integrated circuit used in the Altair. He offered to give away circuit diagrams of his computer to club members, but Jobs suggested that they sell them. Better yet, Jobs suggested that they make the circuit-board computers and sell them. On April 1, 1976, Jobs and Wozniak formed a partnership called Apple Computer to make and sell computers. Jobs developed a reputation as a tough negotiator. He was called "the rejector," because he usually turned down early designs and estimates.

Jobs met an electronics retailer at a Homebrew Club meeting who offered to buy 50 circuit-board computers, called Apple I. Apple Computer needed start-up capital to build them, but no one was willing to lend it to them. Jobs's loan requests were turned down by banks and by his previous employer at an electronics warehouse store. Finally, Jobs found a supplier of electronics parts in Palo Alto who would sell them parts on credit with no interest if they paid within 30 days. When Wozniak designed the next generation computer, Jobs contracted out the insertion of components into circuit boards. The company he chose did not want the work, but Jobs succeeded with his assertive "I'm not going to leave here until you agree" approach.

Until this time in his life, Jobs had been an individual in search of a cause. In promoting the personal computer, he had found his cause. He had a knack for convincing talented people to undertake projects for Apple.

One of Jobs's important early decisions was his choice of an advertising / public relations firm. He was referred to the Regis McKenna Agency. McKenna turned him down. Again Jobs asserted himself; he called McKenna three or four times a day until he agreed to take on Apple as a client.

The fledgling enterprise needed capital to expand. Mike Markkula was recommended as the venture capitalist. Markkula offered to devote four years to Apple and provide money to develop and manufacture the Apple II in return for a one-third ownership in the company. On January 3, 1977, Apple Computer Company was incorporated.

Apple II, because of Wozniak's original design and Jobs's efforts as "rejector," was a work of art. It was easy to produce and it looked good when the cover was raised. Jobs negotiated bargain-basement prices for Apple's components.

In early 1977, Apple II was demonstrated in an attention-gathering booth at a computer fair in San Francisco. Thirteen thousand attendees were captivated by Apple II, and 300 orders were placed. Markkula worked hard to obtain additional capital to fuel Apple's growth. He was amazingly successful.

Apple's next product was an enhanced Apple II, Apple III. In addition to enhancements, the company provided improvements that customers and dealers had requested. Sales of Apple III were less than forecasted. Fortunately, sales of Apple II, which had little competition in 1979, were strong.

Following Apple III's limited success, Jobs needed a new goal. He sought a partner; he considered IBM and Xerox despite the fact that Apple considered IBM the enemy.

Xerox had invested in Apple's second private investment placement. Jobs contacted the Xerox Development Corporation, the company's venture capital unit, and offered to let them invest in Apple if they would give him a tour of their Palo Alto Research Center (PARC). PARC had a talented staff of computer scientists who had made many breakthroughs that Xerox had failed to exploit. Xerox purchased 100,000 shares of Apple at $10.00 and opened their doors to Jobs. The 25-year-old entrepreneur had gotten his way again.

Larry Tesler of PARC demonstrated their Alto personal computer to Jobs and seven Apple developers, who were enthusiastic when they saw the Alto's potential. User interaction with the Alto was revolutionary through the use of icons, menus (action lists), partitions of the screen (windows), and a "mouse." Jobs was moved by what he saw. He shouted: "Why aren't you doing anything with this? This is the greatest thing! This is revolutionary!" After the demonstration, Jobs hired Tesler to work for Apple. Later, Alan Kay, one of PARC's principal computer science visionaries, joined Apple and eventually became an Apple Fellow.

In August 1980, Markkula reorganized Apple into three divisions. Jobs had hoped to be given line authority of a division; instead, he was named Chairman of the Board. On December 12, 1980, Apple Computer Corporation went public. Apple's shares sold out within the first hour.

In 1981, Wozniak crashed his Beechcraft Bonanza light plane and underwent a long recuperation period. He did not return to Apple full time. Jobs and Wozniak made significant contributions to the computer industry. They succeeded where large corporations failed; they pioneered the personal computer revolution. In 1985, President Reagan awarded National Technology Medals to Jobs and Wozniak at the White House.

Without line responsibility in the reorganization of Apple, Jobs was again without a project. He needed a subject for his evangelism. The Macintosh personal computer was the next project to provide an outlet for his zeal. Macintosh was in the R & D phase. Developers planned a "luggable" machine that would be easy to use and would sell for about $1,000. Hardware and software designers would work together from the beginning, and software would be offered as part of the purchase price of the machine. Jobs took over the project and brought in developers from the successful Apple II. Jobs headed the Macintosh Division when it was formed.

Markkula was in a difficult position because his four-year arrangement with Apple was almost over. He looked outside Apple for a new president. He wanted John Sculley, President of Pepsi-Cola USA, who had taken market share from Coca-Cola. Initially, Sculley was not interested in joining Apple. Jobs flew to New York City and courted Sculley. After many long conversations about the future of Apple, Jobs asked Sculley if he intended to sell sugar water to children for the rest of his life when he could be doing something important with personal computers.

Sculley accepted the presidency of Apple and spent many hours learning the technology. Within his first year on the job, he realized that cuts would have to be made. Apple II was carrying the company. He streamlined the organizational structure and eliminated 1,200 jobs to keep the company profitable. Jobs retained his position as manager of the Macintosh Division in addition to serving as Chairman of the Board. Sculley redirected the company from producing most of its own software to increased reliance on outside software developers.

The first disagreements between Jobs and Sculley occurred in 1983. By 1984, when Macintosh sales were considerably below Jobs's estimates, the rift was obvious to everyone. Apple lowered the price of Macintosh, but sales continued to be disappointing. At the Board meeting on April 11, 1985, Sculley dismissed Jobs as manager of the Macintosh Division. Jobs then attempted to have Sculley removed as president and CEO. However, he misjudged Sculley's support from the Board of Directors. Finally, their disagreements became so disruptive that the Board suggested that Sculley force Jobs out of the company.

Jobs founded NeXT, a computer company that produced an expensive computer for academic users. Tim Berners-Lee invented the World Wide Web on a NeXT computer. Nevertheless, the computer had a limited market, so NeXT concentrated on software development. Jobs then founded Pixar, which produced computer-automated cartoons, such as the highly profitable *Toy Story*.

In 1996, Apple bought NeXT to use its software as the foundation for the next-generation MAC operating system. NeXT software became the basis for all future Apple operating systems. Jobs came with the purchase of NeXT. In 1997, Apple's sales and earnings plummeted, and Jobs was appointed interim CEO and led Apple's rebound. He became CEO in 2000.

In 2001, Apple introduced the iPod and became a consumer electronics company and the major company in the media-player market. In 2007, Jobs announced the iPhone, a powerful pocket-sized personal computer, which incorporated a new touch screen and interface and dominated the smart phone market. In 2010, the iPad, a highly successful tablet computer, was introduced by Apple.

In his personal life, Jobs was diagnosed in 2004 with a rare form of pancreatic cancer that could be controlled. He underwent surgery and returned to work.

In 2005, Jobs gave the commencement address at Stanford University. He said, "Your time is limited, so don't waste it living someone else's life. Don't be trapped by dogma, which is living with the results of someone else's thinking. Don't let the noise of others' opinions drown out your own inner voice. And most important, have the courage to follow your heart and intuition. They somehow already know what you truly want to become. Everything else is secondary."

In 2009, Jobs received a liver transplant. He again returned to work. On August 24, 2011, Jobs turned over his CEO responsibilities to Tim Cook, the Chief Operating Officer. Jobs died from complications of pancreatic cancer on October 5, 2011.

In 2011, Apple's market capitalization exceeded that of ExxonMobil, making it the world's most valuable company. Jobs revitalized six industries: personal computers, animated movies, music, telephones, tablet computing, and digital publishing. He also had a significant impact on retailing with the establishment of the Apple retail stores.

Jobs, who considered himself an artist, had a passion for design. He combined art, technology, and ease of use in his products. Jobs did no market research. He did not ask customers what they wanted; rather, he gave them what he thought they should have.

Steve Jobs was the greatest business executive of the late twentieth and early twenty-first centuries. It is thought that historians will rank him with Henry Ford and Thomas Edison.

BILL GATES (1955-) *Cofounder of Microsoft Corporation*

"Bill Gates's philosophy and success are inseparable from the Information Revolution. From the start, he wanted to create 'a tool for the Information Age that could magnify your brainpower instead of your muscle power.' He sees digital tools as the means of augmenting the unique powers of the human being: thinking, articulating thought, working together with other humans to act on thought."

Robert Heller, *Bill Gates*

Young Bill Gates was a very competitive child and a good student. He wasn't disciplined heavily, and his mother, Mary Gates, observed that, to a large extent, he did what he wanted to from the age of eight. By the time Gates was 11, he was ahead of his fellow students in the public schools and needed additional academic challenges.

Gates's parents enrolled him in the Lakeside School, an exclusive private prep school for boys in Seattle. Lakeside was known for its challenging academic atmosphere in which students were encouraged to develop their own interests.

In the spring of 1968, Lakeside provided access to a DEC PDP-10 minicomputer. Gates became a frequent user of the PDP-10. Paul Allen, Gates's future partner, who was two years ahead of him at Lakeside, was also hooked on the new technology. Gates's first programs were written in BASIC (Beginners' All-Purpose Symbolic Instruction Code). Gates, Allen, and two other students formed the Lakeside Programmers' Group to earn money using the computer.

In early 1971, the Lakeside Programmers' Group accepted a contract with Information Sciences, Inc., a Portland timesharing company, to write a payroll program. The four classmates formed a partnership, completed the project successfully, and were paid royalties. Allen graduated from Lakeside in 1971 and enrolled at Washington State University, where he majored in computer science.

During his senior year at Lakeside, Gates was offered a job with TRW Corporation in Oregon to troubleshoot application programs that ran on the PDP-10. Gates immediately called Allen, who had dropped out of Washington State, to work on the project with him. Gates returned to TRW for the summer before entering Harvard University. He became a more professional programmer at TRW.

Gates spent many hours on the PDP-10 at the Aiken Computer Center at Harvard. His schedule was erratic; it included little time for sleep. He accepted a job programming for Honeywell in Boston that summer. He was joined by Allen, who stayed on at Honeywell after Gates returned to Harvard for his sophomore year. One of Gates's residence hall friends was Steve Ballmer, an applied mathematics major, who later played a significant role in the development of Microsoft Corporation.

In December 1974, Allen was walking across Harvard Square to visit Gates when he saw the January issue of *Popular Electronics* at a news kiosk. The cover had a picture of the Altair 8800 with the headline "World's First Microcomputer Kit to Rival Commercial Models." When Allen saw Gates, he told him, "Well, here's our opportunity to do something with BASIC."

The Altair 8800 was developed by Ed Roberts of Micro Instrumentation and Telemetry Systems (MITS) in Albuquerque, New Mexico. It was based on the Intel 8080 microprocessor chip. It had neither a keyboard nor a display. Since a high-level programming language hadn't yet been written for the Intel 8080 microchip, the Altair had to be programmed in machine language by flipping switches on the front panel. It responded by flashing red lights near the switches.

Programming languages available for mainframe and minicomputers at the time included FORTRAN (Formula Translation), which is a scientific language, and COBOL (Common Business-Oriented Language). No BASIC programming language had yet been developed for the Intel 8080 microprocessor. Gates called Roberts to tell him that he and Allen had developed BASIC for the Altair 8800 and would license MITS to sell their software for royalty payments.

After telling Roberts that they had a working BASIC, Gates and Allen worked furiously to develop it. They didn't have an Altair 8800 to use in developing the software so they developed their programs by simulating the Altair 8800 on the PDP-10 in the Aiken Computer Center. Allen observed, "We were in the right place at the right time. Because of our previous experience, Bill and I had the necessary tools to be able to take advantage of this new situation." In late February, Allen delivered the BASIC software to MITS in Albuquerque.

Allen moved to Albuquerque to get BASIC ready for the Altair 8800 and to make enhancements. In effect, he was the entire software development department for MITS; all of the MITS employees were working overtime to fill the high volume of orders for the Altair. The Altair was unreliable and had extremely limited functionality; nevertheless, customers willingly mailed $400 checks to MITS to buy them. Gates worked in Albuquerque during the summer of his sophomore year at Harvard. Gates and Allen realized that they should establish a formal partnership. Microsoft was founded in the summer of 1975.

Gates and Allen signed an agreement giving MITS "exclusive, worldwide rights to use and license BASIC to third parties." The agreement included the key phrase: "The company (MITS) agrees to use its best efforts to license, promote, and commercialize the Program (BASIC)." Gates's father and an Albuquerque lawyer helped Gates draft the agreement, which pioneered software licensing agreements. Although he was only 19, Gates was the principal architect of the groundbreaking agreement.

Gates returned to Harvard in the fall and spent his time attending classes, studying, writing software, and negotiating agreements for Microsoft. Allen stayed in Albuquerque to work with MITS. In January 1977, Gates dropped out of Harvard. His parents weren't happy with his decision.

According to the agreement with MITS, Microsoft had to obtain permission from MITS to sell Intel 8080 BASIC to other companies. Roberts of MITS didn't block these sales unless they were to direct competitors, which initially wasn't a problem. However, as the personal computer industry grew, the agreement limited Microsoft's growth potential.

The Microsoft royalty agreement with MITS included a cap on royalties. Furthermore, Roberts was contemplating selling MITS. Gates realized that Microsoft had to get out of the agreement with MITS. He sent Roberts a letter terminating the agreement for several reasons, including Roberts's lack of success in using his "best efforts to license, promote, and commercialize BASIC." The agreement stipulated that any arguments would be addressed by an arbitrator.

On May 22, 1977, Roberts sold MITS. The new owner notified Gates that "it would no longer market BASIC or allow it to be licensed because it considered all other hardware companies competitors." This was counter to the "best efforts" provision of the agreement with Microsoft. The arbitrator sided with Microsoft in the hearing.

This decision played a significant role in the shaping of the software industry and of Microsoft's role in it. Both MITS and the new owner had underestimated their 21-year-old adversary, Bill Gates.

Gates and Allen realized that New Mexico wasn't the optimal location for a fast-growing software company. They considered two other locations, the San Francisco Bay area and Seattle. San Francisco was the location of Silicon Valley and many computer-related companies; however, Seattle was home. Allen had a strong preference for Seattle, and Gates felt that it would be easy to attract programmers to the Northwest. In December 1978, Microsoft moved to Seattle.

Software had three levels: the operating system; languages, e.g. BASIC, FORTRAN, and COBOL; and application software, such as word processing and spreadsheet applications. The operating system, usually written in a low-level language such as assembly language, performed tasks like selecting the portion of the disk to be written upon. Microsoft licensed the CP/M (Control Program for Microcomputers) operating system from Digital Research to use with their programming language packages.

In 1980, observing the success of Apple Computer and others in the personal computer market, IBM decided to enter the market. In July 1980, IBM contacted Gates to discuss Microsoft's possible participation in its personal computer development effort. IBM met with Gates, Allen, and Steve Ballmer, Gates's friend from Harvard, who had just joined Microsoft as assistant to the president.

In August, at a second meeting with IBM, Gates was asked if he could develop a BASIC program by April 1981. Gates said that Microsoft could do it. In September, IBM asked Microsoft to furnish FORTRAN and COBOL, in addition to BASIC.

In October 1980, Gates and Ballmer met with IBM in Boca Raton, Florida, to discuss a contract for developing software for the

IBM personal computer. The Microsoft cause was aided by a conversation between Don Estridge, who was responsible for IBM's personal computer development, and John Opel, IBM's chief executive officer, several days earlier at lunch. Estridge mentioned to Opel that he was negotiating with Microsoft to develop software for IBM. Opel said, "Oh, that's run by Bill Gates, Mary Gates's son." Opel knew Mary Gates from serving on the national board of the United Way. The contract between IBM and Microsoft was signed on November 6, 1980.

For two years after the IBM personal computer was introduced, MS-DOS (Microsoft Disk Operating System) and CP/M vied for leadership of the operating system market for personal computers. Eventually, the success of IBM's personal computer ensured that MS-DOS would win the race.

On October 28, 1985, the board of directors of Microsoft Corporation met to decide whether to proceed with an initial public offering of Microsoft stock. On March 13, 1986, public trading of Microsoft's stock opened. Two and a half million shares were traded on the first day of trading, and Microsoft's stock was worth $661 million. Gates owned 45 percent of the total shares and Allen owned 28 percent. By March 1987, Gates had become a billionaire at the age of 31.

Microsoft was phenomenally successful throughout the 1980s. In February 1986, Microsoft moved into new facilities in Redmond, Washington. In 1987, Microsoft became the largest microcomputer software company in the world.

Bill Gates was the fundamental factor in Microsoft's success. He focused on addressing the problems and the future of Microsoft.

By 1996, Gates was worth over $14.8 billion and over five to six times that by the end of the decade. However, net worth is not the only measure of success; it certainly isn't Bill Gates's principal measure. He remained focused on the needs of the software industry and persevered in providing the software products to meet those needs.

As the twenty-first century approached, Gates began to withdraw from some Microsoft management activities, although he continued as Chairman of the Board. Gates and his wife, Melinda, founded the Bill and Melinda Gates Foundation, which has contributed billions of dollars to fight poverty and disease.

JEFF BEZOS (1964-) *Founder of Amazon.com*

"Bezos is at once a happy-go-lucky mogul and a notorious micro-manager: an executive who wants to know about everything from contract minutiae to how he is quoted in all Amazon press releases."

Portfolio.com

Amazon.com is a multinational electronic commerce company headquartered in Seattle, Washington, that began as an online bookstore. It diversified into selling DVDs, CDs, video games, software, electronics, clothing, furniture, toys, and jewelry and is the largest online retailer in the world. Amazon also produces consumer products such as the Kindle e-book reader and the Kindle Fire tablet computer and is a major user of cloud computer services in addition to its own storage centers.

Bezos was born Jeffrey Preston Jorgensen on January 12, 1964, in Albuquerque, New Mexico. His mother was Jacklyn Gise Jorgensen and his father was Ted Jorgensen. His mother's ancestors were setters who lived in south Texas. Over many generations they accumulated a 25,000-acre ranch. In March 2015, Bezos was one of the largest landholders in Texas.

Bezos's mother's marriage to Jorgensen lasted just over a year. When Bezos was four, she married Miguel Bezos, a Cuban immigrant. Miguel worked his way through the University of Albuquerque, married Jacklyn, and adopted his stepson Jeff. The family moved to Houston, Texas, where Miguel worked as an engineer for Exxon.

As a child, Bezos spent his summers on his grandfather's ranch in Cotulla, Texas. Preston Gise had retired from his position as regional manager for the Atomic Energy Commission. Bezos was close to his grandfather, who was a significant influence on young Jeff. Gise was technically trained and encouraged his grandson in developing his technical skills and in continuing with his interest in hands-on gadgetry.

The family moved to Miami, Florida. In high school, Bezos participated in the Student Science Training Program at the University of Florida, from which he received a Silver Knight Award in 1982.

He was valedictorian of his high school class and a National Merit Scholar.

Bezos wrote a paper that won a NASA-sponsored student competition. He won a trip to to NASA's Space Flight Center in Huntsville, Alabama. He began to talk about the building of a commercial space station. In his graduation speech as valedictorian, he observed that the colonization of outer space was the way to secure the future of the human race.

Bezos enrolled at Princeton University with a major in physics but changed his major because of his interest in computers. He graduated *summa cum laude* with Bachelor of Science degrees in Electrical Engineering and Computer Science. He was elected to the honor societies Phi Beta Kappa and Tau Beta Pi and was president of the Princeton chapter of the Students for the Exploration of Space.

Bezos graduated from Princeton in 1986 and worked on Wall Street in the computer science field Then he worked on building a network for international trade for Fite, Inc. He relocated to Bankers Trust, where he developed a communications network and later moved to D.E. Shaw & Co., where he worked on Internet-enabled business opportunities.

Bezos met his wife, Mackensie Tuttle, while working at D.E. Shaw. She was a research associate who was an alumna of the Hotchkiss School and Princeton University.

In 1994, Bezos decided to start his own company. He had to decide where to locate it He considered four locations: Portland, Oregon; Boulder, Colorado; Lake Tahoe, Nevada; and Seattle, Washington. Seattle won because of the large number of programmers at companies like Microsoft and Adobe and the excellent reputation of the computer science department at the University of Washington.

In 1994, Bezos wrote the business plan for Amazon.com while driving from New York to Seattle. He left his job at a New York hedge fund when he became aware of significant growth in the use of the Internet. This growth was aided by the U.S. Supreme Court ruling that mail order catalogs were not required to collect sales taxes in States in which they lacked facilities.

Bezos is known as a detail person. He rates customer service as a vital component of his company. It began in a garage on 28th

Street N.E. in Bellvue. He liked to say that they started in a garage like Hewlitt and Packard.

The early years were difficult. Amazon lost $52,000 in 1994 and $303,000 in 1995. Early in 1996, Ramanan Raghavendran, a senior associate with General Atlantic Partners, a large Greenwich, Connecticut, private equity investment firm, discovered Amazon by surfing the Internet and became very interested in it As a venture capitalist, he made the earliest offer of money to expand Amazon.

Amazon received a better offer from Kleiner, Perkins, Caulfield & Byers, the most successful venture capitalist in Silicon Valley, where it had provided start-up money for companies such as Sun Microsystems and Compaq. Once Amazon began to grow, Bezos advocated growing fast.

In going public, Amazon chose Deutsch, Morgan, and Grenfell to represent them. They had had a recently assembled staff and were chosen mainly because of personal contacts.

In 2000, Bezos created Blue Origin, a human spaceflight company. He had been fascinated by space travel since his high school days. In 2006, Blue Origin bought land in west Texas to create a test and launch facility. In 2011, Bezos said that he founded the space company to allow any paying customer to go into space. His two goals were to decrease the cost and increase the safety.

In 2013, Bezos reviewed commercial spaceflight alternatives with Richard Branson, founder of Virgin Group and Virgin Galactic. In 2015, he announced the development of an orbital launch vehicle scheduled for its first flight in the late 2010s.

In 1999, Bezos was named Person of the Year by *Time* magazine. In 2006, he was awarded an honorary doctorate in Science and Technology by Carnegie Mellon University. He was named Business Person of the Year by *Fortune* magazine in 2012. As of July 9, 2015, according to *Forbes* magazine, Bezos was the 15th wealthiest person in the world with an estimated net worth of $39.2 billion.

Bezos and his wife, Mackensie Tuttle Bezos, have four children: three sons and an adopted daughter from China.

LARRY PAGE (1971-   ) *& SERGEY BRIN* (1973-   )
Founders of Google

"The talent of success is to do what you can do well and doing well whatever you do without a thought of fame."

Henry Wadsworth Longfellow

Google began as a research project in January 1996, when Larry Page and Sergey Brin were graduate students at Stanford University. Google's mission statement was "to organize the world's information and make it universally accessible and useful."

Google is a misspelling of the word "googol," the number one followed by one hundred zeros, which was picked to indicate that the search engine would provide large quantities of information. On September 4, 1998, Google was incorporated as a privately held company.

Google's initial public offering occurred on August 19, 2004. Page and Brin own 14 percent of Google stock but control 56 percent of the stockholder voting power via supervoting stock.

Google moved to its new headquarters in Mountain View, California, called the Googleplex, in 2004. On October 2, 2015, Google reorganized as a holding company called Alphabet, Inc. Google became Alphabet's principal subsidiary and the parent for Google's Internet activities.

As of 2007, it was estimated that Google ran more than one million servers in data centers around the world. In 2009, it was estimated that the company processed over one billion search requests per day. In December 2013, google.com was listed as the most visited website in the world.

Larry Page was born in East Lansing, Michigan, on March 26, 1971. His father, Carl Vincent Page, Jr., had a PhD in computer science and was considered a pioneer in computer science and artificial intelligence. He was a professor of computer science at Michigan State University. Page's mother, Gloria, was in instructor in computer programming at Lyman Briggs College at Michigan State University.

Page's home was always full of magazines and books on science and technology. The atmosphere of his home and the attention of

29

his parents nurtured creativity and invention. He became interested in computers at the age of six. His older brother taught him how to take things apart. From an early age, he knew he wanted to invent things.

Page has a Bachelor of Science in computer engineering, with honors, from the University of Michigan, and a Master of Science in computer engineering from Stanford University. He enrolled in a computer science PhD program at Stanford University and began to look for a subject for his dissertation.

Page considered exploring the mathematical properties of the World Wide Web. He wanted to understand its link structure as a large graph. He focused on which web pages link to a particular page. The role of citations in academic publishing would factor in the research.

Sergey Brin, a fellow PhD student, joined Page's research project called "Backrub." Together, they wrote a research paper entitled "The Anatomy of a Large-Scale Hypertextual Web Search Engine." At the time, it was one of the most downloaded scientific documents in the history of the Internet.

John Battelle, cofounder of *Wired* magazine, noted that Page had observed:

> The entire Web was loosely based on the premise of citation—after all, what is a link but a citation? If he could devise a method to count and quantify each backlink on the Web, as Page puts it "the Web would become a more valuable place."

> At the time Page conceived of BackRub, the Web comprised an estimated 10 million documents, with an untold number of links between them. The computing resources required to crawl such a beast were well beyond the bounds of a student project. Unaware what he was getting into, Page began building his crawler (browser of the Web). The idea's complexity and scale lured Brin to the job.

Page and Brin developed the PageRank algorithm to convert the backlink data gathered by BackRub's Web crawler into a measure of importance for a particular Web page. They knew that the PageRank algorithm could be used to develop a search engine far superior to those in use.

Page married Lucina Southworth in 2007. She is a research scientist and a sister of actress and model Carrie Southworth. The Pages have two children, born in 2009 and 2011. They live in Palo Alto, California.

Page received an honorary doctorate from the University of Michigan in 2009. In July 2014, Bloomberg listed Page as the 17th richest man in the world, with an estimated net worth of $32.7 billion. Late in 2014, *Fortune* magazine named Page "Business Person of the Year."

Sergey Brin was born on August 21, 1973, in Moscow, in the Soviet Union. His parents, Mikhai and Yevgenia Brin, are graduates of Moscow State University. His father is a mathematics professor at the University of Maryland, and his mother is a researcher at NASA's Goddard Space Flight Center.

The Brin family immigrated to the United States in 1979, when Sergey was six years old. In May 1993, Sergey Brin received his Bachelor of Science degree in computer science and mathematics from the University of Maryland. Brin received a graduate fellowship from the National Science Foundation for graduate study in computer science at Stanford University.

Brin and Page met at an orientation for new students. They "became intellectual soul-mates and close friends." Brin's contribution to the team's efforts was in developing data mining systems. John Battelle described how Brin and Page began working together on their joint research project:

> [Brin was] A polymath who had jumped from project to project without settling on a thesis topic; he found the thesis behind [Page's] BackRub fascinating: "I talked to lots of research groups around the school," Brin recalls, "and this was the most exciting project, both because it tackled the Web, which represents human knowledge, and because I liked Larry."

Brin and Page used Page's dormitory room as a machine laboratory to develop a device to connect their search engine with the University's broadband campus network. After Page's room was filled with equipment, they made Brin's dorm room into an office and programming center, where they tested their new search engine designs on the Web. The fast growth of their project caused problems for Stanford's computing infrastructure.

Brim married entrepreneur and biotech scientist Anne Wojcicki in May 2007. They had a son in 2008 and a daughter in 2011. They separated in 2013 and were divorced in 2015.

In 2004, Brin and Page won the Marconi Foundation Prize, the "Highest Award in Engineering," and were elected fellows of the Marconi Foundation of Columbia University. In February 2008, Brin was inducted into the National Academy of Engineering. Brin was selected specifically, "for leadership in development of rapid indexing and retrieval of relevant information from the World Wide Web." As of June 2014, according to *Forbes* magazine, Brin was the 30th richest person in the world, with a personal wealth of $30 billion.

Brin and Page are trying to help solve the world's energy and climate problems via Google's philanthropic arm, Google.org. It invests in alternative energy to find wider sources of renewable energy. Their goal is to solve really big problems using technology.

MARK ZUCKERBERG (1984-   ) *Founder of Facebook*

"The secret of the true love of work is the hope of success in that work, not for the money reward, for the time spent, or for the skill exercised, but for the successful result in the accomplishment of the work itself."

Sidney A. Weltmer

Mark Elliot Zuckerberg was born in White Plains, New York, on May 14, 1984. His father is Edward Zuckerberg, a dentist, and his mother is Karen Kempner Zuckerberg, a psychiatrist.

Zuckerberg began writing programs and using computers in middle school. He took a graduate course in computers at Mercy College near his home while still in high school. He liked to write computer programs, particularly for games and communications tools. Some young people played computer games; Zuckerberg built them. He had friends who were artists. He made games out of their art work.

By the time Zuckerberg enrolled at Harvard University to study computer science and psychology, he was already considered a prodigy in computer programming. In January 2004, he began to write the programs for his new Web site.

On January 4, 2004, Zuckerberg launched "Thefacebook," located at the Web site thefacebook.com. Soon after the Web site was launched, three Harvard seniors accused him of misleading them that he would help them build a social network and then using their ideas to construct a competing network. The three filed a lawsuit against Zuckerberg that was settled out of court, for 1.2 million Facebook shares worth $300 million at Facebook's initial public offering

Initially, Facebook was used only at Harvard. With the assistance of his roommate, Dustin Moskovitz, Zuckerberg decided to expand to other colleges. The early expansion was to Ivy League colleges, New York University, and Stanford.

Zuckerberg dropped out of Harvard in his sophomore year to complete Facebook. Looking back in later years, he observed: "I opened up the first version of Facebook; at the time I thought, you know, someone needs to build a service like this for the world. But I just never thought that we'd be the ones to help do it. And I think a lot of what it comes down to is we just cared more."

Zuckerberg moved to Palo Alto, California, along with Moskovitz. Cofounders in addition to Moskovitz were Andrew McCullum, Chris Hughes, and Eduardo Saverin. Subsequently, they located their headquarters in Menlo Park, California.

Zuckerberg met venture capitalist Peter Thiel, who invested in the company. Zuckerberg turned down offers from major corporations to buy the company. Later, he explained: "It's not because of the amount of money. For me and my colleagues, the most important thing is that we create an open information flow for people. Having media corporations owned by conglomerates is just not an attractive idea to me." In 2010, Zuckerberg told *Wired* magazine: "The thing I really care about is the mission, making the world open."

It is well known that registered Facebook users can create a user profile, add other users as "friends," exchange messages, post status updates and photos, share videos and be notified when others update their profiles. Most of Facebook's revenue comes from advertising. Early on, Christopher Matthews of *Time* magazine made an observation about advertising:

> A big part of Facebook's pitch is that it has so much information about its users that it can more effectively target ads to those who will be responsive to the content. If Facebook can prove that theory to be true, then it may not worry so much about losing its cool cachet.

In February 2012, Facebook, Inc., had its first initial public offering of stock. The original peak market capitalization was $104 billion. Facebook became the fastest company on the Standard & Poor's 500 Index to reach a market cap of $250 billion on July 13, 2015. Zuckerberg serves as Chairman and CEO. Sheryl Sandberg is the Chief Operating Officer.

Zuckerberg met his wife, Priscilla Chan, during his sophomore year at Harvard. She was a fellow student. He began dating her in 2003. She is the daughter of Chinese-Vietnamese refugees,who who moved to the United States after the fall of Saigon in 1975.

She was born in Braintree, Massachusetts. On July 31, 2015, Zuckerberg and Chan were married. On that day, they also celebrated Chan's graduation from medical school.

CHAPTER 2

Couples / Teams

"Life affords no higher pleasure than that of surmounting difficulties, passing from one step of success to another, forming new wishes and seeing them gratified. He that labors in any great and laudable undertaking has his fatigues first supported by hope and afterwards rewarded by joy."

Samuel Johnson

EMMELINE (1858-1928) *& CHRISTABEL* (1880-1956) *PANKHURST--Women's Rights Leaders in England*

"The *Daily Mail* called the militant suffragists 'suffragettes,' a name that Christabel liked. In her opinion, the suffragists merely desired the vote, but, if you pronounce the hard g, the suffragettes mean to get it."

Staff writer, London Daily Mail

The women's suffrage movement in England was much more militant than in the United States, and the right of women to vote in England was granted in stages. In February 1917, a bill was proposed to give the vote to women over thirty who were either college graduates, local government electors (owner or tenant householders), or wives of men in the first two categories. The bill was extended to the wives of all voters when it passed in January 1918; it enfranchised 8,500,000 women. In 1928, the vote was extended to all women of voting age.

Emmeline Pankhurst and two of her daughters played a major role in the Women's Suffrage Movement. Emmeline, who was born in 1858, was the handsome, delicate eldest daughter of Robert Goulden, a wealthy Manchester cotton manufacturer. She was sent to finishing school in Paris, where her best friend was Noémie de Rochefort, the daughter of the Marquis de Rochefort, a hero of the Paris Commune of 1871.

After returning from Paris in 1878, Emmeline met Richard Pankhurst, a radical advocate who had been called to the Bar in 1867 after receiving the highest law degrees at London University. In 1865, when Emmeline was only seven years old, Pankhurst had helped found the Woman's Suffrage Society in Manchester. In 1870, he drafted the Married Women's Property Bill that gave women the right to own property and to keep the wages they earned. Also that year, he drafted the first of many parliamentary bills to give women the vote.

Emmeline and Richard fell in love at first sight. She was captivated by his eloquence, his idealism, and his "beautiful white hands." He was a forty-year-old bachelor who lived at home with his mother. When his mother died in 1879, he proposed to Emmeline. Theirs was a happy marriage, partly because they saw each other as kindred spirits ("Every struggling cause shall be ours"). Although she offered to dispense with the legal formalities of marriage to demonstrate their disregard for convention, he was unwilling to expose her to the public response that it would invite.

Four children were born during the first six years of their marriage: Christabel in 1880, Sylvia in 1882, Adela in 1885, and a son who died in childhood. Pankhurst thought of his four children as the four pillars of his house. He told them: "If you do not grow up to help other people, you will not have been worth the upbringing." He continually counseled them that drudgery and drill are important components of life, but that "life is nothing without enthusiasms."

In 1883, Emmeline supported her husband's political campaign when he resigned from the Liberal Association and ran unsuccessfully as an Independent in the Manchester by-election. He advocated the abolition of the House of Lords, establishment of an international court, nationalization of the land and of the mines, reduction in the size of the army and navy, suffrage for adults of both sexes, and the founding of an United States of Europe.

Two years later, Pankhurst ran for office as a Radical candidate in Rotherhithe. This losing effort was Emmeline's first exposure to the heckling and disorder of a brawling campaign. She thought that her husband was able but misunderstood, and that his talent needed a new venue. Emmeline suggested that they move to London, where she would open a shop to support their sagging finances.

At 8 Russell Square, a large double drawing room, which she painted her favorite color (yellow), was the site of her musical afternoons, poetry readings, and suffrage meetings. She invited agitators, anarchists, Fabians, free thinkers, political thinkers, and radicals, including Annie Besant, the brilliant pamphleteer; Tom Mann, the union leader; and William Morris, the artist, craftsman, and poet. Her visitors also included Elizabeth Cady Stanton and her daughter, Harriet Stanton Blatch.

Emmeline didn't believe in sending her daughters to school. Their education was provided by instruction from governesses, by reading, and by visiting museums. The three girls developed very different personalities. Christabel, who inherited her mother's charm and social graces, was an extrovert. Sylvia was introverted and shy; she was also obedient and subject to bouts of depression.

Sylvia developed an interest in drawing and sketching. When they finally were entered into schools, Christabel was happy in her new environment; Sylvia was miserable.

Sylvia was devoted to her mother but was influenced more by her father, whom she called "splendid father." In her autobiography, Sylvia wrote, "Our father, vilified and boycotted yet beloved by a multitude of people in all walks of life, was a standard bearer of every forlorn hope, every popular yet unworthy cause then conceived for the uplifting of oppressed and suffering humanity." She considered her mother his most fervent disciple.

The subject of women's rights was Richard Pankhurst's most zealous activity and the one in which he was a strong influence on his wife and daughters. As one who opposed exploitation of all kinds, he couldn't tolerate half of the population being held back economically and politically. In 1890, when Christabel was ten and Sylvia was eight, the usually calm Pankhurst erupted after a meeting of the Women's Franchise League at their home. He burst out, "Why don't you force us to give you the vote? Why don't you scratch our eyes out?" Christabel and Sylvia were startled by his outburst; Emmeline was astonished at the vehemence of his feelings.

Emmeline's career as a shopkeeper was not successful. Financial problems continued to plague the family. Years of overwork caught up with Pankhurst, and he began to be bothered by gastric ulcers. In order to reduce expenses, the family moved back to Manchester, where the Pankhursts remained politically active. They asserted themselves as Socialists as well as feminists.

Few politicians of the time supported women's rights. The earliest to support the women's cause was Keir Hardie, the first independent working-class Member of Parliament (MP). A former miner, Hardie joined the trade union movement and ran unsuccessfully for office in 1888. In 1892, he was elected as the Radical Association candidate from West Ham. In 1893, he helped to found the Scottish Labour Party and the Independent Labour Party (ILP), which evolved into the Labour Party of today.

In 1894, married women were given the right to vote in local elections and became eligible for election as district councilors and Poor Law Guardians. The following year, Emmeline was elected to the Chorlton Board of Guardians. When she was told that the

Guardians couldn't provide relief to the "able bodied poor," she organized food kitchens with the help of the ILP. She was horrified by conditions in the workhouses and incensed by the treatment of young women with illegitimate babies. Years later, she wrote, "Though I had been a suffragist before, I now began to think about the vote in women's hands not only as a right, but as a desperate necessity."

In 1895, Pankhurst ran unsuccessfully again for Parliament as the ILP candidate from Gorton. The Pankhurst daughters watched helplessly as toughs threw stones at their mother while they celebrated the Tory victory. In 1896, the Manchester Parks Committee ruled that the ILP could no longer use Boggart Clough, a large, municipally-owned field, for their meetings as they had for several years. Speakers were fined and sent to jail unless they paid the fines. Emmeline, as the wife of a senior member of the Bar, surprised the magistrates when she told them she would pay no fine and would continue to attend the ILP meetings there. Eventually, the ban was retracted; controlled agitation, courage, and persistence had won the cause.

In 1898, Richard Pankhurst died suddenly of a perforated ulcer. He had no money to leave the family. The ILP offered to establish an education fund for the Pankhurst children, but Emmeline was too proud to permit it. Pankhurst had frequently asked his children what they wanted to be when they grew up. He advised them, "Get something to work at that you like and can do." However, at the time of his death, the children were not educated or trained to help their mother support the family. Christabel had considered both ballet dancing and dressmaking, but she wasn't encouraged to do either.

Sylvia had taken art lessons from a well-known artist and had displayed a definite talent. When her mother sold their furniture before moving to a smaller house, their old paintings were assessed and the assessor sent some of Sylvia's drawings to the Manchester School of Art. Sylvia was offered a full scholarship to the School. Later, her artwork was frequently used by the suffragists.

Emmeline was offered a position as registrar of births and deaths by the Chorlton Board of Guardians. She also opened another shop, even though she had been unsuccessful with the shop in London. Christabel worked in the shop, but was unhappy with the role of shopkeeper. She enrolled in courses at the University of Manchester, where she participated in discussions. Her perceptive responses brought her to the attention of the Vice Chancellor of the University and of Eva Gore-Booth and Esther Roper of the suffragist movement.

After the death of Lydia Decker, their dynamic leader, the suffragists in England became divided on the amount of political involvement that they should have. Lydia's successor was Millicent Fawcett, a capable leader but one without Lydia's drive. Eva and Esther, who were looking for dynamic women to work in the movement, asked Christabel if she would join their cause. Christabel was flattered and pursued her new duties with vigor. Emmeline's interest in the suffrage movement was increased by her daughter's participation. She gave up her shop and began to work actively for the Women's Rights Movement, thereby establishing an extraordinary mother-daughter partnership.

Christabel discovered that she was a natural leader and speaker. Her intelligence, pleasant appearance, and forceful personality impressed her audiences. Christabel had an internal need to dominate her environment. Sylvia described her sister as being "tenacious of her position." The suffrage movement provided Christabel with a forum to display her strengths.

Sylvia, who had been studying in Venice to further develop her painting, was asked on her return to decorate a hall that the ILP had built in Salford as a memorial to her father. She worked without pay morning, afternoon, and evening for three months to complete the work on schedule, only to find that women could not use Pankhurst Hall because it had a men-only club attached to it. The Pankhurst women were outraged by this rule; they concluded that men were never going to liberate women, and that women must liberate themselves.

In 1903, Emmeline invited ILP women to a meeting at her home and founded the Women's Social and Political Union (WSPU), a name suggested by Christabel. Their motto was "Deeds, not words"; their slogan was "Votes for women." For the next eleven years, it disseminated the views of this remarkable mother-daughter partnership.

Sylvia won a scholarship to the Royal College of Art and studied in London. Her friendship with Keir Hardie was deepening, and they spent every other Sunday together at his sparsely furnished lodgings in Neville Court. Sylvia joined the Fulham branch of the ILP and worked in the women's suffrage campaign at the request of her mother. Sylvia's apartment in Chelsea became a center of WSPU activity.

In 1905, Emmeline and Sylvia heavily lobbied the Members of Parliament to provide a place in their ballot in support of the women's cause. Again, Keir Hardie was their only supporter. Finally, when MP Branford Slack, "at the request of his wife," agreed to introduce a women's suffrage bill, it was scheduled for debate on May 12. Many women attended the debate; some came from as far away as Australia. Unfortunately, filibusters took up most of the available time, and MP Slack was allowed only a half hour. Women's suffrage had not been defeated; debate on it had merely been circumvented.

The women were upset with the government. They realized that relying on private members' bills wasn't the path to success; the government must legislate. Two months later, Keir Hardie led an effort to pass a bill to help the unemployed in an economy in which unemployment was increasing. Prime Minister Balfour's government attempted to postpone the bill. Several thousand destitute workers marched from the East End to Westminster in protest. In Manchester, mobs of enraged unemployed men marched in the streets, and four men were arrested. Ten days later, Arthur Balfour backed down, and the bill became law.

This success was not lost on the women of the WSPU. They had noticed that the threat of violence had caused the Government to act. If a threat of violence was required to get bills passed into law, then they would become increasingly militant. Sylvia observed, "It was only a question of how militant tactics would begin." The Pankhursts were thrust into a nationwide militant movement operating out of Manchester and led by Christabel.

Esther Roper, who was impressed with Christabel's skill in arguing issues, suggested to Emmeline that her oldest daughter should study law. Emmeline asked Lord Haldane to sponsor Christabel as a student at Lincoln's Inn, where her father had studied. Lord Haldane agreed, but her application was rejected because women weren't allowed to practice at the Bar. She enrolled at Manchester University's law school instead, while continuing to participate in suffrage work.

Christabel's coworker, Annie Kenney, wondered, "Where she studied, how she studied is a mystery. She was working for the movement the whole of the day and practically every night." However, as her final examination approached, Christabel said, "Panic prompted concentration, and I withdrew from human society to that of my books." In June 1906, she graduated with honors and used her new skills to support the women's cause. Christabel focused on one overriding cause—obtaining the vote for women. All other causes, including social reform issues, were going to have to wait.

Christabel's first unladylike step occurred in 1904 at a Liberal Party meeting at the Free Trade Hall in Manchester at which Winston Churchill launched the campaign for the general election. When a resolution supporting free trade was agreed upon and the speeches were over, Christabel rose from her chair on the platform and asked the chairman if she could propose an amendment on women's suffrage. The chairman denied her request amid cries from the audience, and Christabel backed down.

Later, she recalled, "This was the first militant step—the hardest for me because it was the first. To move from my place on the platform to the speaker's table in the teeth of the astonishment and opposition of will of that immense throng, those civic and county leaders and those Members of Parliament, was the most difficult thing I have ever done." However, it was "a protest of which little was heard and nothing remembered—because it did not result in imprisonment!" She formed the opinion that she must go to prison to arouse public opinion; she must become a martyr.

In 1905, Christabel and her friend, Annie Kenney, attended a Liberal Party rally in the Free Trade Hall in Manchester. Christabel had told her mother, "We shall sleep in prison tonight." They carried a banner that asked "Will you [the Liberal Party] give votes for women?" Both Annie and Christabel asked the question on their banner. The Chief Constable of Manchester told them that their question would be answered later. It was ignored, so they asked it again. The crowd responded, "Throw them out!"

Stewards bruised and scratched them while attempting to remove them from the hall. Christabel realized that they hadn't done enough to be taken to prison. She knew that she was going to have to do more to be arrested; however, she wasn't sure how to do that with her arms held behind her back. Finally, she was arrested and charged with "spitting at a policeman."

Her account of the incident was, "It was not a real spit, but only, shall we call it, a 'pout,' a perfectly dry purse of the mouth. I could not really have done it, even to get the vote, I think." Christabel was kept in jail for seven days; Annie was jailed for three days. Christabel received the publicity that she sought. Unfortunately, it was not clear that it helped the suffrage cause.

Sylvia and Annie interrupted a speech in Sheffield by Herbert Asquith, Chancellor of the Exchequer, and were jostled by the stewards. Men in the crowd hit them with fists and umbrellas as the women were roughly forced from the hall. The Pankhursts decided to spread their activities to London. They didn't have the finances to do it, however. They were eternal optimists; they thought, "That, too, will come." Annie Kenney was sent to London to spread their version of militant suffrage activity with £2 in her pocketbook. Emmeline Pankhurst instructed her, "Go and rouse London."

The necessary financing did come to them. Frederick and Emmeline ("the other Emmeline") Pethick-Lawrence were visiting South Africa when they heard of the suffragist activities in England. They hurried home to see what they could do to help. The Pethick-Lawrences were philanthropists who had contributed to university settlements and women's hospitals and had founded boys' clubs. They expanded the scope of their monthly newspaper, the *Labour Record*, from supporting the Labour cause to supporting the suffragist movement as well.

Initially, Emmeline Pethick-Lawrence hesitated before backing the Pankhursts. In her autobiography, she observed, "I had no fancy to be drawn into a small group of brave and reckless and quite helpless people who were prepared to dash themselves against the oldest tradition of human civilization as well as one of the strongest governments of modern times." She was moved by Annie Kenney's willingness to "rouse London" with £2 in her pocketbook. "I was amused by Annie's ignorance of what the talk of rousing London would involve and yet thrilled by her courage."

The "other Emmeline" attended a suffragist meeting at Sylvia's lodgings and was impressed with the audacity of the six women who were there. She said, "I found there was no office, no organization, no money—no postage stamps even ... It was not without dismay that it was borne on me that somebody had to come to the help of this brave little group and that the finger of fate pointed to me." Emmeline helped to establish the Central Committee of the WSPU and became its honorary treasurer.

Not only was Emmeline Pethick-Lawrence an effective treasurer, she was also a source of many good ideas. Money began to flow in to the Movement, including generous contributions from Pethick-Lawrence's husband. Collections were taken at WSPU gatherings, and Keir Hardie raised £300 from supporters of the Independent Labour Party. The Pethick-Lawrences allowed the Pankhursts to use their house at Clements Inn as their base of operations, retaining only the upstairs apartment for their own use in addition to one room as an office for the *Labour Record*. They treated Christabel as a favored daughter.

Membership in the WSPU grew rapidly. Middle-class women joined because they were looking for "wider and more important activities and interests." Women of the upper class were drawn to the WSPU for other reasons. Sylvia noted that "daughters of rich families were often without personal means, or permitted a meager dress allowance, and when their parents died, they were often reduced to genteel penury, or unwelcome dependence on relatives." Sylvia decided that with workers of the lower class, the middle class, and the upper class all joining the suffragettes, she was going to have to become a more active participant herself and spend less time on her artistic pursuits.

Sylvia and Christabel began to have different views on the movement. Sylvia advocated social reform along with women's suffrage; Christabel was exclusively focused on the suffragettes' activity. Christabel began to move away from the Labour Party, including Keir Hardie. Sylvia didn't think they should separate themselves from Labour Party support, particularly when Keir Hardie was elected chairman of the group of twenty-nine Labour MPs.

The command of the Movement became a triumvirate: Christabel and the two Emmelines. There was no question as to who was in charge; it was Christabel. Some women were surprised how willingly Emmeline Pankhurst followed the direction of her oldest daughter.

In early 1906, thirty women carrying banners marched in front of the residence of the Chancellor of the Exchequer, Herbert Asquith. The marchers were punched and kicked by police, who attempted to break up the march. Annie Kenney and two other suffragettes were sent to jail for six weeks, and Emmeline Pankhurst was handled roughly for asking a question at one of Asquith's meetings. In October 1906, ten women were arrested for making speeches in the lobby of Parliament.

Sylvia went to their aid at the Cannon Row Police Court and was thrown into the street and arrested for obstruction and abusive language. She spent fourteen days in the Third Division of Holloway Prison. In the Third Division, the lowest division, the women were considered common criminals. They ate prison food, were subjected to coarse treatment, and wore prison clothing. Treatment in the Second Division was marginally better. Prisoners in the First Division enjoyed many privileges, including the right to have friends visit, to wear their own clothing, and to have food, writing materials, and other amenities from the outside world.

In 1907, the triumvirate called a Women's Parliament near Westminster to coincide with the opening of Parliament. When they heard that there had been no mention of women's suffrage in the King's Speech, 400 women stormed Parliament. Sylvia described the activities of the constables:

> Mounted men scattered the marchers; foot police seized them by the back of the neck and rushed them along at arm's length, thumping them in the back, and bumping them with their knees in approved police fashion. Women, by the hundred, returned again and again with painful persistence, enduring this treatment by the hour. Those who took refuge in doorways were dragged down by the steps and hurled in front of the horses, then pounced on by the constables and beaten again.

Fifty women were arrested, including Christabel and Sylvia. Sentences ranged from one to three weeks. This time, the women were placed in the First Division.

Emmeline Pankhurst was asked by the Registrar-General of the

Guardians to give up her suffrage activities. She resigned her position as registrar, giving up her job and the income and pension that accompanied it. She said that she was willing to give up her life, if necessary.

In 1908 at the by-election in Mid-Devon, Emmeline Pankhurst and a fellow suffragist were attacked by a gang of young Liberal toughs, who were unhappy that their candidate had lost to the Tory candidate. Mrs. Pankhurst was knocked unconscious into the mud and injured her ankle. The young toughs were about to stuff her into a barrel and roll her down main street, when she was rescued by mounted police. The effects of the ankle injury persisted for months and motivated her to work harder for the vote.

Christabel decided that the next step was for her mother to go to jail. From a small cart, the injured Emmeline led a delegation of thirteen women who marched on Parliament. All thirteen women were sent to prison for six months in the Second Division. In her first visit to prison, Emmeline tolerated the stripping, the body search, the bath in filthy water, and the patched and stained prison clothing made of coarse material. She knew that the cold cells and the plank bed would be uncomfortable, but she was unprepared for the sobbing and foul language of the other prisoners. In particular, she was affected by the claustrophobic living conditions of many women in a small cell. Within two days, dyspepsia, migraine headaches, and neuralgia caused her to be moved to the prison hospital. Emmeline Pethick-Lawrence proposed that the WSPU should have their own colors and their own flag. Purple, white, and green were selected, and Sylvia designed banners, borders, emblems, and flags displaying these colors. Many of the women wore clothing of the three colors when they marched.

Another march on Parliament was planned. They weren't sure which verb to use. They considered "besiege," "invade," "raid," and "storm," and finally settled on "rush, " which was enough of an action word to provoke the government. They circulated a leaflet with the message, "Men and Women—Help the Suffragettes to Rush the House of Commons," and Christabel, Emmeline, and Flora Drummond (called "the General" because of her efficient methods) spoke in Trafalgar Square. Their call to action was heard by Lloyd George, Chancellor of the Exchequer, and they were charged with "inciting the public to a certain wrongful and illegal act—to rush the House of Commons.... "

Christabel conducted her own defense and that of the other two women in their trial at Bow Street. The magistrate rejected her request for a trial by jury, but she managed to call Lloyd George and Herbert Gladstone, the Home Secretary, as witnesses. The public was captivated by a young woman lawyer cross-examining cabinet ministers. The suffrage movement received much publicity, but, after two days, Emmeline and Flora were sentenced to three months in the Second Division and Christabel to ten weeks.

During the trial, Max Beerbohm was impressed with Christabel. He wrote in the *Saturday Review*: "She has all the qualities which an actress needs and of which so few actresses have.... Her whole being is alive with her every meaning, and if you can imagine a very graceful rhythmic dance done by a dancer who uses not her feet, you will have some idea of Miss Pankhurst's method." Furthermore, he noted "the contrast between the buoyancy of the girl and the depression of the statesman [Lloyd George]."

While her mother and her sister were in jail, Sylvia planned a rally at Albert Hall, where Lloyd George was to speak. She stayed at suffrage headquarters and waited for women to return from the speech. They were bruised and their clothing was in disarray. Some had their corsets ripped off and their false teeth knocked out. One woman had been whipped with a dog whip, and another had a wrist burned by a man using it to put out his cigar while other men struck her in the chest. The Manchester *Guardian* reported that the women had been treated "with a brutality that was almost nauseating."

Muriel Matters of the Women's Freedom League could not be thrown out of Parliament when she rose to speak because she had chained herself to the grille behind which women were required to stand. From then on, only relatives of Members of Parliament were permitted in the gallery.

The more activist members of the movement became impatient with the government's delays. They threw stones wrapped in WSPU literature through the windows of government buildings. When they were arrested, they went on hunger strikes. Women who were prevented from attending public meetings climbed onto the roof of the hall and used axes to chop off slates. One woman was imprisoned for throwing an iron bar through the window of an empty railroad car on the train carrying the Prime Minister back to

London.

The women were given sentences ranging from two weeks to four months. Many of them went on hunger strikes. The Home Secretary ordered that they be forcibly fed using rubber tubes through their mouth or nose. In one case, the feeding tube was accidentally passed into the trachea instead of the esophagus, and the woman developed pneumonia from broth forced into her lung.

Sylvia described being forcibly fed in graphic terms. She experienced shivering and heart palpitations when told that she was going to be forcibly fed. Six big, strong wardresses pushed her down on her back in bed and held her by her ankles, knees, hips, elbows, and shoulders.

A doctor entered her room and attempted unsuccessfully to open her mouth. He then tried to push a steel gag through a gap between her teeth, making her gums bleed. Next, two doctors thrust a pointed steel instrument between her jaws, which were forced open by the turn of a screw, and forced a tube down her throat. While Sylvia panted and heaved, she tried to move her head away. She was almost unconscious when they poured the broth into her throat. As soon as the tube was withdrawn, she vomited. She said: "They left me on the bed exhausted, gasping for breath, and sobbing convulsively." The women were subjected to this treatment twice a day.

Women began to die for their beliefs in the women's cause. In December 1910, Celia Haig, a sturdy, healthy woman, died of a painful illness from injuries incurred when she was assaulted at a public gathering. Mary Clarke, Emmeline Pankhurst's sister, died of a stroke after being released from prison "too frail to weather this rude tide of militant struggle." Henria Williams, who had a weak heart, died in January 1911 from injuries suffered during a rally.

Early in 1912, Emmeline broke several windows at the Prime Minister's residence at 10 Downing Street. She went to jail for two months with 218 other women. In March 1912, the police raided WSPU headquarters and arrested Emmeline and Frederick Pethick-Lawrence. Christabel had recently moved into an apartment and wasn't at Clements Inn when the police arrived. It was obvious to Christabel that the "ringleaders" were being rounded up. She fled to France so that the movement's leaders weren't all in jail. Annie Kenney became her link with Clements Inn.

Frederick and the two Emmelines were sent to prison for seven months in the Second Division. Emmeline Pankhurst refused to be treated as she had been on her first trip to prison. Sylvia described the scene: "Mrs. Pankhurst, ill from fasting and suspense, grasped the earthen toilet ewer and threatened to fling it at the doctors and wardresses, who appeared with the feeding tube. They withdrew and the order for her release was issued the next day." Emmeline Pethick-Lawrence was forcibly fed once, and her husband for five days; they, too, were released early.

The militant wing of the Movement began to set fire to buildings. Sylvia suspected that Christabel was behind this phase of their effort. They burned down churches, historic places, and empty buildings. They tried to set fire to Nuneham House, the home of Lewis Harcourt, an anti-suffragist Minister. Mary Leigh and Gladys Evans attempted to burn down the Royal Theatre in Dublin, where Herbert Asquith was scheduled to speak.

Christabel's mother convinced her that increased militancy was the direction in which they should move. This caused a rift with the Pethick-Lawrences, who preferred a more moderate approach. When they returned from a trip to Canada, the couple who had contributed so much effort and money to the campaign found that they had been frozen out of the leadership.

Frederick Pethick-Lawrence commented on their falling out in unselfish terms. "Thus ended our personal association with two of the most remarkable women I have ever known.... They cannot be judged by ordinary standards of conduct; and those who run up against them must not complain of the treatment they receive." He realized that the Pankhursts shared a common characteristic: "their absolute refusal to be deflected by criticism or appeal one hair's breadth from the course they had determined to pursue."

Emmeline Pethick-Lawrence didn't accept the split with the Pankhursts as easily as her husband did. She observed, "There was something quite ruthless about Mrs. Pankhurst and Christabel where human relationships were concerned." The couple recognized Christabel's intelligence and political acumen as well as her appeal to young men and young women. They also appreciated Mrs. Pankhurst's ability to move an audience with her appeals to their emotions by modulating her voice.

The level of destruction caused by the suffragettes stepped up as they became increasingly frustrated with the delay in obtaining the vote. It included:

- widespread burning with acid of the message "votes for women" on golf greens
- cutting telephone wires
- burning of boathouses and sports pavilions, including the grandstand at Ayr racecourse
- slashing of thirteen paintings at the Manchester Art Gallery and the Rokeby *Venus* at the National Gallery
- destroying with a bomb a home being built for Lloyd George
- smashing the glass orchid house at Kew Gardens
- breaking a jewel case in the Tower of London
- burning three Scottish castles and the Carnegie Library in Birmingham
- flooding the organ in Albert Hall
- exploding a bomb in Westminster Abbey

Emmeline Pankhurst was charged with "counseling and procuring" the blowing up of the house being constructed for Lloyd George at Walton-on-the-Hill. That bombing was done by Emily Wilding Davison, one of the most impulsive suffragettes. To protest not being granted the vote, Davison waited at the turn at Tattenham Corner and committed suicide by throwing herself under the King's horse at the Derby. During her imprisonment, Emmeline Pankhurst experienced a new government tactic, implementation of the Prisoners Temporary Discharge Bill—the "Cat and Mouse Act." Prisoners who refused to eat would be released when their health began to be affected, and then imprisoned again when they were at least partially recovered. Mrs. Pankhurst was released nine times after hunger and thirst strikes, only to be returned to prison.

The militancy of the movement in England ceased with the outbreak of World War I. Christabel moved back to England, confident that the government would have more on its mind than pursuing her. She announced, "This was national militancy. As suffragettes we could not be pacifists at any price. We offered our service to the country and called upon all our members to do likewise."

Christabel supported Asquith in the war effort as fervently as she had opposed him prior to the war.

In August 1916, Asquith surprised the House of Commons by declaring that if the voting franchise were expanded, women had an "unanswerable" case for being offered the vote. He observed that "during this war the women of this country have rendered as effective a service in the prosecution of the war as any other class of the community."

In February 1917, a committee recommended that the vote be granted to all men over twenty-one and women over thirty who were university graduates or local government electors (owners or tenant householders), or the wives of both. Sylvia was upset by this discrimination. The bill was extended to the wives of all voters and became law in January 1918. Eight and a half million women were enfranchised. Ten years later, the remaining political limitations on women were removed.

Emmeline Pankhurst died in June 1928, a month before her seventieth birthday. Christabel wrote, "The House of Lords passed the final measure of Votes for Women in the hour her body, which had suffered so much for that cause, was laid in the grave. She, who had come to them in their need, had stayed with the women as long as they might still need her, and then she went away."

Christabel became a Second Adventist and in 1936 was made a Dame Commander of the British Empire for "public and social services." She moved to the United States and died in Santa Monica, California, in 1958. Sylvia was involved in the Bolshevik Revolution after World War I and later moved to Ethiopia. She died in Addis Ababa in 1960. The Emperor attended her funeral.

The Pankhursts were a family of achievers. Perhaps the characteristic that led to their many accomplishments was best summarized by Frederick and Emmeline Pethick-Lawrence: "Their absolute refusal to be deflected by criticism or appeal one hair's breadth from the course they had determined to pursue... Men and women of destiny are like that."

LILLIAN GILBRETH (1878-1972) & *FRANK GILBRETH* (1868-1924) *Motion Study Pioneers*

"To state that it is in the field of human relationships that Lillian Gilbreth's personal contribution to management will endure is not to detract from her earlier work with her pioneer husband in motion study. That she was one of the pioneers, too, in building management securely into the field of ... engineering adds both strength and scope to her contribution. Engineering needed, for its own professional development, emphasis in the human factors in work."

Edna Yost, *Frank and Lillian Gilbreth*

The story of Lillian Gilbreth cannot be told without also telling the story of her husband, Frank Gilbreth. Lillian and Frank Gilbreth, management consultants and specialists in motion study, were classic examples of two halves that make up the whole, or, more accurately, perfect the whole. He was not college educated; she had a Ph.D in psychology. He began his working career as a bricklayer and moved into motion study from the trades.

Before they married, Frank told Lillian of his intention to teach her all facets of his construction business and of his consulting activities. Although her undergraduate and masters degrees were in liberal arts, she did not question his plan. She concentrated on the people side of their contracts and consulting work, thus compensating for one of his shortcomings.

Lillian and Frank Gilbreth, "efficiency experts," were an incredible team in scientific management, which ultimately became part of the field of industrial engineering. Frank's specialty was motion study, which he describes in the foreword of his 1911 book, *Motion Study, A Method for Increasing the Efficiency of the Workman:*

> The aim of motion study is to find and perpetuate the scheme of perfection. There are three stages in this study:
> 1. Discovering and classifying the best practice
> 2. Deducing the laws

3. Applying the laws to standardize practice either for the purpose of increasing output or decreasing the hours of labor, or both

Lillian's strength was the application of psychology to scientific management in optimizing the human factors, or the "people" component of their projects. Individually, Lillian and Frank were both missing part of the total package. Together, because they complemented each other extremely well, they provided the total package to their clients.

In the Introduction to Lillian's and Frank's 1917 book, *Applied Motion Study*, George Iles describes the authors:

> Frank B. Gilbreth is a versatile engineer, an untiring observer, an ingenious inventor, an economist to the tips of his fingers; first and chiefly, he is a man.... Every page [of this book] has taken form with the aid and counsel of Mrs. Gilbreth, whose *Psychology of Management* is a golden gift to industrial philosophy. And thus, by viewing their facts from two distinct angles we learn how vital phases of industrial economy present themselves to a man and to a woman who are among the acutest investigators of our time.

In the foreword of Edna Yost's book, *Frank and Lillian Gilbreth, Partners for Life*, A. A. Potter, Dean of Engineering at Purdue University, summarized the personal characteristics of the Gilbreths:

> The outstanding characteristics of Frank Bunker Gilbreth were: an alert and incisive mind; great ability to observe, analyze, synthesize, and correlate quickly and soundly; an insatiable intellectual curiosity and inquisitiveness; unbounded enthusiasm, zeal, courage, and determination; marked optimism, great vitality, deep foresight, and a most remarkable manner of inspiring others to accept his ideas.

54

> Lillian Moller Gilbreth, like her husband-partner, has an innate urge for the best and the first-rate, has unusual courage and optimism, loves people and work, has a talent for winning cooperation, and is a person of few antagonisms. Lillian Gilbreth not only won high recognition for her own contributions in motion study and applied psychology, but has preserved, enhanced, and increased the appreciation on the part of industry of the pioneering work of both Gilbreths in the field of management.

Frank Gilbreth was born on July 7, 1868 in Kendall's Mills, Maine, to Hiram and Martha Bunker Gilbreth. Young Frank was confident and willing to work hard. He wanted to earn money immediately — not in four years after graduating from college. Also, although his mother could afford to send him to college, he was not comfortable attending school while she worked. She was disappointed when he decided to skip college to learn the construction contracting business from the bottom up.

In July 1885, Frank joined the Thomas J. Whidden Company, contractors and builders, to learn the bricklaying trade. Shipbuilding was the only field that paid higher wages than the building trades. Because of its relatively high wages, construction attracted a higher grade of workmen than most of the other trades. Frank's first contacts were with these workers, and it influenced his attitude favorably toward his fellow workmen.

In his training for a supervisory job, Frank had the opportunity to learn other construction skills, such as carpentry, stone masonry, concrete work, roofing, tinsmithing, cast-iron work, and black-smithing. However, bricklaying was his specialty. He was promoted to assistant foreman within two and a half years and then to foreman. His goal was to be a partner in the business within ten years. Thomas Whidden had given him the impression that the goal was attainable.

In 1892, Frank patented a scaffold for bricklayers that used platforms resting on adjustable frames at three levels. In a later design, it was suspended from jacks. His scaffold kept the rising wall at the same height for the bricklayer, thus minimizing stooping and stretching to lay bricks. He submitted other patents, including one for the Gilbreth Waterproof Cellar to prevent leaky cellars due to the daily rising of the tide in the Boston area.

At the age of twenty-seven, Frank realized that becoming a partner of the Whidden Company in the short term was unlikely. Applications of his two inventions were not receiving the attention that they required, so he left Whidden to establish his own business. He supported his mother and his Aunt Kit; however, he had no reservations about starting out on his own. His first employees were J. W. Buzzell, a civil engineering graduate of Worcester Polytechnic Institute, who became his second in command, and Anne Bowley, who efficiently ran his office.

Frank's third invention was a portable concrete mixer that relied on gravity to move concrete through a trough. This mixer was effective on small construction jobs, and the invention generated income to use on other projects. It also sold well in England.

Frank traveled widely, but he had time for meeting and dating young women. He was full of energy and had a good sense of humor; he was a popular bachelor. His cousin, Minnie Bunker, arrived in Boston with three young women whom she was chaperoning on a trip to Europe. Lillian Moller was one of Minnie's responsibilities. Frank met his future bride and partner when he gave Minnie and her charges a sightseeing tour of Boston.

Lillian Evelyn Moller, the oldest surviving child of William and Annie Delger Moller, was born in Oakland, California, on May 24, 1878. Annie was never in strong health after her firstborn child died in infancy. Lillie learned the responsibilities of caring for children and maintaining a home at an early age. Although she was born into a well-to-do family, her personality was shaped by the responsibility that was thrust upon her in her youth.

Lillie's childhood was a happy one in a family steeped in discipline of the children. She earned good grades in school. In high school, she studied music with composer John Metcalfe and wrote poetry. She wanted to attend the University of California at Berkeley, but her father initially disapproved because he believed she would never have to support herself.

Finally, her father was willing to let her matriculate at Berkeley. Lillie majored in modern languages and philosophy and also enrolled in history, mathematics, and science courses. She performed in student-produced plays in college and surprised herself with her confidence on the stage. She earned a Phi Beta Kappa key and was selected as the first woman Commencement Day speaker at the University.

Lillie earned an M.A. at Berkeley and planned to continue with courses leading to a Ph.D degree. The summer she received her M.A. degree was reserved for the planned trip to Europe with Minnie Bunker. The four women visited New York and Boston before boarding their ship bound for Europe. Frank gave the young women from California a grand tour of Boston in his new Winton-six motorcar. He included many new buildings on his tour, and his conversation was sprinkled with observations such as "ready for occupancy forty-nine days after the contract was signed."

The Winton's engine quit on the trip, and Frank was confronted with a gathering of children taunting him about his shiny, new car that would not run. Lillie was impressed with Frank's smiling, unruffled response to their teasing. Lillie kept the children's attention with stories while Frank obtained help fixing the car. He was impressed with Lillie's ability to keep the children occupied.

Frank suggested that she use her literary background to help him write about his many experiences in the construction business. It was obvious to both of them that they were on the same wavelength. They knew that they would see each other again when Lillie returned from Europe.

1903 was an important year in Frank's personal life and his business life. The fields of management and industrial engineering were not well-defined at the time. Frederick W. Taylor presented his classic paper number 1003, "Shop Management," to the American Society of Mechanical Engineers that year. Taylor's specialty was time study, but the field became known generically as scientific management.

When Lillian returned from Europe, Frank met the ship and was introduced to her parents, who were impressed with him. He spent the Christmas holidays with Lillian and her family in Oakland. When he proposed to her, he made it clear that he expected her to participate in his business activities, and that his mother and his Aunt Kit would live with them after they were married. Although they were engaged for ten months, Frank and Lillian spent only six days together between her return from Europe and their marriage in the Moller home in California on October 19, 1904.

Frank agreed with Lillian's continuing her work on a doctorate, but he suggested that she change her minor in psychology to her major. He recognized the future importance of the application of psychology in industry.

Lillian realized very early in their marriage that she had signed up for both a marital and a business partnership for life. Frank immediately began to educate her about his business. He started by saying: "First I want to teach you about concrete and masonry. 'Bond' is the term we use to express the relationship of joints in masonry." Then he made a sketch so that she could understand the concept clearly.

Lillian had some adjustments to make. She was brought up in a sufficiently wealthy family that women were not expected to have a job. Frank had the reverse experience. His mother supported the family when his father died, and the wife of one of his fellow contractors ran her own contracting firm and even competed for contracts with her husband.

Frank's mother, Martha, was in charge of the household, and he was frequently away on business trips. It was difficult for Lillian not to be mistress in her own home, but she had the personality to deal with it. Both Frank and Lillian wanted a large family, but she was surprised to hear that he wanted twelve children. She was not dismayed by this; Lillian was the oldest of nine children. Her background of playing second fiddle to her attractive, personable younger sister and her fears as a young woman that she was not attractive to men probably helped her adapt to life with her strong-willed husband.

In addition to pursuing demanding careers, Lillian and Frank had twelve children, one of whom died in childhood. In 1948, two of their children, Frank Gilbreth, Jr. and Ernestine Gilbreth Carey, published the story of their family in *Cheaper by the Dozen,* which was made into a movie.

Frank was accused by his friends as having more children than he could keep track of. In one of the family stories, Lillian was out of town giving a lecture and left Frank in charge of their brood. When she returned, she asked him how everything had gone in her absence. He responded, "Did not have any trouble except with that one over there, but a spanking brought him into line." Lillian pointed out, "That is not one of ours, dear; he belongs next door."

No one in the family remembers this actually happening. They attribute it to the fact that the only thing Frank liked more than telling a story about Lillian was telling one about himself. However, the children remembered that two redheaded children lived next door, and all of the Gilbreth children were either redheads or blondes.

Frank applied his motion study concepts at home as well as on his construction projects. He buttoned his vest from the bottom up because it took only three seconds; from the top down took seven seconds. He installed process charts in the bathrooms for the children to initial in the morning after they had brushed their teeth, taken a bath, combed their hair, and made their bed. At night, the children initialed a work sheet after they had weighed themselves, completed their homework, washed their hands and face, and brushed their teeth. It was regimentation, but Frank thought that discipline was important in shepherding twelve offspring through their day.

Lillian was a quick study in the construction business. Sometimes her opinions differed from his, particularly on the people side of the business. He thought that workmen always wanted to do what he thought they should do; she realized that this was not always true.

Their work became a joint effort that was not divided into her contribution and his contribution; it was their effort. The contracting and construction aspects of the business did not really appeal to her. The people side of the business interested her, and she was a vital contributor in documenting her husband's thoughts on management—the planning of work and the efficient accomplishment of projects.

Their business grew substantially. They had construction sites around the country, including many on the West Coast. As their family grew, Frank disliked being away from home frequently. He conveyed these thoughts to Lillian in many "Dear Chum" letters.

In December 1907, Frank met Frederick Taylor, the "Father of Scientific Management." Taylor concentrated on time study, and Frank specialized in motion study. Frank thought that if a job were done in its most efficient way, the time that it took would be at a minimum. Later, the two specialties would merge into time and motion study.

Taylor, who was ten years older than Frank, became Chief Engineer for the Midvale Steel Company in the 1880s. He had an imaginative and probing mind. While others worked to improve the technology of producing steel, Taylor concentrated on making the workers who produced the steel more efficient.

Management training at the time was accomplished by apprenticeship programs. Taylor was the first to apply the inductive method to the challenges of managing a factory. His initial emphasis on time study was a means of reducing the pay of nonproducers. Eventually, he applied the inductive method to both the administration and the operation of a factory. He divided work into two distinct functions, planning and execution; also, he set finite, standardized tasks for all workers to allow the application of a bonus or a penalty to each worker's pay.

One of the differences in the outlooks of Taylor and Frank was their viewpoint about unions. Taylor had had mainly negative experiences with unions of lower skilled workers; Frank had experienced principally positive experiences with unions of higher skilled workmen. A shortcoming of Taylor's landmark paper, "Shop Management," is that he advocated time study of existing methods. He did not stress the improvement of those methods. Doing tasks more efficiently was the goal of Frank's motion study approach.

Although Lillian had three babies in the first three years of their marriage, she worked actively in the business, including climbing scaffolds when necessary. Frank's influential book, *Bricklaying System*, was published in 1909, one year after he published *Concrete Construction*. In 1911, he published *Motion Study: A Method for Increasing the Efficiency of the Workman*. Lillian's help was vital to Frank in compiling and editing his thoughts in preparing the books for publication.

Lillian observed that Frank had a good relationship with his workers and informally was using the little-understood principles of psychology as they existed at the time. She suggested combining these principles of psychology with the practice of management. Frank considered her "a very remarkable woman," who had moved from being his student / assistant to his junior partner and was moving up to even greater responsibility.

In 1911, Frederick Taylor published his seminal work, *The Principles of Scientific Management*. Although Taylor gave credit to others who contributed to the development of his principles, it was becoming apparent that he was not going to credit Frank as a contributor to the subject of motion study.

In his book and in a paper published in *Engineering* in London that was reprinted in the *American Society of Mechanical Engineering Transactions*, Taylor observed that "motion study has been going on in the United States with increasing volume." Taylor also observed that his colleague in time study, Sanford Thompson, was "perhaps the most experienced man in motion study and time study in the country."

In 1912, a difficult year for Frank and Lillian, the Gilbreth business was operating under financial stress because Frank did not want to apply for additional loans and be controlled by bankers. Also that year, the two oldest daughters, Anne and Mary, contracted diphtheria at school. Six-year-old Anne was able to fight off the disease, but her younger sister succumbed. Mary's death devastated Frank and Lillian. After her death, both parents had difficulty talking about the loss of their daughter.

When she recovered from this blow, Lillian completed her doctoral dissertation, "The Psychology of Management," at the University of California at Berkeley. The University approved her dissertation, but required her to complete an additional year of resident study before awarding her Ph.D.

Lillian and Frank had the dissertation published serially in the periodical *Industrial Engineering*. In 1914, Sturgis and Walton published it in book form—by L. M. Gilbreth as cited in *Industrial Engineering*. If the fact that the author was a woman was known, it was not publicized. When Frank was asked if L. M. Gilbreth was related to him, he responded, "Only by marriage."

Frank's next construction project was in Providence, Rhode Island, home of Brown University. Brown offered a Ph.D program in Applied Management that fit Lillian's needs precisely. She was now a full partner with Frank in developing scientific motion study methods. The move to Providence had the additional benefit of getting the children away from their home in Montclair, New Jersey, where their sister Mary had died.

With six children at home, the Gilbreths had to establish a regimen that permitted Lillian to complete her studies while Frank spent long hours on his construction projects. They hired a housekeeper, a handyman, and a Pembroke College student who served as an au pair girl for the children. Frank's mother was in her late seventies but was in excellent health and helped with the household duties.

At Brown University, Lillian continued to develop the concept of micro-motion techniques and also studied the elimination of fatigue. Fatigue in the workplace was mental as well as physical, and she sought ways of combining the psychological aspects with the concept of motion study. Both Lillian and Frank participated in a series of summer programs at Brown. Frank undertook assignments with companies in Europe, and he was returning from one of those jobs when Lillian received her Ph.D from Brown University. The Gilbreths moved back to Montclair, New Jersey, after Lillian finished her studies.

In the United States, Frank and Lillian applied their motion study techniques at companies such as Cluett Peabody, Pierce Arrow, U.S. Rubber, and Eastman Kodak. Lillian usually accompanied Frank on the first plant visit for their projects when they were sizing up the task ahead. Gilbreth Associates had managers capable of directing projects, including their first employee, J. W. Buzzell; however, Lillian was Frank's only partner. In his letters to her at this time, his salutation had evolved from "Dear Chum" to "Dear Boss."

The Gilbreths believed that a maximum of seventeen elements were required to complete a motion cycle:

• Search	• Dissemble	• Wait, unavoidably
• Find	• Inspect	• Wait, avoidably
• Select	• Transport, loaded	• Rest, necessary for
• Grasp	• Pre-position for	overcoming fatigue
• Position	next operation	• Plan
• Assemble	• Release load	
• Use	• Transport, empty	

In the spring of 1921, an honorary membership in the Society of Industrial Engineers was awarded to Lillian in Milwaukee. For the first time in his life, words failed Frank. He was so happy for her that no words came out when he was called upon to speak. The resulting applause rescued him. She claimed that the honorary membership was due to Frank's overstressing her contributions, but her own book, *Psychology of Management*, was highly regarded and frequently quoted.

In 1924, the Gilbreths planned to attend the World Power Conference in London and the International Management Congress in Prague. Early one morning, Frank prepared to go to Manhattan to have their passports renewed. He called from the railroad station in Montclair to tell Lillian that he had forgotten to bring the passports with him. She left the telephone to look for them and when she returned, there was no one on the line. The police asked a neighbor to come to her house and tell her that Frank had dropped dead in the telephone booth.

Lillian and the family were heartbroken. They were a close-knit family, and all of the children revered their father. According to his wishes, he had a simple funeral service with no music or flowers. Several days later, Lillian sailed for Europe as Frank would have advised her to do. She attended the World Power Conference in London and then traveled to Prague for the International Management Congress. She read the paper that they had prepared for Frank to read in Prague, chaired the session at which he was scheduled to preside, and was made an honorary member of the Masaryk Academy in his place. She controlled her emotions with difficulty as members of the Congress paid many tributes to her husband.

When she returned home, she consulted with the eleven Gilbreth children about their future. Frank and Lillian had placed a priority on college education for all of the children, and she intended to honor that plan. Lillian's mother invited her and the children to move in with her and to take advantage of the California educational system. However, consulting opportunities for Lillian were greater on the East Coast, where she was better known.

Lillian listed her goals for the future:

- Provide a home, a living, and love for the family.
- Maintain Frank's work. Teach his ideals and techniques to younger people who would keep them alive and progressing.
- Push forward cooperative research projects in the areas of his interests, especially the motion study aspects of problems affecting the health and efficiency of human beings in industry.

Her first project was a request from Johnson & Johnson to establish a facility to train employees in motion study techniques. This task meshed with an activity that she and Frank had already planned. She continued Frank's ongoing projects and began work on a new assignment for R. H. Macy and Company. When she had spent the insurance money and the money received from selling their car, she had to borrow from her mother to help pay for living and school expenses. All of these loans were eventually repaid in full.

Lillian faced significant challenges. At the age of forty-six, she had to venture out on her own without the backing and advice of her strong-willed husband. However, Lillian had inner strengths that she drew upon. She needed these strengths at a time when women were not universally accepted in industry.

Initially, she was faced with providing the necessary discipline for her teenage children, particularly her sons. Then she had to cope with providing for forty-four years of college education, four years for each of her eleven children. In time their eleven bachelors degrees included three from the University of Michigan and two from Smith College.

In October 1930, with the country struggling with the Great Depression, Lillian was asked to head the women's unit of the President's Emergency Committee for Employment. She devised a plan to use women's clubs and other national organizations to conduct job surveys and to determine how to use the unemployed.

The Chairman of the Committee for Employment credited Lillian with "conceiving a new method to apply to an old evil ... a brilliant conception and carried through with speed and skill."

Following her success with this program, she was asked to serve with the President's Organization on Unemployment Relief.

In 1935, Lillian was invited by President Elliott of Purdue University and Dean Potter of its Engineering School to join the Purdue faculty. They offered her an appointment as Professor of Management that allowed her time for outside consulting. This appointment provided her with the opportunity to pass on the principles of motion study to younger people and gave her more employment stability than consulting provided during the Depression.

Initially, she was required to be away from Montclair, where her younger children were still in school, for three weeks out of every four. Her Purdue experience was very rewarding for her; she retained her appointment there until her retirement in 1948. Lillian remained in good health as she grew older. She followed the physical exercise program that Frank had devised for her to use after the births of their children.

In 1931, Lillian was awarded the first Gilbreth Medal by the Society of Industrial Engineering "for distinguished contribution to management." She received many honors, including an honorary Master of Engineering degree from the University of Michigan and an appointment as the only woman delegate to the World Engineering Congress in Tokyo.

One of her greatest honors was awarded at an annual joint meeting of the American Society of Mechanical Engineers and the American Management Association: "To Dr. Lillian Moller Gilbreth, and to Dr. Frank B. Gilbreth posthumously ... the 1944 Gantt Medal, in recognition of their pioneer work in management and their development of the principles and techniques of motion study." Lillian was considered the First Lady of Engineering in her later years.

BETTY COMDEN (1917-2006) & *ADOLPH GREEN* (1914-2002) *Songwriters / Playwrights*

"Perhaps the greatest wonder is the joint career of Betty Comden and Adolph Green, merry-andrews and collaborators extraordinary. For twenty-two years, Comden and Green have amicably and successfully collaborated as performers with other performers; as lyricists with several different composers, choreographers, and librettists; as librettists with a half-dozen directors and producers, as authors with a swarm of temperamental stars; and, needless to say, with each other. It is a record of harmony unique in the theater."

Peter Lyon in "The Antic Arts: Two Minds That Beat As One," *Holiday* magazine, December 30, 1961.

Betty Comden and Adolph Green collaborated on films, musicals, and revues for over fifty years. Neither wrote a libretto, lyric, or screenplay without the other. They thought as one person, and one was rarely mentioned without the other. In fact, they were treated as one person in their contracts. After over fifty years of collaboration, they had the ability to speak virtually as one person. One started a sentence, and the other finished it.

They seldom disagreed about their work. Their main personal difference was about being on time. Betty was always on time, and Adolph was usually late, although he became more punctual as he grew older. Betty was calm and under control, in contrast to Adolph, who was always restless and moving around. Betty had a vivid imagination, a strong sense of humor, and a sharp wit, which she rarely used to be unkind. Adolph, who also had a brilliant imagination, had an encyclopedic mind and a zany, unpredictable sense of humor. Their personal strengths were amazingly complementary. They accomplished together what they couldn't have done alone.

Betty Comden and Adolph Green are known as the prolific librettists / lyricists for many Broadway musicals, including *On the Town, Wonderful Town, Bells Are Ringing, Do Re Mi, Fade Out— Fade In, Hallelujah,* and *Applause.* They are also known for writing screenplays and lyrics for movies, including *On the Town, Singin' in the Rain,* and *The Band Wagon.* They were the recipients of the Writers Guild Award for *On the Town,* 1949; *Singin' in the*

Rain, 1952; and *Bells Are Ringing,* 1960.

Betty Comden and Adolph Green began their collaboration in the late 1930s. Their first joint effort was in preparing material for The Revuers, a quintet of comedians and singers with whom they performed at the Village Vanguard. They looked for material for their act and were told that they would have to pay royalties, which they couldn't afford. Betty and Adolph began to write all of the material for their acts, including music, lyrics, and skits.

Comden and Green worked every day, usually in Betty's apartment. Initially, Adolph described their methods: "Sometimes when you're on a project, you go all day and all evening. Sometimes you just work only a short time. It depends on what stage the project is in."

Betty said that "Adolph and I have lots of old, outdated references and phrases we have mutually piled up over the years. There is a kind of radar between us, knowing what the other is thinking based on stuff we have both read or shared."

In *Off Stage,* Betty describes Adolph: "The mythic character of my life, my partner, Adolph Green, it seems to me must have sprung full-blown from his own head. There is no other head quite capable of having done the job. Only his head has the antic, manic imagination and offbeat creative erudite plus childlike originality to conceive of such a person."

Comden and Green placed considerable emphasis on structure in writing the story for a musical or a screenplay. Adolph observed: "What we find most effective is structuring the book as much as we can before writing any songs. The more structure you have, the better off you are, and the more tightly the plot will mesh." They were extremely successful in incorporating the songs into the storyline, something that was not emphasized until they did it. Two of their early successes at doing this were *Singin' in the Rain* and *The Band Wagon.*

According to Betty: "That doesn't mean that you don't start working on the score before the book is written. People like Leonard Bernstein, Jule Styne, Cy Coleman are dramatists, and they always write for the theater, for situation and character. It's collaborative, flexible." Comden and Green remembered vividly the constantly changing approach used in creating *On the Town.* "Sometimes Leonard [Bernstein] had some melody that he decided should be used, and we put words to it. Other times we came with a full lyric, and he'd work on it. Still other times we'd have an idea and start working on it together. And we'd use patterns of other songs and start putting a few lines of lyric to them, just to get a start."

Comden and Green always used experiences from their own lives in their work. Early in their careers, they went to Hollywood, and the movie for which they were to write the screenplay was cancelled. They weren't able to find other work in Hollywood. Betty returned to New York first, and then Adolph returned because his mother was ill. Betty met him at Grand Central Station carrying a sign that read "The Adolph Green Fan Club" when he returned.

They used that idea in *The Band Wagon,* when Fred Astaire, playing an actor whose career was fading, walked slowly and dejectedly up the railroad station ramp singing "By Myself." He was met by two friends, played by Oscar Levant and Nanette Fabray, carrying "fan club" signs that cheered him up.

One of their hit songs was "Just in Time" from *Bells Are Ringing,* which starred Judy Holliday. Jule Styne wrote a simple melody for which no lyrics were written for several months. They referred to it as "Da-Da-Da." Finally, they found a situation in the storyline that provided them with the title, "Just In Time." Their creative process encompassed many variations on a theme. They were pragmatic. If it worked, they used it.

Another technique they employed was to listen to the audience. Betty observed: "You listen to what they're saying, not necessarily to the critics. We like the idea of going out of town. You have to listen to the audience, plus keep in mind what your own intention was."

On occasion, the collaborators encountered "second act trouble." Adolph commented on that phenomenon: "That's probably because the story isn't spreading itself out in inevitable fashion, which is what you strive for. Very often the problems are in the first act. The second act has to play off whatever you've set up in the first."

Because they were so successful, the impression is sometimes given that it was an easy road. Adolph described the creative process as "agony." He explained their way of generating an idea. "Just read, think, kick around things, meet every day and stare at each other and say no to something for a year, then suddenly say, 'Let's try it.' Sometimes other people you're involved with get enthusiasm and pull you along, and suddenly you say, 'Well, this can work.'"

Comden and Green always collaborated with each other. In careers that spanned over fifty-five years, neither of them worked with another collaborator. They were once asked if either of them had ever considered working on their own. They both quickly responded: "Never! Unthinkable!"

Betty summed up the reasons for their success:

> We write with humor about basically serious things. We like to think we're expressing something of ourselves, something of what we feel is important in the world today. At the same time, we try to help audiences feel the way they should when they leave the theater—that is, glad to be alive. That windows have been opened, fresh air has been let in, and they're leaving as happy people.

They certainly accomplished their goal of making people— thousands of people— happy. It is difficult to imagine what the world of the Broadway musical and musical films would be like without the contributions of Comden and Green.

Betty Comden was born Betty Cohen on May 3, 1917, in Brooklyn, New York, to Leo and Rebecca Sadvoransky Cohen. Her first acting experience came at the age of eleven when she was cast as Rebecca in Sir Walter Scott's *Ivanhoe* in the seventh grade at the Brooklyn Ethical Culture School. After graduating from Erasmus Hall High School, she majored in drama at New York University. She graduated with a B.S. degree in drama in 1938 and began acting in theater groups.

Adolph Green was born on December 2, 1914, in the Bronx, New York, to Daniel and Helen Weiss Green. In grammar school, he wrote poetry and acted in plays. He grew up loving music, and, although he did not receive formal training in music, he developed an encyclopedic musical memory. In 1934, he graduated from DeWitt Clinton High School and attended college, but he didn't complete the courses required for a degree. During the day, he worked as a runner on Wall Street and then as an installer for a carpet company; in the evenings, he participated in little theater groups.

Comden and Green met through a mutual friend while Betty was at New York University. Their paths crossed again while they were acting in the theater. Their first break came during the summer of 1938 when Judy Tuvim, later Judy Holliday, saw Green perform and was impressed with his energy and humor.

Holliday met Max Gordon, the proprietor of the Village Vanguard, and asked him to consider hiring a group that did songs and skits. Holliday asked Green if they could get a group together, and, when Green saw Comden at an audition, he asked her if she would be interested. They both knew an actor who was looking for a job, and five of them, including Judy Holliday, formed a group called "The Revuers."

Initially, each member of the group earned $5.00 for one show a week. They couldn't afford to pay royalties for outside material, so they wrote their own—skits, music, and lyrics. The five performers met to "brainstorm," and Betty recorded the ideas that were generated. When they identified a good idea, they improvised on it. It was a cooperative effort, and no one kept a record of who contributed what. Their shows were humorous, satirical skits about the social mores of the 1930s. Eventually, they did two shows, five nights a week. A favorable review by Dick Manson of the New York *Post* increased their audience significantly.

In November 1939, The Revuers performed at the Rainbow Room on the top floor of Rockefeller Plaza. They did their well-developed impersonations of Noel Coward, Joan Crawford, Queen Victoria, and Oscar Wilde, as well as sketches of Broadway, Hollywood, and the New York World's Fair. Patrons at the Rainbow Room were conservative, and what worked at the Village Vanguard didn't work there. They received respectable reviews, but they thought that they had "bombed."

In October 1940, The Revuers performed five times a day for three weeks at Radio City Music Hall. In December, they returned to the Village Vanguard. They were disappointed, because it seemed that they were back where they started. The following year they toured the country as far west as St. Louis.

In 1942, Irving Caesar, the lyricist who wrote "Swanee" and "Tea for Two" cast The Revuers in a musical called *My Dear Public*. The play had a short run in New York, so The Revuers returned to the nightclub circuit. They had a long engagement at the Blue Angel, Max Gordon's cabaret on the east side of Manhattan, and then went on a road tour, which included an engagement at the Blackstone Hotel in Chicago.

On January 4, 1942, Betty Comden married Siegfried Schutzman, who subsequently changed his name to Steven Kyle. He was an artist about to enter the U.S. Army. Later, they had two children; Susanna was born in 1949, and Alan was born in 1953. Their friend Leonard Bernstein wrote "Anniversary for Susanna Kyle" to celebrate the birth of their first child.

During the summer of 1942, The Revuers went to Los Angeles, where Hollywood agent Kurt Frings had obtained roles for them in the film version of the popular radio show, *Duffy's Tavern*. However, upon their arrival in Hollywood, they were told that the film had been cancelled.

The Revuers obtained an engagement at the Trocadero night club; they opened to rave reviews. Agents offered Judy Holliday movie contracts, but none of the other members of The Revuers received any offers. Holliday didn't want to accept a contract with Twentieth Century Fox unless the other members of The Revuers were included. Comden and Green told her that she would be foolish not to take the studio's offer.

On completion of their engagement at the Trocadero, Comden returned to New York, where her husband was on leave from the Army. She planned to return to Hollywood when Kyle's furlough was over, but Adolph called her to tell her that he was coming to New York to visit his mother who was ill. Temporarily, they were unemployed.

Comden and Green, without the rest of The Revuers, returned to perform at Max Gordon's Blue Angel in Manhattan. From this point onward in their careers, they continued to perform but became more creators than performers. In between performances at the Blue Angel, they were visited by Leonard Bernstein, Paul Feigay, and Oliver Smith. The three men were motivated by the success of the ballet, *Fancy Free,* which Bernstein and Jerome Robbins had presented with the Ballet Theatre.

Oliver Smith, who had designed the set for the ballet, and Paul Feigay wanted to produce a musical about three sailors on leave in New York; the ballet version had premiered at the Metropolitan Opera House on April 18, 1944, to rave reviews. They asked Betty and Adolph to write the script and the lyrics for the musical. During the summer that year, Comden and Green wrote the libretto and the lyrics while Bernstein wrote the music.

In the summer of 1937, Green had played the Pirate King in *The Pirates of Penzance* at Camp Onata, a boys' summer camp near Pittsfield, Massachusetts. The music counselor that summer was a young Harvard music student, Leonard Bernstein. Bernstein sat down at the piano and played a practical joke on Green. He mentioned that he was going to play a Shostakovich prelude. Green asked, "Which one?" Bernstein responded, "This one," but instead he played a series of dissonances. Green told him that it wasn't any of Shostakovich's preludes. Bernstein laughed; he had played the trick many times before, and the listeners always had claimed to recognize the music.

They both possessed a knowledge of music and a sense of humor, and they became close friends. Bernstein's younger brother, Burton, wrote that Green was "capable of performing—a capella and with every orchestral instrument outrageously imitated—just about any symphonic work, classical or modern, down to the last cymbal crash."

In June 1939, Leonard Bernstein graduated from Harvard University and moved to New York to look for a job. He shared an apartment in Greenwich Village with Green and occasionally filled in as the pianist for The Revuers. Frequently, Bernstein played the piano at the parties that he and Green attended. At one of these parties, Betty Comden met Bernstein. She went home, awakened her mother from a sound sleep, and told her, "I met a real genius tonight."

Bernstein discussed his future with Dimitri Mitropoulos, who told him that he had all the necessary skills to be a conductor. Bernstein applied to the Julliard School in September but was told that no more applications were being accepted. He enrolled at the Curtis Institute in Philadelphia and was on his way to becoming famous.

In 1942, The Revuers were cast in a musical called *My Dear*

Public, which played in Philadelphia before opening in New York. Leonard Bernstein had completed his conductor training at the Curtis Institute but was unable to find a steady job so he hung out with the cast of *My Dear Public.* Bernstein impressed Irving Caesar, who had done the casting for the play. He compared the young man to George Gershwin. Caesar found Bernstein a job in New York making piano arrangements for a music publishing company.

The following year, Artur Rodzinski was appointed conductor of the New York Philharmonic and appointed Bernstein his assistant. On November 14, 1943, Bruno Walter, the guest conductor, was ill, and Maestro Rodzinski was snowed in at his Stockbridge farm. Twenty-five-year-old Bernstein conducted the New York Philharmonic that evening and made the most of the opportunity. The performance was broadcast nationally on radio, and Bernstein woke up the next morning a famous man. However, he and Comden and Green continued to collaborate on musicals.

In June 1944, Bernstein entered the hospital to have an operation for a deviated septum to relieve his chronic sinus problems. At the same time, Adolph had his enlarged tonsils removed. They were operated on the same day by the same doctor and shared a hospital room, so that they could continue to work on the musical, *On the Town.* As they recuperated, Betty worked with them in their room. When friends visited they became a bit rowdy, which irritated the hospital staff. One nurse upset by Bernstein's antics commented, "He may be God's gift to music, but I'd hate to tell you where he gives me a pain."

In August, Bernstein accompanied the Ballet Theatre to California to conduct *Fancy Free.* He composed the music for *On the Town* en route and while he was in California. He wrote the first major number, "New York, New York," as the train sped across the flat farmland of Nebraska. *On the Town* was completed that autumn and opened at the Adelphi Theatre on December 28, 1944. Critics praised the book by the young writing team, Comden and Green, and called the work "fresh." In particular, they liked the integration of the storyline with the choreography and the songs. Comden and Green maintained their friendship and collaboration with Leonard Bernstein over the years.

Comden and Green wrote lively parts for themselves into the

73

script of *On the Town*. They had to audition, but they were chosen for the parts. Adolph was one of the three sailors, Ozzie, and Betty played Claire de Loone, an anthropologist. Claire is fascinated by Ozzie because, in her opinion, his appearance is that of a prehistoric man. The storyline is about three sailors pursuing "Miss Turnstiles," whose picture they had seen on a poster in a subway train. The success of the musical was virtually assured when George Abbott agreed to direct the play. He was the only one of the creators of the musical who was over thirty years old.

The team that created *On the Town*, except Bernstein, who was not available, immediately started work on another musical. Morton Gould wrote the music for *Billion Dollar Baby*, which opened at the Alvin Theatre on December 21, 1945. The musical, which starred Joan McCracken, was about the roaring twenties. It was only moderately successful, but Comden and Green now had two successful plays to their credit. They wanted to return to Hollywood to work on a film.

Metro-Goldwyn-Mayer gave them an offer to write a screenplay based on the Broadway musical about college life, *Good News,* working with the producer Arthur Freed. Initially, Comden and Green weren't enthusiastic about the project, which was a revision of a 1930 film. They wrote a new screenplay that incorporated most of the songs from the original script. However, they added to the original lyrics and wrote a catchy song, "The French Lesson," about the subject that the football hero was flunking. June Allyson, Peter Lawford, and Joan McCracken starred in the film. *Good News* was considered the best college-theme musical produced in the 1940s.

Comden's and Green's second screenplay was *The Barkleys of Broadway,* starring Fred Astaire and Ginger Rogers. It was about a married couple, an acting and dancing team, who danced well together but whose off-stage relationship was stormy. It was one of the top-rated films of 1949, and it received a nomination for a Screenwriters Guild Award.

Comden's and Green's next Hollywood project was to write the lyrics for four songs for *Take Me Out to the Ball Game,* starring Gene Kelly and Frank Sinatra. The story was written by Gene Kelly and his assistant and friend, Stanley Donen. Gene Kelly was one of the few people in Hollywood that Betty and Adolph knew when they moved west. They had met Kelly in 1939 when they had performed at the Westport Country Playhouse. *Take Me Out to the Ball Game,* which was released in 1949, was another successful movie.

Comden's and Green's greatest success in 1949 was the movie made from their Broadway musical, *On The Town,* which was co-directed by Gene Kelly and Stanley Donen. The producer, Arthur Freed, considered Bernstein's music too avant-garde, so he asked Roger Edens to write the music and Comden and Green to write the lyrics for eight new songs.

Only four songs of Bernstein's original Broadway score were used in the film. The three sailors on the town were played by Gene Kelly, Frank Sinatra, and Jules Munshin, the same trio from *Take Me Out to the Ball Game. On The Town,* which premiered at Radio City Music Hall on December 30, 1949, earned Comden and Green a Screenwriters Guild Award.

In 1951, Comden and Green received an urgent call from Metro-Goldwyn-Mayer to return to Hollywood to write an original story, screenplay, and lyrics for a new musical film. The screenplay was about the transition from silent movies to the talkies. The lead character, who began his career in vaudeville, was to be shown making the successful transition from silent films.

They were to work for producer Arthur Freed in the Thalberg Administration Building. At their first meeting with Freed, they were told that they had been assigned to write the story and screenplay, but that the songs used would be ones already written by lyricist Arthur Freed (the producer) and composer Nacio Herb Brown. The movie was to be called *Singin' in the Rain.*

Comden and Green erupted. They had been told that they were to write the lyrics, and, furthermore, their previous agent had told them that their contract stated that they were to create the lyrics unless the music was written by Irving Berlin, Cole Porter, or Richard Rodgers and Oscar Hammerstein. They stomped off the job and threatened to return to New York. They accused Freed of breaking his promises; the strained relations continued for two weeks.

Finally, their new agent, Irving Lazar, suggested that they read their contract. The clause about Berlin, Porter, and Rodgers and Hammerstein wasn't there. Lazar told them "anyone can write lyrics for your picture: Berlin, Porter, Rodgers and Hammerstein,

Freed, Karloff, Lugosi, Johnny Weissmuller—you name it. My suggestion is you write 'Singin' in the Rain' at the top of a page, followed by 'Fade-in,' and don't stop until you come to 'That's All, Folks.'"

Roger Edens, the associate producer and music director, played the songs as the collaborators searched for a storyline. Initially, they had difficulty coming up with a usable plot. For example, the song, "The Wedding of the Painted Doll," might have suggested a story about a painted doll who got married. Many of the songs are now well-known, including "Broadway Melody," "Fit as a Fiddle," "You Were Meant for Me," and the title song, "Singin' in the Rain." The only song in the movie for which Comden and Green wrote the lyrics was "Moses Supposes His Toes-es Are Roses."

They also had difficulty deciding on the time period in which the movie should be set. Many of these songs had been written between 1929 and 1931 for the first musical movies made. Instead of placing the story in contemporary times or a period like the gay nineties, they decided to use the time during which the songs were written.

Knowing who would play the lead was important, because that would affect the storyline. Initially, Howard Keel was considered for the role. Freed wanted Gene Kelly for the starring role, but Kelly was busy filming *An American in Paris*. Because of the delays in getting started on the story and screenplay, Gene Kelly became available. Kelly was so enthusiastic about the plans for *Singin' in the Rain* that he agreed to co-direct the film with Stanley Donen.

After the first month of planning the screenplay, Comden and Green had three possible openings:

- the premiére of an important silent movie in New York
- an action sequence from the silent movie being pre-miéred in New York, with the star meeting a girl in New York, losing her, and returning to Hollywood
- an interview for a magazine, with the star in Hollywood relating a fantasized life story.

Comden and Green couldn't decide which opening to use. The work just wasn't moving along smoothly; they were depressed.

They seriously considered returning the money that MGM had given them, packing up, and returning to Manhattan.

About that time, Betty's husband, Steve Kyle, arrived from New York. He wasn't surprised to see them slumped over in near despair. He had seen them this way before on earlier projects that weren't going well. Steve wasn't a writer; he was an artist with a successful merchandising business. However, they frequently used him as a sounding board, and he had been a valuable source of ideas. He laughed when he read the material. They asked him which opening they should use; he suggested that they use all three openings. Steve's suggestion resulted in the realization that all of the action could take place on Hollywood Boulevard instead of on Fifth Avenue in New York. The final approval was given by Dore Schary, who had recently replaced L. B. Mayer as head of MGM.

Meetings began with Gene Kelly and Stanley Donen in which they applied their skills in integrating the various elements of the musical. Comden and Green realized that the success of the film would be to a large extent due to what they referred to as the "four-way mental radar" among them. Kelly and Donen were professionals who excelled at the execution of the performance while sustaining a light, carefree air.

They all knew from their first reading that the musical involved a scene that took place in the rain. What none of them realized was that "here Gene Kelly performs the most notable solo musical number of his career," or, in other words, "miracle happens here." The song, "The Wedding of the Painted Doll," was replaced with "Make 'Em Laugh," in which Donald O'Connor pulled out all the stops and did a classic, upbeat vaudeville / clown number.

Comden and Green returned to New York after completing the screenplay for *Singin' in the Rain* to write sketches and lyrics for *Two on the Aisle*. They were in Philadelphia, helping to whip that revue into shape prior to playing on Broadway, when they received an urgent call from Kelly and Donen. They were asked to drop everything and write a romantic scene in an empty sound stage where Kelly would sing one song and do one dance with Debbie Reynolds. This was to replace a lengthy love scene in which Kelly and Reynolds danced and did a medley of songs involving multiple sets.

Comden and Green unplugged themselves from a frantic effort

to finish *Two on the Aisle* and projected themselves back to the atmosphere of *Singin' in the Rain*. Their efforts clicked, and the movie was wildly successful. It is consistently rated as one of the ten best musical films; in one rating, it is considered to be third best. Critic Pauline Kael wrote: "This exuberant and malicious satire of Hollywood in the late twenties is perhaps the most enjoyable of all movie musicals—just about the best Hollywood musical of all time."

Comden and Green won their second Screenwriters Guild Award for the movie, which opened at Radio City Music Hall on March 27, 1952. The film on which the writers of the screenplay almost gave up and went home—not once, but twice—turned out to be one of the best ever.

After finally completing work on *Singin' in the Rain,* Comden and Green returned to New York to finish revising the skits and the lyrics for the revue *Two on the Aisle,* which starred Bert Lahr and Delores Gray. Lahr, a talented comedian, is remembered mainly for his role as the Cowardly Lion in *The Wizard of Oz*. Delores Gray, an accomplished singer and comedienne, had her first success starring in the role of Annie Oakley in *Annie Get Your Gun* in London. *Two on the Aisle* was the first of many musicals in which Comden and Green collaborated with composer Jule Styne.

Their next screenplay was *The Band Wagon,* which starred Fred Astaire and was directed by Vincent Minnelli. The movie was based on the 1931 Broadway revue starring Fred Astaire and his sister, Adele. It was about a film star whose career was fading being invited to New York by friends, a writing team much like Comden and Green, to star in a Broadway musical. The film, which received an Academy Award nomination, debuted at Radio City Music Hall in July 1953.

Comden's and Green's next musical, *Wonderful Town,* opened at the Winter Garden Theatre on February 25, 1953, to rave reviews. It was based on the 1940 play, *My Sister Eileen,* which, in turn, was based on Ruth McKenney's stories about herself and her lively sister in New York in the 1930s. Rosalind Russell starred as Ruth, as she had in the 1940 movie version.

Comden and Green were pleased to be working again with their friend, Leonard Bernstein, who wrote the music for the play. George Abbott directed the musical, which won a Tony Award for

Outstanding Musical of the Year. Rosalind Russell won the award for Outstanding Musical Actress and Comden and Green won a Donaldson Award for *Wonderful Town,* which played for 559 performances.

In May 1956, Comden and Green reviewed the first draft of *Bells Are Ringing* with Judy Holliday and enticed her to star in the play. The story was about a switchboard operator at an answering service who takes a personal interest in the service's customers. The music was written by Jule Styne, and the musical was directed by Jerome Robbins. It opened at the Shubert Theatre on November 29, 1956, and ran for 924 performances. Judy Holliday won a 1957 Tony Award for her role.

Phyllis Newman met Adolph Green when she was Judy Holliday's understudy in *Bells Are Ringing.* Adolph visited the theater frequently because he was a friend of both Judy Holliday and the leading man, Sydney Chaplin, the son of Charlie Chaplin. Phyllis was attracted to Adolph, but she was intimidated by "his age, his reputation as an intellectual, his success, and, most of all, by his mind-boggling eccentricity." In her book, *Just in Time,* Phyllis commented about Adolph: "He always looks suspicious and guilty, as though he has just done something he shouldn't have. He rarely looks you straight in the eye. He seems to be hiding something, but I have never found out what it is."

Adolph and Phyllis dated, and she was intimidated again—this time by his famous friends, such as Lauren Bacall and Leonard Bernstein. She realized that she was in love with Adolph after seeing him and Betty perform in *A Party With Betty Comden and Adolph Green* at the Westport Playhouse in Connecticut. Phyllis and Adolph were married on January 31, 1960.

Work on the film version of *Bells Are Ringing* began on October 6, 1959. Judy Holliday reprised her role as the switchboard operator; Vincent Minnelli directed. The movie opened at Radio City Music Hall on June 23, 1960. Betty and Adolph won their third Screenwriters Guild Award for the screenplay.

Also that year, Comden and Green wrote the lyrics for *Do Re Mi,* a musical based on the novella by Garson Kanin. Jule Styne wrote the music. Phil Silvers starred as Hubie Cram, a nobody with aspirations of fame and fortune. Comedienne Nancy Walker contributed a memorable performance as Mrs. Cram. The play opened on December 26,

1960, at the St. James Theatre and ran for over 400 performances. The song, "Make Someone Happy" by Comden, Green, and Styne, was the hit song from the musical.

Comden's and Green's hit of the 1970s was *Applause,* which opened at the Palace Theatre on March 30, 1970, with Lauren Bacall in the leading role. They wrote the book; the music was by Charles Strouse and the lyrics were by Lee Adams. When Bacall was asked by the producers about Comden and Green doing the book she hesitated because they were good friends, and she didn't want to mix friendship and career. She ultimately agreed because "they were so smart and funny, and talented."

Applause was based on the film *All About Eve,* which starred Anne Baxter and Bette Davis. The musical won the Tony Award for Best Musical in 1970, and Bacall won the Award for Best Actress in a Musical. Comden, Green, Adams, and Strouse all won Tony Awards that year. *Applause* ran for 840 performances on Broadway.

On March 17, 1980, Betty and Adolph were voted into the Songwriters Hall of Fame. In 1981, they were selected by drama critics and editors for entrance into the Theatre Hall of Fame. Requirements for membership are a Broadway career of at least twenty-five years and more than five major credits. They continued to write plays and lyrics into the 1990s, in addition to teaching at New York University's Tisch School of the Arts.

On May 29, 1991, Betty and Adolph were presented with the Johnny Mercer Award for Lifetime Achievement by the Songwriters Hall of Fame. On December 8, 1991, the collaborators were awarded the Kennedy Center Honors for Lifetime Achievement in the Performing Arts, a fine career capstone.

PALO ALTO RESEARCH CENTER   *Personal Computer Pioneers*

"The scientists at PARC created more than a personal computer. They designed, built, and used a complete system of hardware and software that fundamentally altered the nature of computing itself. Along the way, an impressive list of digital 'firsts' came out of PARC. In addition to the Alto computer, PARC inventors made the first graphics-oriented monitor, the first hand-held 'mouse' inputting device simple enough for a child, the first word processing program for inexpert users, the first local area communications network, the first object-oriented programming language, and the first laser printer."

Douglas K. Smith and Robert C. Alexander, *Fumbling the Future*

In 1973, over three years before Steve Wozniak of Apple Computer designed and built the Apple I, Xerox's Palo Alto Research Center (PARC) created the first computer dedicated to the use of one person. PARC did more than design and build a computer. Its developers introduced a comprehensive system of hardware and software that changed the environment of computing. PARC called their computer Alto and its environment "personal distributed computing": "personal" because it was designed for use by an individual and "distributed" because it was connected via a network to shared resources, such as printers and other computers.

PARC was unable to convince anyone within Xerox to exploit the technology. PARC was a development and research center, not a manufacturing and marketing organization. The technology languished. Xerox failed to capitalize on their dramatic developments. Apple Corporation promoted the technology and became associated with the introduction of the personal computer. After Apple's initial success, Xerox introduced the Star computer, which was too late and too expensive. Xerox had missed the opportunity.

Xerox established PARC in 1970 as part of the company's plan to acquire or develop digital capability. IBM was entering the copier business, and Xerox knew that they had to expand into the computer business to remain competitive. However, Xerox didn't plan to take on IBM in large mainframe computers. Their goal was to fight it out with IBM in developing products for the "office of the future." In other words, they would develop and market equipment and systems to be used by managers and secretaries as well as by production and sales personnel.

Peter McColough, who had succeeded founder Joe Wilson as CEO of Xerox in 1968, decided to buy and expand an existing computer company rather than form a start-up. He approached Control Data Corporation, Digital Equipment Corporation, and the Burroughs Corporation, but no mutually beneficial agreements could be reached. In 1969, Xerox paid $900 million for Scientific Data Systems (SDS), a California-based company that had sales of $100 million in the previous year. Most of the SDS customers were in technical computing, but McColough planned to reorient his new acquisition to commercial computing markets.

SDS had no independent development laboratory. Jack Goldman, who succeeded John Dessauer as director of research at Xerox in 1968, recommended to McColough that Xerox establish a digital research and development center. McColough approved the request, and a talented team of scientists and engineers was assembled at Palo Alto to provide Xerox with future-oriented digital capability. Goldman chose George Pake, a well-regarded physicist with experience in both academia and industry, to establish and manage the new center.

Both Goldman and Pake believed in hiring highly capable people and then following a "bottom up" rather than a "top down" approach to research. Overall goals were conveyed to the researchers, but it was left up to them to tell their managers what they had to do to accomplish them. After all, development of the "architecture of information" involved in moving to the "office of the future" wasn't immediately obvious to high-level managers.

Pake divided the lab into three components:

- The General Science Laboratory (GSL)—conducted research in physics and other basic sciences
- The Systems Science Laboratory (SSL)—was responsible for broad "systems" research in engineering, information, mathematics, operations, and statistics
- The Computer Science Laboratory (CSL)—focused on computer systems

Pake managed the GSL in addition to the laboratory as a whole. Bill Gunning, who had twenty years of computer science experience, was appointed to manage SSL. Jerry Elkind was selected to head CSL. Elkind had worked for NASA and for the computer consultant that designed ARPANet, the first nationwide computer communications network, for the Advanced Research Projects Administration (ARPA) of the Department of Defense. Bob Taylor, who had served as ARPA's chief administrator of computer funding, was named associate director of CSL.

With the high cost of mainframe computers and minicomputers that cost over $100,000, time-sharing was a popular tool. Many users at different terminals were connected to one central computer and shared its use.

Computers were considered fast and people were considered slow, so this was viewed as a good arrangement. However, it caused many computer scientists to work odd hours, such as the middle of the night, to gain access to the central computer. Developers' schedules were slaves to the computer's schedule. As the cost of computers came down due to the increased use of integrated circuits and microprocessors, an alternative to time-sharing was sought. Taylor recommended a "one computer, one person" solution to the problem.

CSL computer scientist Alan Kay had described a tool called FLEX in his 1969 doctoral dissertation that fit Taylor's concept. It was an interactive tool. "It must be simple enough so that one doesn't have to be a systems programmer to use it, and it must be cheap enough to be owned. It must do more than just be able to recognize computable functions." FLEX was an "idea debugger" and, as such, it was hoped that it was also an "idea media." Kay proposed that PARC develop a FLEX-like computer called "Dynabook," which he referred to as a "dynamic media for creative thought." When the Dynabook project was turned down by Xerox management, he countered with a project called "interim Dynabook."

Interest in the project began to build within the CSL, and Taylor obtained approval to develop a computer that met the "one person, one computer" criterion. It was called Alto. CSL scientist Butler Lampson described it as having an enhanced display monitor, being virtually as powerful as a minicomputer, operating in a network of distributed machines, and being affordable. He referred to the use of such a computer as "personal computing." Computer scientist Chuck Thacker had some ideas on putting it together. Their goals were to make it both better and cheaper than a minicomputer.

Lampson and Thacker used some of the tools developed by Douglas Englebart, an early advocate of interactive computing, including an input device called a "mouse" and displays that could be divided into multiple "windows." Englebart's mouse was a bulky analog device that was converted into a digital tool and made smaller and more reliable.

Lampson and Thacker planned to improve Englebart's displays. They favored a technique called bit-mapping, which associated each picture element (pixel) with a specific bit of computer memory. Specific binary bits are programmed to be "on "(one) while others are "off" (zero); in combination the bits create a character on the screen and retain it in memory for later use. Unfortunately, this one-to-one relationship of pixels on the screen with bits in the computer's memory required a large storage capacity and was expensive.

Another Alto innovation was multitasking, which allowed one processor to operate as many. A task was performed according to its priority. Multitasking slowed Alto down because the bit-mapped display used the processor two-thirds of the time, but provided more functionality for less cost. In April 1973, after four months of work, the first Alto was completed. Ten Altos were built by the end of the year, and forty were completed by the following summer.

However, hardware alone doesn't make a computer system. Still needed to obtain benefit from the machine were an operating system, programming languages, and application software. As the software became available, three applications were emphasized: communications, printing, and word processing.

The communications tool developed by Robert Metcalfe was called Ethernet, which didn't use telephone lines but relied on local cable runs within a building. Ethernet connected an Alto to shared equipment, such as printers and other Altos. PARC also developed the xerographic laser printer. Laser printers were expensive, but sharing them reduced the cost to individual computer users.

Lampson and CSL scientist Charles Simonyi developed a word processing application called "Bravo," which allowed the word image on the screen to be the same as that which was output by the printer. This feature, which was called "wysiwyg" for "what you see is what you get," wasn't available on earlier word processing packages. Subsequently, a more user-friendly version, called "Gypsy," was developed. Alto was used successfully in an experiment at Ginn & Company, a Xerox textbook publishing subsidiary, to streamline the publishing process.

The Alto effort seemed to be prepared for takeoff. Thacker observed, "It was certainly from my own experience the largest piece of creative effort I have seen anywhere. And it was like being there at the creation. A lot of people worked harder than I have ever seen, or have seen since, doing a thing they all felt was worthwhile, and really thought would change the world." However, no attempt was made to translate PARC's developments into products.

Xerox faced many challenges at the time. In 1972, the Federal Trade Commission (FTC) claimed that the company was monopolizing the plain paper copier market. The FTC accused Xerox of manipulating patent laws, setting prices that were discriminatory, insisting on leases over sales of equipment, and exploiting the market by using joint ownership arrangements with Rank in England and Fuji in Japan. In July 1975, the FTC discontinued the antitrust action. In order to comply with FTC demands, Xerox had to give up its patents, change its pricing policies, and allow supplies such as toner to be sold by other companies.

In late 1973, CEO McColough and president Archie McCardell, a Ford Motor Company financial executive who had joined Xerox in 1971 upon the death of Xerox founder Joseph Wilson, formed a team of four people to plan the future strategy of Xerox. The team was headed by Michael Hughes, who had a corporate planning background, and included George Pake, who had been assigned to corporate headquarters after directing PARC for three years.

The team evaluated four distinct strategies for Xerox and recommended the alternative that pursued the office of the future. They suggested combining computers, copiers, and word-processing typewriters with PARC's innovations in communications, microcircuitry, and software. No action was taken on their recommendation by Xerox management.

Xerox research director Goldman thought that PARC's inventions would be brought to market by SDS. When SDS hemorrhaged financially during the first half of the 1970s, he realized that another avenue would have to be used to capitalize on PARC's innovations. As the emphasis on financial analysis practiced by ex-Ford executives became prevalent at Xerox, Goldman's influence as the senior technical person waned.

In January 1973, Bob Potter became the General Manager of Xerox's Office Products Division, which was responsible for developing and manufacturing office products other than copiers. The division had few successes other than developing a popular facsimile machine. Potter wanted to move the division from Rochester, New York, to another location. Dallas and Silicon Valley were two of the favored locations. Goldman lobbied strongly for Silicon Valley because PARC was located there. However, Dallas was chosen for strictly financial reasons, such as lower costs for labor, taxes, and transportation. The financial types had won again; PARC was to remain isolated from the rest of the company. In Goldman's opinion, this decision had the greatest negative impact of any single decision on the future of digital technology at Xerox.

Potter visited PARC and observed the Alto technology, but decided to concentrate on word processing technology. Although his background was in both technology and operations, he thought that PARC's ideas were too futuristic. Also, he was influenced by the Xerox financial people, who emphasized short-term profits.

PARC was disappointed that the word "software" didn't enter into Potter's plans for Dallas. They thought that products that weren't programmable, such as Potter's electro-mechanical devices, would fail. Within a year and a half of entering the market, Potter's word-processing typewriter was out of date because of its display and communications shortcomings. Xerox's Display Word Processing Task Force recommended that the new word processor be Alto-based. However, a team from Dallas recalculated PARC's estimates for the new product and concluded that the Alto would take longer to build and cost more than the estimates. The task force's recommendation was ignored. Next, Goldman proposed that a small entrepreneurial team be formed to produce a general-purpose workstation using the Alto. That idea was also rejected.

The recession in 1974-75 impacted Xerox. The company found that customers made as many copies in bad times as in good times, but they made them with existing machines. They didn't buy or lease new copiers during a slowed economy. However, the greatest negative impact on Xerox was the staggering loss from the

Scientific Data Systems acquisition. Taking on IBM head-to-head in the "office of the future" wasn't working.

Combining the copier and the computer businesses in a functional organization grouped by design and manufacturing, marketing and service, and planning had removed the focus of the computer business. In effect, SDS drifted without a general manager. In July 1975, CEO McColough admitted that the SDS acquisition had been a mistake. No buyer for SDS could be found. Xerox took a write-off of just under $1.3 billion and left the computer business.

In 1975-76, the Office Products Division began to manufacture the laser printer developed at PARC; a patent was received for Ethernet; and the Systems Development Division (SDD) was formed to translate PARC inventions into products. Some PARC-developed products were entering the marketplace. However, Xerox wasn't prepared to exploit the advances made on the Alto.

In 1976, PARC researcher John Ellenby was authorized to produce hundreds of Altos for use with laser printers within Xerox. He thought that at last technology transfer from the lab to the users was beginning to happen. In August 1976, Ellenby submitted a proposal on Alto to the Xerox task force determining new product strategies for the company. No action was taken on his proposal.

Ellenby was pleased when he was asked to organize the 1977 "Futures Day," at which Xerox showcased its new products within the company. His team worked hard and thought that they had made a strong case for proceeding with the Alto. By this time, McCardell had left Xerox to become CEO of International Harvester, and David Kearns from IBM had taken his place as president and chief operating officer. Ellenby was informed that Kearns had decided not to go into production with the Alto.

In 1979, a Xerox investment unit contacted Steve Jobs about investing in Apple. Jobs requested and received a tour of the PARC facility. Larry Tesler demonstrated Alto for Jobs, who saw its potential immediately. He asked, "Why isn't Xerox marketing this? You could blow everybody away." Once Jobs knew that it could be done, he set out to duplicate it at Apple. He hired Tesler immediately and later Alan Kay, who eventually became an Apple Fellow. Most of the "look and feel" of the Alto that provided its ease of use eventually was incorporated into the Apple Macintosh. Xerox was amazingly open with their technology.

In 1978, Xerox combined the Office Products Division in Dallas with other non-copier units. General Manager Potter left to join McCardell at International Harvester as chief technical officer. In 1979, the Office Products Division was again made independent, and Don Massaro hired from Shugart Associates to be Potter's replacement as General Manager. Massaro, who was known as an entrepreneurial type, announced a new word processor, readied two facsimile machines for the market, announced PARC's Ethernet as a product, and started an electronic typewriter project within the first year. Soon he became interested in Star, a product that had evolved from the Alto.

Massaro asked Xerox management for $15 million to make and sell the Star and was turned down. He scaled down his request and was turned down again. He proceeded on his own using his division's budget. The Star's strength, like Alto's, was its "user interface," including the contents of the screen and the tools provided to work with the display. The Star used icons, action choice menus, and multiple screen windows along with electronic file cabinets, in and out boxes, and wastebaskets. The Star was designed to be used by managers.

Much of the software had already been designed when a decision was made to replace the processor. Hardware is usually designed before software, and compromises had to be made that slowed the speed of the machine to incorporate the new processor. It was the first personal computer to offer the bit-map screen, a laser printer, the mouse, combined text and graphics in the same document, and "what you see is what you get" word processing.

However, it had limitations in addition to its slow speed:

- Because it was a distributed system, it was more expensive than a stand-alone computer. ($16,595 for the workstation, five times the cost of a stand-alone personal computer).
- It didn't offer a spreadsheet.
- Its design was based on a closed architecture, not an open architecture, and suppliers could not make and sell components to be used with it.
- Its programming language wasn't available to the public (only Xerox employees could write application software for it).
- It wasn't compatible with other computers.

In April 1981, the Star was introduced—eight years after the invention of the Alto. It wasn't a successful product; however, the Star (the Xerox 820) was the first personal computer introduced by a Fortune 500 Corporation.

Mishandling the introduction of the personal computer by Xerox was a classic case of missing an opportunity. Unfortunately for Xerox, the technology developed at PARC was exploited by others and Xerox didn't receive the benefit of its labors. An incredible body of talent had been assembled at PARC during the 1970s. Some of the key people seeded the laboratories of other companies: for example, Charles Simonyi was hired by the Microsoft Corporation. Butler Lampson, Bob Taylor, and Chuck Thacker joined the Systems Research Center of the Digital Equipment Corporation. In 1984, they received the System Software Award from the Association of Computing Machinery for the invention of personal distributed computing. In 1987, President Reagan awarded George Pake the National Medal of Science for the notable accomplishments of PARC.

SIR JONATHAN IVE'S RESEARCH TEAM
Chief Designers for Apple, Inc.

[Jony Ive] has more operational power than anyone else at Apple, except me. There's no one who can tell him what to do, or to butt out. That's the way I set it up."

Steve Jobs

Sir Jonathan Ive, a native of Great Britain, is the Chief Designer at Apple Inc. He has been responsible for the Industrial Design Group and provided direction for the Human Interface software teams. His team has designed many Apple products, including the MacBook Pro, iMac, MacBook Air, Mac mini, iPod, iPod Touch, iPhone, iPad, iPad Mini, Apple Watch, and the iOS operating system. Steve Jobs considered him his "spiritual partner" at Apple.

Ive was born in Chingford, London, on February 27, 1967. His father was a silversmith lecturer at Middlesex Polytechnic Institute. Ive attended the Chingford Foundation School and then Walton High School in Stafford. He was very interested in cars in school and considered going into automobile design.

Ive studied industrial design at Newcastle Polytechnic Institute (now Northumbria University}. He decided on a career in product design. He worked at the London design agency Roberts Weaver Group, which was his college sponsor. Ive graduated with a first class Bachelor of Arts degree in 1989. He was familiar with Apple products and was impressed with the mouse-driven system.

In 1988, while an undergraduate, Ive married British writer and historian Heather Pegg. They have twin sons and live in the Pacific Heights district of San Francisco.

After a year with Roberts Weaver, Ive joined a new design agency called Tangerine, where he designed products such as microwave ovens. Tangerine wasn't particularly impressed with his work and he wasn't impressed by their supervision. While at Tangerine, he consulted with Apple Inc., and created the initial PowerBook designs. Apple not only appreciated his work, but tried for two years to hire him.

During Ive's consulting activity with Apple, he worked for Robert Brunner, Apple's Chief of Industrial Design. Ive became a full-time employee of Apple in 1992 and designed the second generation of the Newton and the MessagePad 220.

In 1997, Ive became the Senior Vice President of Industrial Design after the return of Jobs to Apple and became head of the team responsible for most of Apple's hardware products. His first design assignment was the iMac, followed by designs, such as the iPod, iPhone, and iPad.

Jobs made design his main focus, which led to products that were functionally uncomplicated, aesthetically pleasing, and extremely popular. In *Time,* March 17, 2014, Ive described his working relationship that had existed with Jobs:

> When we were looking at objects, what our eyes physically saw and what we came to perceive were exactly the same. And we would ask the same questions, have the same curiosity about things. Ive described Jobs as "so clever" with "bold" and "magnificent ideas.

In 2011, Fortune.com cited some observations from Ive about the fragility of ideas:

> Steve used to say to me—and he used to say this a lot—"Hey, Jony, here's a dopey idea." And sometimes they were. Really dopey. Sometimes they were truly dreadful. But sometimes they took the air from the room and they left us both completely silent. Bold, crazy, magnificent ideas. Or quiet, simple ones, which in their subtlety, their detail, they were utterly profound . . . And just as Steve loved ideas, and he loved making stuff, he treated the process of creativity with a rare, wonderful reverence. You see, I think he knew better than anyone that while ideas ultimately can be so powerful, they begin as fragile, barely formed thoughts, so easily missed, so easily compromised, so easily squashed.

Ive runs his own laboratory at Apple. Only top executives and his core team, consisting of fifteen people from America, Australia, Britain, Japan, and New Zealand, who have worked together for twenty years, have access to his laboratory. On May 26, 2015, Ive was promoted to Chief Design Officer. He is the third C-level executive at Apple, along with CEO Tim Cook and CFO Luca Maestri.

In 2006, Ive was appointed Commander of the Order of the British Empire (CBE) for services to the design industry. In the 2012 New Years Honors, he was elevated to Knight Commander of the British Empire for "services to design and enterprise." He was knighted by Princess Anne at Buckingham Palace in a May 2012 ceremony. He said he was "both humbled and sincerely grateful." As of early 2014, Ives was a patent holder of over 730 U.S. design and utility patents, as well as many more patents around the world.

In 2014, Ive was quoted as saying:

> We are at the beginning of a remarkable time, when a remarkable number of products will be developed. When you think of technology and what it has enabled us to do and what it will enable us to do in the future, we're not even close to any kind of limit. It's still so new . . . At Apple, there's almost a joy at looking at your ignorance and realizing, "Wow," we're going to learn about this and, by the time we're done, we're going to really understand and do something great. Apple is imperfect, like every collection of people. But we have a rare quality. There is this almost pre-verbal, instinctive understanding about what we do, why we do it. We share the same values.

CHAPTER 3

Reformers / Activists

"These three things—work, will, success—fill human existences. Will opens the door to success, both brilliant and happy. Work passes through these doors, and at the other end of the journey success comes in to crown one's efforts."

Louis Pasteur

FREDERICK DOUGLASS (1818-1895) *Abolitionist Leader and Publisher*

"It rekindled the few expiring embers of freedom and revived within me a sense of my own manhood. It recalled the departed self-confidence, and inspired me again with a determination to be free. He can only understand the deep satisfaction which I experienced, who has himself repelled by force the bloody arm of slavery. I felt as I never felt before. It was a glorious resurrection, from the tomb of slavery to the heaven of freedom. My long-crushed spirit rose, cowardice departed, bold defiance took its place, and I now resolved that, however long I might remain a slave in form, the day had passed forever when I could be a slave in fact." (Frederick Douglass, upon winning a fight with a "slave breaker")

Douglas T. Miller, *Frederick Douglass and the Fight for Freedom*

Frederick Douglass was born Frederick Bailey in February 1818, in Talbot County on the eastern shore of Maryland. His mother, Harriet Bailey, was a slave, and his father, whom he never met, was a white man. His master was Captain Aaron Anthony.

In March 1826, Frederick was sent to live with a member of Anthony's family, Hugh Auld, in Baltimore. Living in Baltimore was a good experience for Frederick; he had many opportunities to learn.

Thomas Auld, Frederick's legal owner, brought him back to rural slavery in 1833. He was not obedient, so Auld hired him out to an overseer who had reputation as a "slave breaker." After he had endured six months of flogging and other mistreatment, he turned on the slave breaker in a two-hour fight that he won. After that, the overseer didn't bother Frederick, who was even more committed to winning his freedom. Thomas Auld sent him back to Hugh Auld in Baltimore. Frederick became an experienced caulker in a boatyard, where competition for jobs was fierce between poor white immigrants and slaves. He was attacked and badly beaten because he was thought to have taken a job from a white immigrant.

Frederick continued his self-education by joining the East Baltimore Mental Improvement Society, a debating club. An argument with Hugh Auld motivated Frederick to board a northbound train and escape. Despite some tense moments when he saw two local men who could identify him as a slave, he arrived in Philadelphia safely and continued on to New York City.

Frederick stayed with David Ruggles, publisher of the anti-slavery quarterly, *The Mirror of Slavery*. Ruggles, who was active in the Underground Railroad, suggested that he move farther north. Frederick traveled to New Bedford, Massachusetts, where he hoped to find work as a caulker, and lived with Nathan Johnson and his wife. Johnson suggested that because Frederick was an escaped slave, he should change his name. Johnson had just finished reading Sir Walter Scott's *Lady of the Lake*; he suggested the surname of "Douglass," the name of the Scottish lord and hero. Frederick Bailey became Frederick Douglass.

When Douglass looked for work as a caulker, he found that prejudice existed in the North as well as the South. White caulkers did not want to work with African Americans. He was forced to take odd jobs as a common laborer. One day he found a copy of William Lloyd Garrison's antislavery newspaper, *The Liberator,* and it changed his life. Garrison was a strong-willed abolitionist. In addition to being an editor, Garrison had helped to establish the New England Anti-Slavery Society. Douglass subscribed to Garrison's paper and was moved by it.

Douglass attended the annual meeting of the New England Anti-Slavery Society in New Bedford on August 9, 1841, and a meeting the next day on the Island of Nantucket. At the second meeting, Douglass was asked to speak. Although he was nervous, he spoke movingly about his life as a slave and was well-received.

Douglass was asked to become a full-time lecturer for the organization. He reluctantly accepted a three-month assignment and stayed for four years. He improved his oratorical skills and became one of the Society's most popular lecturers.

It was a dangerous time to be an abolitionist. On September 15, 1843, Douglass was severely beaten in Pendleton, Indiana. He escaped with a broken wrist and bruises. Abolitionist newspaper editor Elijah Lovejoy was killed in Alton, Illinois, while defending his press from an incensed mob. William Lloyd Garrison was dragged through the streets of Boston with a rope around his waist and almost lost his life.

During the winter and early spring of 1844-45, Douglass left the lecture circuit to write an autobiography, *The Narrative of the Life of Frederick Douglass, an American Slave*. In August 1845, he went on a successful lecture tour of England, Ireland, and Scotland.

One month after Douglass's return to America, two English women raised money and negotiated for his freedom. They contacted American agents to buy his freedom from the Aulds for $711.66. The deed of manumission was filed at the Baltimore Chattel Records Office on December 13, 1846, and Douglass was a free man.

Douglass returned to England for a lecture tour in 1847. Upon his return to America, he published an antislavery newspaper. His British friends raised money to help him get started. He was surprised when Garrison advised against it. Garrison did not want competition for his own newspaper.

Douglass started his newspaper despite Garrison's counsel against it. He knew that he would have to choose a base far from Garrison's in New England. Douglass chose Rochester, New York, a booming city of 30,000 on the Erie Canal, where he had been well-received on the lecture circuit in 1842 and 1847. Douglass moved his family there on November 1, 1847.

In December 1847, the first edition of his newspaper, *North Star*, was published. He named it *North Star* because the North Star was the guide that the slaves used when escaping from the South to freedom.

Douglass supported the Women's Rights Movement. On July 14, 1848, his *North Star* carried the announcement: "A convention to discuss the Social, Civil, and Religious Condition and Rights of Women will be held in the Wesleyan Chapel at Seneca Falls, New York, the 19th and 20th of July instant." The masthead that Douglass used for the *North Star* was: "RIGHT IS OF NO SEX— TRUTH IS OF NO COLOR."

In 1851, the *North Star* merged with the *Liberty Party Paper;* the resulting paper was called *Frederick Douglass's Paper*. In 1858, Douglass began publishing *Douglass's Monthly* for British readers. The weekly ran until 1860; he stopped printing the monthly in 1863, thus ending a 16-year publishing career.

Douglass served as a Rochester stationmaster on the Underground Railroad. He hid hundreds of escaping slaves at the *North Star* printing office and at his home and made arrangements for them to travel to Canada.

In January 1871, President Grant appointed Douglass to a commission to Santo Domingo (Dominican Republic). Douglass moved to Washington, D.C., because he thought that more federal appointments would be offered. In 1877, President Rutherford Hayes appointed him United States Marshal for the District of Columbia. He served in that position until 1881, when President James Garfield appointed him Recorder of Deeds for the District of Columbia. He held that office until 1886.

In September 1889, President Benjamin Harrison appointed Douglass Minister-Resident and Consul-General to the Republic of Haiti, where he served until July 1891. Douglass, one of the strongest antislavery voices of his time, died of a heart attack in Washington, D.C., on February 20, 1895.

FLORENCE NIGHTINGALE (1820-1910) *Nursing and Medical Pioneer*

"It was not by gentle sweetness and womanly self-abnegation that she had brought order out of chaos in the Scutari Hospitals, that, from her own resources, she had clothed the British Army, that she spread her dominion over the serried and reluctant powers of the official world; it was by strict method, by stern discipline, by rigid attention to detail, by ceaseless labor, by the fixed determination of an indomitable will."

Lytton Strachey, *Eminent Victorians*

Florence Nightingale is known principally for her work at military hospitals during the Crimean War. However, her contributions were much greater than that. She was the driving force in the reform of British Army medical services during and after the Crimean War in designing hospitals with the patient in mind, in the establishment of a school of nursing with higher standards than previous ones, and in the administration of medical services for the army in India.

This effort involved guiding those in positions of power in the British government, choosing chairmen for key committees, and generally steering medical and hospital reform, both military and civilian, for over 40 years. Nightingale provided direction for the careers of many Members of Parliament and advice to every Viceroy of India before he left England to assume his new duties.

Virtually all of Nightingale's girlhood friends were contented to become wives, mothers, and hostesses whose principal interests in life were social activities. She was bored with the social whirl and felt obliged to do something meaningful with her life. She viewed this as a call and entered this note in her diary: "On February 7, 1837, God spoke to me and called me to His service."

However, Nightingale did not know what form this service was going to take; she knew that it was going to have something to do with ministering to the sufferings of humanity. It did not become clear to her for seven years that her call was caring for the sick.

In the fall of 1842, while visiting the Baroness and Baron von Bunsen, the Prussian Ambassador to Great Britain, Nightingale asked them what a person could do to relieve the suffering of those who cannot help themselves. The Baron told her about the work at

Kaiserswerth, Germany, where Protestant deaconesses were trained in the institution's hospital to nurse the poor who were sick. Nightingale had not considered nursing as a way of serving those in need, and she did not follow up on this suggestion at the time.

By the spring of 1844, however, Nightingale was certain that her life's work was with the sick in hospitals. Thirteen years later she wrote, "Since I was 24 . . . there never was any vagueness in my plans or ideas as to what God's work was for me."

In June 1844, Dr. Ward Howe, the American philanthropist, visited the Nightingales at Embley. Nightingale asked Dr. Howe: "Do you think it would be unsuitable and unbecoming for a young Englishwoman to devote herself to works of charity in hospitals and elsewhere as Catholic sisters do?" Dr. Howe replied: "My dear Miss Florence, it would be unusual, and in England whatever is unusual is thought to be unsuitable; but I say to you 'go forward.' If you have a vocation for that way of life, act up to your inspiration and you will find there is never anything unbecoming or unladylike in doing your duty for the good of others. Choose, go on with it, wherever it may lead you and God be with you."

Nightingale considered how to present to her parents her plan to spend three months in nursing training at nearby Salisbury Infirmary, where the head physician was Dr. Fowler, a family friend. She broached the subject with her parents in December 1845, during a visit by Dr. Fowler and his wife.

The Nightingales were strongly opposed and could not understand why Florence wanted to "disgrace herself." She wrote later: "It was as if I had wanted to be a kitchen-maid."

Nightingale was distressed because she knew what she had to do, but she was prevented from doing it. Lytton Strachey, in *Eminent Victorians,* observed: "A weaker spirit would have been overwhelmed by the load of such distresses — would have yielded or snapped. But this extraordinary young woman held firm and fought her way to victory. With an amazing persistency, during the eight years that followed her rebuff over Salisbury Hospital, she struggled and worked and planned."

While continuing to perform her social obligations, Nightingale studied hospital reports and public health material. She built up a detailed knowledge of sanitary conditions that ultimately allowed her to become the foremost expert in England and on the Continent in her subject.

Finally, Nightingale was given the opportunity to receive nursing training at Kaiserswerth. Her spartan life started at five o'clock in the morning and the work was hard; but, in her words, "I find the deepest interest in everything here and am so well in body and mind. This is life. Now I know what it is to live and to love life, and I really should be sorry to leave life . . . I wish for no other earth, no other world than this."

Nightingale met Dr. Elizabeth Blackwell, the first woman medical doctor in modern times, in the spring of 1851 in London, where Blackwell had come for further medical training. Nightingale talked with Blackwell about the strength of her own commitment to hospital nursing.

In April 1853, Nightingale heard of an opportunity that suited her parents' expectations. The Institution for the Care of Sick Gentlewomen in Distressed Circumstances had encountered problems and was to be reorganized and moved to another location. Nightingale took charge and was responsible not only for the management of the institution but also its finances.

Nightingale had one year of nursing experience in March 1854, when England and France declared war on Russia. In June, the British Army landed at Varna on the Black Sea. When they embarked from Varna for the Crimea there was a shortage of transport ships, so they had to leave hospital tents and regimental medicine chests behind. On September 30, the British and the French defeated the Russians in the Battle of the Alma with heavy casualties on both sides.

British casualties did not receive proper care, since there were no litters or hospital wagons to transport them to a site to receive medical attention. When the wounded were carried by their comrades to receive the care of a doctor, no bandages or splints were available, nor were there any anesthetics or painkillers.

William Russell's dispatches to the London *Times* brought the conditions of the casualties to the attention of the British public. Two weeks after the Battle of the Alma, he wrote, "It is with feelings of surprise and anger that the public will learn that no sufficient preparations have been made for the care of the wounded. Not only are there not sufficient surgeons . . . not only are there no dressers and nurses . . . there is not even linen to make bandages."

Russell visited the French Army to see how their wounded were being treated. He found that their medical facilities and nursing care were excellent, and that 50 Sisters of Charity had accompanied their army. In another article for his newspaper, he asked, "Why have we no Sisters of Charity? There are numbers of able-bodied and tender-hearted English women who would joyfully and with alacrity go out to devote themselves to nursing the sick and wounded, if they could be associated for that purpose and placed under proper protection."

The Secretary for War during the Crimean War was Sidney Herbert, a good friend of Nightingale and her family. He wrote to ask if she would go to the Crimea to organize and superintend the nurses to care for the wounded.

Nightingale immediately began interviewing candidates and ultimately selected 14 nurses who, along with 10 Catholic Sisters and 14 Anglican Sisters, accompanied her to Scutari. She was appointed Superintendent of the Female Nursing Establishment of the English General Hospitals in Turkey. This title caused her problems, since it was construed to restrict her authority to Turkey and to exclude her from the Crimea in Russia.

Nightingale arrived at the military hospital in Scutari on November 4, 1854, 10 days after the Battle of Balaclava, where the Light Brigade was decimated by pitting cavalry against artillery, and 10 days before the Battle of Inkerman. She encountered a medical support system in total collapse, due to insufficient planning, poor execution of the few plans that did exist, and generally inadequate administration hampered by bureaucratic constrictions.

The Commissariat was responsible for the procurement, financing, transporting, and warehousing of hospital supplies. The Purveyor was responsible for food for the sick but did not procure it; the Commissariat did, and the organizations did not work well together.

Barrack Hospital, with four miles of beds, was not big enough. Nightingale had to plan, equip, and finance accommodations for 800 additional patients when the casualties from the Battles of Balaclava and Inkerman began to arrive. Open sewers, which ran under Barrack Hospital, were filled with lice, rats, and other vermin. Ventilation was poor and the stench was horrible. Working in these conditions is an indication of the strength of Nightingale's empathy for her patients. She became a purveyor of hospital supplies and a supplier of clothing to the patients.

Finances available to Nightingale were money sent to her from private sources in England and funds collected by the London *Times* for aid to the sick and the wounded. An eyewitness wrote, "I cannot conceive, as I now look back on the first three weeks after the arrival of the wounded from Inkerman, how it would have been possible to have avoided a state of things too disastrous to contemplate had not Miss Nightingale been there, with the aid of the means placed at her disposal."

Although Nightingale complied with regulations, her active style offended Dr. John Hall, Chief of the Medical Staff of the British Expeditionary Army. He found ways to obstruct her efforts. In particular, he was initially able to prevent her from supporting the two large hospitals in the Crimea by a strict interpretation of her title, Superintendent of the Female Nursing Establishment in *Turkey*. He claimed that her responsibility did not extend to the Crimea. She had to overcome Dr. Hall's obstructions.

Coworkers were in awe of Nightingale. Dr. Sutherland said, "She is the mainspring of the work. Nobody who has not worked with her daily could know her, could have an idea of her strength and clearness of mind, her extraordinary powers joined with her benevolence of spirit. She is one of the most gifted creatures God ever made."

Nightingale worked incredibly long hours and gave personal attention to the patients, even those with infectious diseases. The administrative load was overwhelming, and she had no secretary to share the paperwork burden. By spring 1855, she was physically exhausted. Nightingale was becoming a legend in England. She received a letter from Queen Victoria:

> You are, I know, well aware of the high sense I entertain of the Christian devotion which you have displayed during this great and bloody war, and I need hardly repeat to you how warm my admiration is for your services, which are fully equal to those of my dear and brave soldiers, whose sufferings you have had the privilege of alleviating in so merciful a manner.

In August 1856, Nightingale returned home from Scutari. Within a few weeks of her return, she visited the Queen and the Prince Consort at Balmoral Castle and made an excellent impression. The Prince wrote in his diary: "She put before us all the defects of our present military hospital system and the reforms that are needed." The Queen observed, "Such a head! I wish we had her at the War Office."

Nightingale became an influential person, and she knew how to use that influence. She negotiated Sidney Herbert's appointment as chairman of a royal commission whose function was to report on the health of the army.

During six months of extremely hard work, Nightingale assembled and wrote in her own hand "Notes Affecting the Health, Efficiency, and Hospital Administration of the British Army." This comprehensive 800-page document contained farsighted recommendations for reform in the areas of hospital architecture, military medical requirements, sanitation, and medical statistics.

In December 1859, Nightingale published a nursing guide, *Notes on Nursing.* In 1860, she opened the Nightingale Training School for Nurses at St. Thomas Hospital and became known as the founder of modern nursing. She did this concurrently with her ongoing efforts for medical and sanitary reform, which continued for over 40 years. Administration was her strength; she established a cost accounting system for the Army Medical Services between 1860 and 1865 that was still in use over 80 years later.

In November 1907, King Edward VII bestowed the Order of Merit on Nightingale, the first such award given to a woman. She died on August 13, 1910, after serving others for virtually her entire adult life.

During the time when Nightingale was pleading unsuccessfully with her parents to allow her to undertake nursing training, her mother confided her concerns to her friends. As noted by Lytton Strachey in *Eminent Victorians,* "At times, indeed, among her intimates, Mrs. Nightingale almost wept. 'We are ducks,' she said with tears in her eyes, 'who have hatched a wild swan.' But the poor lady was wrong; it was not a swan that they had hatched; it was an eagle."

MOHANDAS GANDHI (1869-1948) *Promoter of Passive Resistance*

"When he died, Gandhi was what he had always been: a private citizen without wealth, property, title, official position, academic distinction, or scientific achievement. Yet the chiefs of all governments . . . and the heads of all religions paid homage . . . Men and women and children knew, or felt, that when Gandhi fell by the assassin's three bullets the conscience of mankind had been left without a spokesman. Humanity was impoverished because a poor man had died. No one who survived him had faced mighty adversaries at home and abroad with the weapons of kindness, honesty, humility, and nonviolence, and, with these alone, won so many victories."

Louis Fischer, *Gandhi, His Life and Message for the World*

Mohandas Gandhi accomplished more by the use of civil disobedience and passive resistance in achieving his goals than many generals of armies and heads of government achieved. Albert Einstein said, "In years to come men will scarce believe that such a one as this ever in flesh and blood walked on this earth." Gandhi observed, "Men say I am a saint losing myself in politics. The fact is I am a politician trying my hardest to be a saint."

Gandhi attended college in India and law school in London. In 1893, he moved to South Africa to undertake civil cases for a company controlled by a group of Muslim merchants.

In 1901, Gandhi returned to India, where he was greeted as a hero because of his social work in South Africa. He was asked to return to South Africa by the Natal National Congress because many of the reforms that he had implemented to protect the rights of Indians living in South Africa were eroding. Gandhi opened a law office in Johannesburg. He published a weekly newspaper, *Indian Opinion*, to provide a voice for the Indian community and to give advice on self-improvement. He believed "The good of the individual is contained in the good of all; that is, the more one gives to society, the more one gains personally."

Gandhi adhered to three principles in his life: to be celibate, to practice ahimsa—absence of violence and satyagraha—truth-force or love-force. Ahimsa is more than non-violence; it is the respect for life and a positive reaching out to life in all of its forms. Gandhi's definition of satyagraha was "the vindication of truth not by the infliction of suffering on the opponent but on one's self." One doesn't use violence on an adversary, but self-control is used since the opponent must be "weaned from error by patience and sympathy." His meaning is more than passive resistance, since satyagraha requires an ongoing interaction between adversaries in working out their differences.

In September 1906, the government of Transvaal passed the Asiatic Law Amendment Ordinance requiring all Indians to register, to carry a registration card at all times, and to submit to being fingerprinted. Gandhi addressed a meeting of 3,000 Indians in Johannesburg in which he described the "Black Act," and proposed that all Indians refuse to obey the law.

Gandhi and the other leaders were given a two-month jail sentence. He read Thoreau's *Civil Disobedience* during his stay in jail. He agreed with Thoreau's view that it is more moral to be right than to abide by an unjust law. In Thoreau's words: "The only obligation which I have the right to assume is to do at any time what I think is right." Gandhi and Thoreau knew that a minority, if sufficiently determined, can overrule the majority.

The restrictions imposed upon Indians by the South African government included restrictions on moving freely between provinces. In 1913, Gandhi planned another satyagraha civil disobedience. Gandhi went to Newcastle to convince the mine workers, along with women and children—over 2,000 people in all—to march with him to Transvaal and, probably, prison. The government ignored his requests to repeal the unjust laws, so he marched with the crowd. He was arrested and given a nine-month jail sentence.

The British Parliament reacted when they heard that thousands of the government's subjects, including many children, had been sentenced to hard labor in the prison camps. A commission of inquiry was instituted about the time that Gandhi was released from prison. Gandhi planned a march to protest prison conditions, but a strike by the white South African railway workers began before he could start the march. This strike threatened to pull down the government, so he called off his march.

Prime Minister Botha and General Smuts appreciated Gandhi's decision and negotiated with him, even though Gandhi held no official office. On July 18, 1914, Gandhi returned to India. General Smuts commented, "The saint has left our shores; I hope forever."

Smuts also wrote: "It was my fate to be the antagonist of a man for whom even then I had the highest respect . . . He never forgot the human background of the situation, never lost his temper or succumbed to hate, and preserved his gentle humor in the most trying situations. His manner and spirit, even then, as well as later, contrasted markedly with the ruthless and brutal forcefulness which is in vogue in our day." Gandhi's emotional control could not be described any better.

In January 1915, Gandhi arrived in Bombay. He found that living conditions hadn't improved in his absence, and that Hindus and Moslems were still antagonists. He worked to improve living conditions in India to prepare for independence from the British Empire. Gandhi was asked to arbitrate a demand for a pay increase for workers at a textile mill in Ahmedabad. He had friends on both sides of the conflict. The mill owners were heavy contributors to his commune; he knew them well. He suggested a compromise, which the owners rejected. The mill was temporarily shut down.

Many workers, who were now starving, were eager to accept the owners' terms. Gandhi urged them to hold out. One worker said to Gandhi that it was easy for him to hold out—he had plenty to eat. Gandhi wrote later, "The light came to me. Unbidden, the words came to my lips." He decided not to eat until the dispute was resolved, preferably by the owners' agreeing to his compromise. He would "fast until death" if required. The owners knew he was serious, and they didn't know how the workers would react if Gandhi died. After Gandhi had fasted for three days, they gave in, and the workers were given the compromise increase.

Incidents and atrocities in the Punjab brought Gandhi into politics in a way he hadn't planned. He became a leader of the Indian National Congress and the Indian Nationalist Movement. Previously, he had advocated dominion status for India, similar to the status of Canada and Australia in the British Commonwealth. Now he wanted the British out of India.

Gandhi participated in the drafting of a new constitution and opened up the membership of the Congress. He promoted the increased participation of the Moslem minority and stated a policy of noncooperation with the British. He organized a National

Volunteer Corps, which consisted mainly of student activists, to help spread the concept of a satyagraha of noncooperation throughout India. One of his student volunteers was Jawaharlal Nehru, the son of Molital Nehru, president of the Indian Congress.

One goal was to become less dependent on imported British textiles. Initially, the British weren't worried by the noncooperation campaign, but as people burned their foreign-made clothes and picketed British clothing stores, it disrupted British control. Leaders of the National Congress and National Volunteers were arrested. By March 1920, 30,000 had been jailed, including Gandhi and the whole Nehru family. Gandhi was sentenced to six years in jail. He served just under two years, from March 1922 to February 1924, in solitary confinement.

With the leaders in jail, the Swaraj, or home rule movement, had languished and had become a struggle between the Hindu faction and the Moslem faction. When riots between Hindus and Moslems occurred in the Northwest Frontier Province, Gandhi began a fast scheduled for 21 days that would end with an improvement in Hindu-Moslem relations or with his death. Their relations improved during the fast, which became known as his "Great Fast," and groups composed of Hindus and Moslems visited him at his bedside. He fasted the entire 21 days; unfortunately, the improvement in Hindu-Moslem relations lasted only two years.

On January 1, 1930, Jawaharlal Nehru began his first term as president of the Indian Congress. Gandhi proposed protest activity against British rule. On March 2, 1930, he wrote to the Viceroy, noting that he held British rule to be a curse because "It has impoverished dumb millions by a system of progressive exploitation and by a ruinous, expensive military and civilian administration which the country could never afford. It has reduced us politically to serfdom. It has sapped the foundations of our culture. And it has degraded us spiritually." To demonstrate his displeasure, he announced that he would disregard the Salt Law.

The Salt Law established taxes on all salt consumed and prohibited the manufacture, sale, or consumption of salt not imported from England. The government was concerned by Gandhi's proposed action, but, once again, he had chosen a cause that was just. Salt is a necessary ingredient of the human diet for both peasants and the wealthy. However, the peasants were less able to pay the tax on a commodity that was available along India's shoreline.

On March 12, Gandhi and 78 of his followers began the 200-mile march from Sabarmati Commune to the coast. Twenty-four days later, 60-year-old Gandhi, wearing only a loincloth, waded into the Arabian Sea, reached down and picked up a small piece of salt from the beach, and ate it. By this act of eating one of God's gifts that the resident foreign government had forbidden him to eat, he had broken the law. It was precisely the type of gesture that the peasants could understand; furthermore, it caused injury to no one.

The Salt March gained attention not only all over India, but all over the world via press and radio. All of India began to break the Salt Law. Many were imprisoned, but there wasn't enough jail space for everyone. The government arrested Gandhi. Gandhi, Nehru, and many other leaders were jailed without a trial, and were held "at the pleasure of the government" under a little-used 1827 law. In late May, 2,500 National Volunteers advanced on the government-run Dharansa Saltworks. This unarmed mass faced 400 Indian police armed with lathis, steel-tipped bamboo clubs. A United Press staff writer reported:

> They marched steadily, with heads up, without the encouragement of music or cheering or any possibility that they might escape serious injury or death. The police rushed out and methodically and mechanically beat down the column. There was no fight, no struggle; the marchers simply walked forward until struck down.

The saltworks weren't damaged, but there was considerable damage to the world's view of British law enforcement.

Gandhi launched another civil disobedience campaign and was arrested on January 4, 1932; he was sent again to jail. By March, 35,000 Indians were in jail.

Britain's attention was diverted from India at the beginning of World War II in September 1939. When two neighbors of India were invaded by Japan, Britain knew that India had to be defended and reacted by taking away the few liberties that the Indians had.

Another passive resistance campaign began, causing jail sentences for Gandhi, Nehru, and 400 other Indian leaders. Twenty thousand resisters were in jail by 1941, but were released by year end. Nehru and Gandhi offered to help the British, but only as a free nation. Britain offered dominion status at the end of the war.

In 1942, the leaders of Congress began a "Quit India" campaign and were jailed again. Gandhi left prison on May 6, 1944; he spent 2,338 days of his 77-year life in prison.

In February 1947, Lord Louis Mountbatten became the last Viceroy of India. His assignment was to withdraw from India. The Moslems threatened civil war if they weren't given the northeast and northwest territories. Congress had no alternative, and the two territories became Pakistan. (The northeast territory became Bangladesh in 1971). This concession triggered widespread rioting.

Approximately 500,000 Indians were killed trying either to leave or to enter the new country of Pakistan; 15 million people were homeless. Gandhi began another fast until death. Moslems knew that they would be blamed for his death, so Moslem representatives joined with Hindu representatives at the bedside of the 77-year-old Mahatma. He ended his fast after four days.

On January 20, a bomb exploded near Gandhi while he was at prayer. It was thrown by a radical Hindu who disapproved of Gandhi calling Moslems his brothers and giving them two large sections of India. Gandhi told his friends, "If I die by the bullet of a madman, I must do so smiling. Should such a thing happen to me, you are not to shed one tear . . . if someone shot at me and I received his bullet in the bare chest without a sign and with Rama's [God's] name on my lips, only then should you say that I was a true Mahatma."

At about five o'clock the next evening, as Gandhi climbed the steps to his raised garden and walked toward an assembled crowd, Naturam Godse, a Hindu extremist, bent down to kiss Gandhi's feet. When he was pulled up, he fired three shots from a revolver into Gandhi's chest and stomach. Gandhi slumped to the ground, said "Hai Rama!" (Oh God) and died.

Gandhi left a great legacy to the world, including his saintliness and his nonviolent approach to the problems of life. His view of life was "I can wait 40, or 50, or 400 years—it is the same to me. Life goes on forever—we all persist in some form and inevitably victory is ours." It is difficult to think of a better example of emotional control than Mahatma Gandhi.

NELSON MANDELA (1918-2013) *First Native South African President*

"During my lifetime, I have dedicated myself to this struggle of the African People. I have fought against white domination, and I have fought against black domination. I have cherished the ideal of a democratic and free society in which all persons live together in harmony and with equal opportunities. It is an ideal which I hope to live for and to achieve. But if needs be, it is an ideal for which I am prepared to die."

Nelson Mandela

Nelson Mandela spent over twenty-seven years in the Union of South Africa's prisons for political activism in striving to eliminate racial segregation and to improve the living and working conditions of blacks in South Africa. In February 1990, he was released from prison and was overwhelmed by the fervor with which he was greeted by the people. In April 1994, for the first time in the history of South Africa, black people voted to elect leaders of their choice. On May 19, 1994, Nelson Mandela was inaugurated as the first black President of the Union of South Africa.

Nelson Rolihlahla Mandela was born on July 18, 1918, at Qunu in the Transkei reserve on the east coast of South Africa. He was the eldest son of Henry and Nonqaphi Mandela, members of the royal family of the Thembu, a Xhosa-speaking people. His Xhosa name, Rolihlahla means "stirring up trouble." Henry Mandela was the chief counselor to the leader of the Thembu people and served on the Transkeian Territories General Council.

Young Nelson worked on the family farm plowing the fields and tending the cattle and sheep. He attended the local school run by white missionaries. When Nelson was twelve, Henry Mandela became ill and sent his son to live with the Chief of the Thembu. Nelson was raised with the Chief's son and attended the Methodist High School.

In 1936, Mandela enrolled in Fort Hare College, a Methodist college in eastern Cape Province. At Fort Hare, he met many future activist leaders, including Oliver Tambo, who later became the leader of the African National Congress. Mandela's political leanings took shape in college. After three years of college, he was suspended for boycotting the Students' Representative Council, of which he was a member, because the college administration had reduced the powers of the council.

Mandela returned to the Transkei. The Chief was disappointed in him; he encouraged him to cooperate with the college administration. Mandela moved to Johannesburg, the center of the gold-mining region in the Transvaal, to avoid the arranged marriage that the Chief had planned for him.

Cosmopolitan Johannesburg was a shock to Mandela, who was used to rural and small-town life. Like all "Bantus," the white name for black South Africans, he lived in a township on the outskirts of the city with no electricity or sewers. Initially, he worked as a guard at a mining compound. In the township of Alexandra, he met Walter Sisulu, owner of a real estate agency, who loaned him money to complete his college degree.

Sisulu also helped Mandela find a job with a Johannesburg law firm to finance his law studies at the University of Witwatersrand. While studying for a law degree, he met a young nurse, Evelyn Mase, whom he married. They lived in Soweto (Southwest Townships) in Orlando Township. Sisulu, a member of the African National Congress (ANC), suggested that Mandela join their organization, which had been formed by journalists, lawyers, teachers, and tribal chiefs to work to end segregation. They wanted to be able to buy property and to be elected to parliament.

In 1943, Mandela joined the Youth League of the ANC. The Youth League planned to push the ANC to fight white domination by participating in protests against the white government and by spurring blacks into militant action. In September 1944, Anton Lembede was elected president of the ANC, and Mandela, Sisulu, and Tambo (Mandela's friend from college), were appointed to the executive committee.

The ANC stated their philosophy: "The Congress must be the brains-trust and power-station of the spirit of African nationalism; the spirit of African self-determination, the spirit so discernible in the thinking of our youth. It must be an organization where young African men and women will meet and exchange ideas in an atmosphere pervaded by a common hatred of oppression."

In 1946, black African mine workers held a strike for better wages in which 70,000 workers participated. Seven mines were shut down; the country's booming economy was slowed. The government reacted violently. Police, aided by army units, cut off all food and water to workers' living quarters, arrested the leaders of the strike, and used batons to beat protesters who would not return to work. After some workers were killed, the strike was broken within a week. The ANC learned lessons from the strike. They realized that in numbers alone they had the power to make social change happen. Mandela said, "We have a powerful ideology capable of capturing the masses. Our duty is now to carry that ideology fully to them."

In 1949 at the ANC annual conference, the Youth League implemented a new policy of action employing strikes, civil disobedience, and noncooperation. They were convinced that they had to become more militant and had to use mass action to fight apartheid, the government's program of racial separation and white supremacy. In 1950, the ANC became allied with the Indian National Congress in South Africa, which was better financed than the ANC. Mandela learned about the passive resistance campaigns waged by Mohandas Gandhi in Africa earlier in the twentieth century. He respected the Indians' hard work and dedication to their cause, but he felt that the African movement should be separate. The Indian National Congress worked closely with the South African Communist Party. Mandela noted, "It is clear that the exotic plant of communism cannot flourish on African soil."

Also in 1950, Mandela completed his law studies and set up a a law practice in Johannesburg with Oliver Tambo. Most of their cases involved victims of apartheid laws. Tambo observed: "South African apartheid laws turn innumerable innocent people into 'criminals.' Every case in court, every visit to the prison to interview clients, reminded us of the humiliation and suffering burning into our people."

On May 1, 1950, the ANC scheduled a one-day national work stoppage. Over half of native South African workers stayed home. The strike was successful; however, nineteen Africans were killed in Johannesburg when police attacked demonstrators. Mandela commented: "That day was a turning point in my life, both in understanding through firsthand experience the ruthlessness of the police, and in being deeply impressed by the support African workers had given to the May Day call."

In 1951, as newly elected national president of the Youth League, Mandela was asked to lead a Defiance Campaign. He toured the country to sign up volunteers. In June 1952 in Port Elizabeth, the Defiance Campaign began their "defiance" by singing African freedom songs, calling out freedom slogans, and using the "Europeans only" entrances to post offices and railroad stations.

In Johannesburg, Sisulu, Mandela, and fifty Defiance Campaign volunteers were arrested for violating the 11:00 p.m. curfew. A volunteer broke his ankle when a guard pushed him down a flight of stairs; he was then refused medical attention. When Mandela protested to the policeman, he was beaten with a nightstick. By the end of December 1952, over 8,000 Defiance Campaign volunteers had been arrested.

Mandela and other ANC leaders were tried in December 1952. Mandela and over fifty of the ANC's most capable leaders were prohibited from participating further in the organization. Mandela was forbidden to travel outside of Johannesburg for two years, and he was not permitted to attend political meetings. By year-end 1952, ANC membership had grown to 100,000.

Mandela was away from home most of the time, putting considerable strain on his marriage. Evelyn was raising their children by herself, and, with his commitment to the ANC, she could foresee no improvement in their relationship. He was never out of the view of undercover police. She moved with the children to Natal. Finally, Mandela and Evelyn were divorced.

On December 5, 1956, 156 people, including Mandela, Sisulu, and Tambo, were arrested and charged with treason as members of "a countrywide conspiracy, inspired by communism, to overthrow the State by violence." The "Treason Trial" lasted for six years, during which time Mandela, who helped to prepare the defense, was alternately in jail and out on bail. During one of the times that he was out of jail, Mandela was introduced to Winnie Nomzamo Madikizela by Oliver Tambo and his fiancée, Adelaide Tsukudu.

Winnie's Xhosa name, Nomzamo, means "she who strives." Winnie, whose parents were both teachers, graduated from Shawbury High School and enrolled in the Jan Hofmeyr School of Social Work in Johannesburg. Upon graduating with honors from the Hofmeyr School, she won a scholarship to study for an advanced degree in sociology in the United States. Instead, she accepted a position at the Baragwanath Hospital in Soweto and became the first black medical social worker in South Africa.

Mandela was thirty-eight when he met Winnie. She was nervous because he was a national figure sixteen years older than she. A white resident of Cape Town observed: "I noticed people were turning and staring at the opposite pavement and I saw this magnificent figure of a man, immaculately dressed. Not just blacks, but whites were turning to admire him." While they were dating, Winnie commented: "Life with him was a life without him. He did not even pretend that I would have a special claim on his time."

In June 1958, Mandela and Winnie were married. They moved into a home in the Orlando West township of Soweto. Winnie joined the ANC and enrolled in a course in public speaking. Soon after their marriage, they were awakened in the middle of the night by security police who searched their home but found nothing incriminating.

At a mass demonstration organized by the Women's League of the ANC, Winnie and 1,200 other female protesters were arrested and imprisoned. Winnie, who was pregnant, was struck several times and almost lost her baby. Upon her release from prison, Winnie was told that she had been fired from her position at the hospital. She found a job with the Child Welfare Society.

In 1959, a militant group split off from the ANC because they did not want to cooperate with other racial groups; they advocated "Africa for Africans" and called themselves the Pan Africanist Congress (PAC). In the following year, the PAC planned a campaign against the requirement for all blacks to carry a pass.

On March 21, 1960, in Sharpeville, 10,000 protesters gathered in peaceful support of the ban on passes. The police panicked and fired into the unarmed crowd, killing sixty-seven Africans, including eight women and ten small children. Most were shot in the back as they were running away.

Later, the police fired into a peaceful crowd in the township of Langa, outside of Cape Town, killing fourteen and wounding many others. The government of the Union of South Africa was universally condemned by world opinion. The United Nations Security Council spoke out against the government of the Union of South Africa for the first time. The ANC decided to send one of their leaders outside of the country, beyond the jurisdiction of the police of South Africa. Oliver Tambo was chosen to go.

In March 1961, the chief judge announced a verdict of not guilty in the treason trial. Spectators cheered and shouted "Nkosi Sikelel' iAfrika" (God Bless Africa). Mandela had conducted the defense, cross-examined witnesses, and given testimony himself. He emphasized that the ANC through their Defiance Campaign had conducted nonviolent activities and maintained that, in the long run, civil disobedience would free all Africans. His defense brought him an international reputation and increased his standing within the ANC; he was now considered its strongest leader.

Mandela had responded to the accusation that the freedom of the ANC was a threat to Europeans (whites): "No, it is not a direct threat to the Europeans. We are not non-white; we are against white supremacy and in struggling against white supremacy we have the support of some sections of the European population. We said that the campaign we were about to launch was not directed at any racial group. It was directed against laws we considered unjust."

After spending a brief time with his family, Mandela went on the road. His first stop was the All-in-Africa Conference in Pietermaritzburg, where he was the keynote speaker. He was elected head of the National Action Council. He decided to go underground to plan further protests.

Mandela became known as the "black pimpernel," modeled on the fictional English Scarlet Pimpernel who always eluded his enemies during the French Revolution. He stayed underground for a year and a half, surfacing only for meetings. On one occasion, he had to climb down a rope from an upstairs window in the back of a house while police entered the front.

Winnie would be given a message to meet someone in a car at a certain location. She would change cars frequently: "By the time I reached him I had gone through something like ten cars. The people who arranged this were mostly whites. I don't know to this day who they were. I would just find myself at the end of the journey in some white house; when we got there they were deserted."

One day at work, Winnie was told to drive to a particular corner of the city. She described the incident: "When I got there, a tall man in blue overalls and a chauffeur's white coat and peaked hat opened the door, ordered me to shift from the driver's seat and took over and drove. That was him. He had a lot of disguises and he looked so different that for a moment, when he walked toward the car, I didn't recognize him myself."

By June 1961, the ANC realized that the tactic of nonviolence had failed. They were going to have to "answer violence with violence." A new organization was formed, the Umkhonto we Sizwe (Spear of the Nation, or MK), to conduct violent attacks against the government. The MK was not a terrorist organization; they limited their attacks to sabotage, mainly of power plants, railroad freight cars, and transmission lines where innocent bystanders wouldn't be injured. If caught, MK saboteurs faced the death penalty. The police stepped up their search for Mandela.

In January 1962, Mandela traveled out of South Africa for the first time. Oliver Tambo asked him to speak at the Pan African Freedom Conference in Addis Ababa, Ethiopia. He was moved by the open environment outside of South Africa: "Free from white oppression, from the idiocy of apartheid and racial arrogance, from police molestation, from humiliation and indignity. Wherever I went, I was treated like a human being."

Mandela returned to South Africa. For leaving the country without a passport, Mandela was charged with an additional "crime." As the result of a tip from an informer, on August 5, 1962, he was captured returning to Johannesburg from a meeting in Natal. He was accused of inciting a strike in 1961 and of leaving the country illegally. At his trial in Pretoria, Mandela shouted to the gallery, "Amandla!" (power), and the crowd in the gallery answered "Ngawethu!" (to the people).

Mandela told the court: "I consider myself neither legally nor morally bound to obey laws made by a parliament in which I have no representation. In a political trial such as this one, which involves a clash of the aspirations of the African people and those of whites, the country's courts, as presently constituted, cannot be impartial and fair." He was found guilty on both charges and sentenced to ten years of hard labor. He was imprisoned in Pretoria, where he sewed mailbags, and then transferred to the maximum-security prison on Robben Island in the Atlantic Ocean, seven miles off Cape Town.

On July 12, 1963, the police raided the ANC's Rivonia farm and captured Walter Sisulu. They found many ANC documents, including Mandela's diary of his tour of Africa and incriminating evidence that documented his role in the MK violence. On trial, he stated to the court: "I do not deny that I planned sabotage. I did not plan it in a spirit of recklessness, nor because I have any love of violence. I planned it as a result of a calm and sober assessment of the political situation that had arisen after many years of tyranny, exploitation, and oppression of my people by the whites."

On June 11, 1964, Mandela was sentenced to life imprisonment. A staff writer for the New York *Times* wrote, "To most of the world, the Rivonia defendants are heroes and freedom fighters, the George Washingtons and Ben Franklins of South Africa." The London *Times* added, "The verdict of history will be that the ultimate guilty party is the government in power."

On Robben Island, Mandela had a small cell without electricity or sanitary facilities. It was furnished with a mat, a bedroll, two light blankets, and a bucket. He was issued cotton shorts, a khaki shirt, and a light jacket. The guards told him that he was going to die there. He rejected the offer of a special diet and did not use his international reputation to obtain special privileges. All prisoners at Robben Island considered him their leader and spokesperson. He worked in a limestone quarry, chained to another prisoner.

Every six months, prisoners were permitted one half-hour visit and were allowed to mail one letter of 500 words and to receive one letter. On Winnie's first visit, she was instructed that they could not speak in the Xhosa language, and that political subjects could not be discussed. She could not bring any presents, and their daughters could not visit their father until they were fourteen. They communicated with microphones and headsets through a glass partition that gave a distorted view of the other party.

Winnie was forced to leave her job at the Child Welfare Society. To support her family, she worked at menial jobs—in a dry cleaners, a furniture store, and a laundry—but lost the jobs when the security police threatened the owners with reprisals. Spies and informers were everywhere she went, and the police maintained an ongoing program of harassment.

The children suffered. Winnie was frequently in jail, and friends and neighbors had to care for the young girls. On one occasion, she spent seventeen months in jail; the first five months were spent in solitary confinement in filthy living conditions. She believed that this treatment made her a stronger person. Finally, she sent their daughters to Swaziland to attend school. She lived on the charity of her friends and her supporters.

On June 16, 1976, during a mass protest in Soweto, the cruelty of the government was again displayed. A Soweto leader observed:

> I saw a stream of schoolchildren marching past my house. They had just reached the Orlando West school when the police tried to stop them marching any further. The children kept on walking so the police released dogs. Then the police panicked and fired into the mass of children. I will never forget the bravery of those children. They were carrying [trashcan] lids to protect themselves and deflect the bullets. The police had dogs and tear gas and batons, but they chose instead to use bullets against those unarmed kids. The saddest sight anyone can see is a dying child crippled by bullets.

The people of Soweto responded with an uprising. Over 1,000 protesters died, and over 4,000 were wounded. Across South Africa, over 13,000 were arrested, 5,000 of whom were under eighteen. The government of the Union of South Africa was condemned in world news. The government did not respond to international opinion. In September 1977, Steve Biko, the leader of the Black Consciousness Movement, died in jail from beatings and torture.

In May 1977, Winnie Mandela was banished to Brandfort in the Orange Free State, where she lived for ten years, in an attempt to minimize her role as a national leader. She was moved into a three-room concrete-block house without running water, electricity, or a sewer system. It had a dirt floor; access was by openings in the front and side walls that could not be closed. Communication was difficult. Local people spoke only the African languages, Sotho and Tswana; Winnie spoke English and Xhosa. To communicate with the outside world, Winnie began to use the international press.

Winnie received an honorary doctor of laws degree from Haverford College, and two Scandinavian newspapers awarded her the Freedom Prize. In January 1985, U.S. Senator Edward Kennedy visited Winnie at Brandfort while on a trip to South Africa.

While Winnie was receiving international attention, Nelson Mandela continued to lead even while in prison. The United Democratic Front stated their opinion: "You [Nelson Mandela] are a true leader of the people. We will not rest until you are free. Your release and the release of all political prisoners is imperative. Your sacrifice for your people is affirmed. We commit ourselves anew to a free South Africa in which the people shall govern." Bishop Desmond Tutu said, "The government has to come to terms with the fact that the black community now says, 'Our leader is Nelson Mandela and any other persons are just filling in.'"

The government offered to release Mandela if he would reject violence unconditionally. He responded, "Only free men can negotiate. Prisoners cannot enter into contracts. I cannot and will not give any undertaking at a time when I and you, the people, are not free. Your freedom and mine cannot be separated. I will return."

Samuel Dash, chief counsel for the U.S. Senate Watergate Committee, observed on a visit that the guards treated Mandela "as though he were their superior, unlocking gates and opening doors on his command as he led me on a tour of his building." When Dash commented on the whites' fear of the black majority, Mandela pointed out that "unlike white people anywhere else in Africa, whites in South Africa belong here—this is their home. We want them to live here with us and to share power with us."

Dash noted: "I felt that I was in the presence not of a guerrilla fighter or radical ideologue, but of a Head of State." Mandela reiterated the principles of the ANC to Dash:

• A unified South Africa without artificial "homelands"
• Black representation in the central parliament
• One man, one vote

On February 11, 1990, Nelson Mandela was released from prison. His first speech to the people was given in Cape Town at the Grand Parade, a large square in front of the old City Hall.

Mandela greeted the reception committee and the huge crowd. "Friends, comrades, and fellow South Africans. I greet you all in the name of peace, democracy, and freedom for all! I stand here before you not as a prophet but as a humble servant of you, the people. Your tireless and heroic sacrifices have made it possible for me to be here today. I therefore place the remaining years of my life in your hands."

In late February, Mandela traveled to Lusaka to attend a meeting of the National Executive Committee of the ANC. He enjoyed being reunited with comrades that he hadn't seen in many years. He also spoke with heads of State of other African countries, including Angola, Botswana, Mozambique, Uganda, Zambia, and Zimbabwe. After the conference, Mandela traveled around Africa and visited the Egyptian president, Hosni Mubarak, in Cairo. While in Egypt, Mandela stated at a press conference that the ANC was "prepared to consider a cessation of hostilities." This was a message for the government of South Africa.

Upon Mandela's return to South Africa, the ANC leadership, including Mandela and Walter Sisulu, met with government officials in a first round of talks to discuss their differences. In early June, Mandela went on a six-week trip to Europe and North America. He met with world leaders in France, Switzerland, Italy, Ireland, and England as well as the United States and Canada. After visiting Memphis and Boston, he traveled to Washington and addressed a joint session of Congress.

Upon his return to South Africa, Mandela realized that violence was continuing to obstruct the peace process. He traveled around the country in an attempt to soothe some of the ill feelings. On December 20, 1991, the first serious negotiations, called the Convention for a Democratic South Africa (CODESA), started between the ANC, other South African parties, and the government.

On June 3, 1993, negotiations resulted in setting a date for the first non-racial, one-person-one-vote national election in South Africa on April 27, 1994. For the first time in the history of South Africa, black voters could elect the leaders of their choice. In 1993, Mandela and President de Klerk shared the Nobel Peace Prize. Mandela accepted the prize on behalf of the people of South Africa. He acknowledged that Mr. de Klerk had made a serious, vital contribution to the peace process.

Mandela and de Klerk had one television debate before the presidential election. In his remarks, Mandela looked at de Klerk and said, "Sir, you are one of those I rely upon. We are going to face the problems of this country together." Mandela extended his hand to de Klerk and added, "I am proud to hold your hand for us to go forward." The gesture surprised de Klerk, but he agreed to work together.

Mandela won the election with 62.6 percent of the vote. He realized that now he would have to heal the country's wounds, to promote reconciliation, and to instill confidence in the leadership of the government. At his inauguration, Mandela declared:

> We have, at last, achieved our political emancipa-
> tion. We pledge ourselves to liberate all our people
> from the continuing bondage of poverty, depriva-
> tion, suffering, gender, and other discrimination.
> Never, never, and never again shall it be that this
> beautiful land will again experience the oppression
> of one by another. The sun shall never set on so
> glorious an achievement. Let freedom reign. God
> bless Africa.

After his swearing-in ceremony, the ranking generals of the South African Defense Force and the security police saluted the new president and affirmed their loyalty as jet fighters, multi-engine aircraft, and helicopters of the South African Air Force flew overhead. Ceremonies were concluded with blacks singing "Die Stem van Suid-Afrika," the anthem of the republic, and whites singing "Nkosi Sikelel' iAfrica."

In *Long Walk to Freedom*, Nelson Mandela wrote:

> I have walked that long road to Freedom. I have
> tried not to falter; I have made missteps along the
> way. But I have discovered the secret that after
> climbing a great hill, one only finds that there are
> many more hills to climb. I have taken a moment
> to rest, to steal a view of the glorious vista that sur-
> rounds me, to look back on the distance I have
> come. But I can rest only for a moment, for with
> freedom comes responsibilities, and I dare not
> linger, for my long walk is not yet ended.

MARTIN LUTHER KING, JR. (1929-1968) U.S. Civil Rights Activist

"A final victory is an accumulation of many short-term encounters. To lightly dismiss a success because it does not usher in a complete order of justice is to fail to comprehend the process of achieving full victory."

Martin Luther King, Jr.

On February 25, 1948, Martin Luther King, Jr., was ordained a minister and became assistant pastor of Ebenezer Baptist Church in Atlanta, his father's church. After graduating from Morehouse College, King enrolled at Crozer Seminary. While at Crozer, King attended a lecture by the president of Howard University, who had just returned from a visit to India. He talked about the role of Mohandas Gandhi in freeing India from British rule by using non-violent means. He also discussed civil disobedience and passive resistance and made a profound impression on young King.

King thought what he had heard "was so profound and fascinating that I left the meeting and bought a half dozen books on Gandhi's life and works." Later, he wrote in his book *Stride Toward Freedom*, "Not until I entered Crozer Theological Seminary . . . did I begin a serious intellectual quest for a method to eliminate social evil."

In 1951, King graduated first in his class from Crozer. He gave the valedictory address at commencement, won the Plafker Award as the most outstanding student, and received a fellowship to Boston University's School of Theology. In Boston, King met Coretta Scott, a voice student at the New England Conservatory of Music. They were married by Martin Luther King, Sr., on June 18, 1953.

King knew what he was going to do with his life. He explained his goal to his wife: "I'm going to be pastor of a church, a large Baptist church in the South . . . I'm going to live in the South because that's where I'm needed."

In April 1954, the Dexter Avenue Baptist Church in Montgomery, Alabama, offered King the position of pastor. He and Coretta moved to Montgomery in August when she graduated from the conservatory. King continued to work on his doctoral dissertation and received his Ph.D in Theology on June 5, 1955.

On December 1, 1955, an incident of national significance occurred in Montgomery. Rosa Parks, an African-American seamstress at a local department store, was riding home on a public bus after a busy work day. The bus driver asked her to give up her seat to a white passenger who had just boarded the bus. She was sitting in the first row of the African-American section of the bus, one row behind the white section; her feet hurt and she was carrying packages, so she refused to move. The driver asked her again to move. She responded again, firmly, "No."

The driver called the police; Parks was taken to the police station where she was booked for a violation of a city bus ordinance. She called E. D. Nixon, a member the National Association for the Advancement of Colored People (N.A.A.C.P.) to request bail. Nixon cheered when he heard that Rosa had been charged with violating the local bus segregation law. The N.A.A.C.P. was looking for a test case to challenge the blatantly unfair ordinance as far as the U.S. Supreme Court, if necessary. Nixon suggested a boycott of the city bus service using car pools. The boycott was virtually 100 percent successful on the first day.

Rosa Parks was found guilty and fined; the N.A.A.C.P. had their case. A new organization, the Montgomery Improvement Association (M.I.A.) was established to direct the boycott, and King was elected president. This surprised him, since he was new to the city and only 26-years old. He expected an older person to be nominated, but he willingly accepted the position.

Early in the boycott, King gave a rousing speech at a rally at the Holt Street Baptist Church. He said to the gathering, "If we protest courageously, and yet with dignity and Christian love, when the history books are written in the future, somebody will have to say, 'There lived a race of people, of black people, of people who had the moral courage to stand up for their rights. And thereby they injected a new meaning into the veins of history and civilization.'"

King received many life-threatening phone calls—as many as 30 to 40 calls a night. One evening he became depressed; he thought that he could no longer cope with his burden. He said later, "At that moment I experienced the presence of the Divine as I had never experienced Him before." He heard an inner voice that directed him to "Stand up for righteousness, stand up for truth, and God will be at your side forever."

On January 30, 1956, King spoke at an M.I.A. meeting at the First Baptist Church. Coretta was home with their daughter, Yolanda, when they heard something hit the front porch. They moved quickly from the front room to the back of the house as a bomb exploded; it destroyed part of the front porch and sent shards of glass all over the room they had just left.

King hurried home from the meeting. A crowd of African Americans, armed with clubs, knives, and guns, gathered in front of their home ready to retaliate for the bombing. He dispersed them by telling them to put away their weapons and to pursue a path of non-violence. He said, "I want you to love your enemies. Be good to them. This is what we must live by. We must meet hate with love."

The city government tried to stop the bus boycott by enforcing a little-known law banning boycotts. Almost 100 M.I.A. members were charged, and King was the first one to be tried. He was found guilty; his sentence was a $500 fine or 386 days of hard labor. His attorney appealed the decision.

The city passed an injunction to stop the use of car pools by declaring them a public nuisance. King was in court in November when he was told that the U.S. Supreme Court had ruled that Alabama's State and local bus segregation laws were unconstitutional.

King was gaining national attention. In February 1957, he became a national celebrity when his picture was on the cover of *Time* magazine and the cover article was about him. King was now viewed as the leader of 16 million African Americans.

A bill was sent to Congress to establish a civil rights commission to investigate violations of African-American rights, including their right to vote. The bill became the Civil Rights Act of 1957.

In early 1957, King and other African-American clergymen and leaders met to found the Southern Christian Leadership Conference (S.C.L.C.). King was elected president. He wrote the book that Harper and Brothers asked him to write, *Stride Toward Freedom*, a combination of an autobiography and a description of the Montgomery boycott.

Activity in the civil rights movement increased. On February 1, 1960, four African-American students from North Carolina

Agricultural and Technical State University in Greensboro occupied stools at a segregated lunch counter at a Woolworth store. They weren't waited on, so they opened their books on the counter and began to study.

On the following day, six times their number engaged in a sit-in at the same Woolworth store. Within a week and a half, sit-ins occurred in South Carolina, Virginia, and other areas of North Carolina. By year-end, over 125 Southern towns had desegregated their lunch counters. The Student Non-violent Coordinating Committee (S.N.C.C.) grew out of the lunch-counter sit-ins.

Older adults continued what the students had started, and on October 19, 1960, King and 35 other African Americans were arrested in Rich's department store in Atlanta for trespassing when the waiters in the Magnolia Room refused to wait on them. Mayor William Hartsfield didn't like keeping King in the Fulton County jail; nevertheless, all except King were released promptly.

King had been arrested earlier in DeKalb County, Georgia, for driving with an expired license, fined, and placed on probation for a year. Fulton County officials complied with DeKalb County's request to turn King over to them. He was found guilty of violating his parole, denied bail, and sentenced to four months of hard labor at the State penitentiary at Reidsville, a prison for hardened criminals.

On October 25, Coretta received a call from Senator and presidential candidate John F. Kennedy, who offered his help in releasing her husband. Robert Kennedy, who managed his brother's presidential campaign, called the judge who sentenced King and expressed his thoughts about the injustice to King. He was released on bail within three days of JFK's call to Coretta.

On December 13, 1961, King spoke in Albany, Georgia, at a rally for an ongoing voter registration campaign sponsored by the S.N.C.C. Late the following day, he led a march to the City Hall. He and the other marchers were jailed for obstructing traffic, released within two days, and jailed again when they refused to pay a fine. Again, they were released after a short stay.

The S.C.L.C. chose Birmingham, Alabama, as the next target for a civil rights demonstration because of its history of segregation. The S.C.L.C. issued a demand to integrate public facilities and hire blacks for positions for which they hadn't been hired previously.

The Commissioner of Public Safety arrested and jailed 20 African Americans engaged in sit-ins in department stores. The following day, King led a group of 50 marchers on city hall. King was jailed again and subjected to abusive treatment.

Coretta called President Kennedy, and Kennedy talked to Birmingham officials about King's release. While in jail, King wrote his 6,400-word "Letter from Birmingham Jail." He wrote it in the margins of newspapers and on toilet paper and smuggled it out of jail. It was published as a pamphlet by the American Friends Service Committee and later published in a magazine with a circulation of a million copies. After eight days, King was released on bail and recruited more marchers.

On May 2, over 1,000 marchers were greeted with high-pressure fire hoses that knocked them to the ground and into walls. Marchers were also attacked by snarling German shepherd police dogs. President Kennedy sent troops to Birmingham to assist in maintaining order.

On August 28, 1963, a high point of King's role as leader of the civil rights movement in the United States occurred on the mall between the Washington Monument and the Lincoln Memorial in Washington, D.C. A march on Washington was led by African-American civil rights organizers to demonstrate the widespread support for the recently introduced civil rights legislation. Organizers anticipated a crowd of 100,000; however, the size of the crowd approached 250,000.

At 3:00 p.m., the last speaker of the rally was introduced, a man referred to as "the moral leader of the nation." King began to give his prepared speech, but the responsiveness of the crowd, which clapped in cadence with his speech, caused him to set aside the prepared text and speak extemporaneously from his heart—drawing on previous speeches he had given. The result was his famous "I have a dream" speech:

- I have a dream that one day on the red hills of Georgia the sons of former slaves and the sons of former slave owners will be able to sit down together at the table of brotherhood. . . .

• I have a dream that my four little children will one day live in a nation where they will not be judged by the color of their skin, but by the content of their character. . . .

• And when we allow freedom to ring, when we let it ring from every State and city, we will be able to speed up that day when all of God's children—black men and white men, Jews and gentiles, Catholics and Protestants—will be able to join hands and to sing in the words of the old Negro spiritual, "Free at last, free at last, thank God almighty, we are free at last."

After the rally, President Kennedy invited the leaders of the march to the White House, where he promised his support in moving the civil rights legislation through Congress.

President Kennedy was assassinated on November 22, 1963. Fortunately, his successor, President Lyndon Johnson, was also a supporter of the civil rights movement, and the legislation was passed within a year. Enforcement of that legislation took much longer. *Time* magazine designated King "Man of the Year" for 1963.

On July 2, 1964, President Johnson signed the Civil Rights Act, authorizing the integration of public facilities and public schools. Civil rights leaders were invited to the White House for the signing ceremony in the East Room.

In October 1964, the Norwegian Parliament selected King for the Nobel Peace Prize. At 35, he was the youngest recipient to date of one of the most prestigious honors in the world, awarded for contributions to international peace.

The civil rights leaders were pleased with the passage of the Civil Rights Act and pushed for a Voting Rights Act. In some areas of the deep South, blacks were terrorized at polling places.

The S.C.L.C. chose Selma, Alabama, where only 383 of 15,000 African Americans were registered to vote, as the site for voting rights activity. The sheriff arrested 226 African Americans merely for attempting to register to vote. On March 7, 1965, the S.C.L.C. marched from Brown Chapel to the Edmund Pettus bridge over the Alabama River, where they were attacked by the sheriff's troopers. Almost 80 of the 600 marchers were treated for broken ribs and collar bones, fractured skulls, head cuts, and many other injuries on what was called "Bloody Sunday."

These incidents motivated President Johnson to push for voting rights. He stated that "This time, on this issue, there must be no delay, no hesitation, and no compromise with our purpose." African Americans were entitled to "the full blessing of American life," and "their cause must be our cause, too." Everyone must strive to "overcome the crippling legacy of bigotry and injustice. And . . . we shall . . . overcome." On August 6, 1965, the Voting Rights Act was signed into law by President Johnson.

King and his followers next turned their attention to the economic inequality faced by African Americans. Initially, their efforts were concentrated in Chicago. However, when the striking garbage collectors of Memphis requested King's help, he went to Tennessee for a rally on April 3, 1968.

On April 4, King was joined at the Lorraine Motel by his brother, A. D., and several friends. Just after 6:00 p.m., King stood on the balcony outside room 306 with Hosea Williams, Jesse Jackson, and Ralph Abernathy. As they prepared to leave to go to dinner, King was shot in the neck and lower right side of his face by a single bullet fired by James Earl Ray from a rooming house across the street.

King died at about 7:00 p.m. His body was returned to Atlanta for his funeral at the Ebenezer Baptist Church on April 9, 1968. Over 60,000 people attended the funeral service, 800 inside the church and the rest outside, who listened to the service on loudspeakers. He was buried in South View Cemetery in Atlanta, where his paternal grandfather was buried. The epitaph on his crypt is "Free at last, free at last. Thank God Almighty, I'm free at last." During the course of his struggle, he said, "If you are cut down in a movement that is designed to save the soul of a nation, then no other death could be as redemptive."

CHAPTER 4

Songwriters / Composers

Success involves every facet of life: your relationships with others, your ability to make in the business word, the health you need to preserve, and the happiness that you enjoy. It also involves a security that goes well beyond financial security. I'm talking about the security of knowing that you have love, trust, and support not only of family but of friends and associates as well.

Zig Ziglar, *Success for Dummies*

COLE PORTER (1891-1964) *Popular Songwriter and Composer*

"As an undergraduate, you first won acclaim by writing the words and music to two of Yale's perennial football fight songs. Since then, you have achieved reputation as a towering figure in the American musical theater. Master of the deft phrase, the delectable rhymes, the distinctive melody, you are, in your own words and your own field, the top. Confident that your graceful, impudent, inimical songs will be played and sung as long as footlights burn and curtains go up. Your alma mater confers upon you the degree of Doctor of Humane Letters."

Norman S. Buck, Provost, Yale University, 1960.

Cole Porter was born on June 9, 1891, to a wealthy family in Peru, Indiana. His maternal grandfather was a coal and timber speculator who expected his grandson to become a lawyer. Cole attended law school but knew that it wasn't for him. He wanted to write songs for the musical theater.

Porter's musical abilities weren't initially recognized. His success began in the 1920s, and by the 1930s he was one of the most popular songwriters on Broadway. Unlike George Gershwin and Richard Rodgers, Porter wrote the lyrics as well as the music.

In 1937, Porter had a very serious horseback riding accident that left him disabled and in constant pain. He continued to write songs but his shows of the 1940s did not measure up to those of the 1920s and 1930s. However, in 1948, he wrote what many consider his finest musical, *Kiss Me, Kate,* based on Shakespeare's *Taming of the Shrew.* It won the first Tony Award for Best Musical.

Among Porter's many musicals are *Anything Goes, Can-Can, Fifty Million Frenchmen,* and *Silk Stockings.* His many hit songs include "Begin the Beguine," "Night and Day," "What Is This Thing Called Love?," "You Do Something To Me," and "In the Still of the Night." Porter also composed scores for films from the 1930s to the 1950s, including *Born to Dance* (1936) with "You'd Be So Easy to Love," *Rosalie* (1937) with "In the Still of the Night," *High Society* (1956) with "True Love," and *Les Girls* (1957).

Porter was an only child born to Samuel Porter, a druggist, and Kate Cole Porter, the daughter of James Omar "J. O." Cole, "the richest man in Indiana." J. O. Cole dominated the family. Kate Porter strongly encouraged her son's musical training. He learned the violin at age six, the piano at eight, and with help from his mother wrote his first operetta at ten. Porter's father was a vocalist, a pianist, and an amateur poet. He may have been a minor influence on his son's talents in rhyme and meter. However, the father and son relationship was not close.

In 1905, Porter enrolled in Worcester Academy in Massachusetts. He was class valedictorian when he graduated in 1909, the year he entered Yale University. At Yale, he majored in English, minored in music, and also studied French. He was a member of Scroll and Key and Delta Kappa Epsilon fraternity and contributed to the humor magazine, *The Yale Record*. He was a member of the Wiffenpoofs singing group. In his senior year, Porter was elected president of the Yale Glee Club and was its main soloist.

Porter wrote 300 songs at Yale, including student songs, such as "Eli Yale" and "Bulldog":
:

> Bull Dog! Bull Dog! Bow, wow, wow
> Eli Yale '
> Bull Dog! Bull Dog! Bow, wow, wow
> Our team can never fail.

They are still sung at Yale today.

Porter also wrote music for his fraternity, the Yale Dramat (the Yale dramatic society), and while attending Law School at Harvard University. He enrolled in Harvard Law School in 1913 but soon switched to the Music School, where he studied harmony and counterpoint with Pietro Yon. J. O. Cole was not told of this move.

Porter's first song on Broadway was "Esmeralda" from *Hands Up* in 1915. This first success was followed by the failure of his first Broadway show in 1916, *See America First,* a "patriotic comic opera." It folded after two weeks.

In 1917, when the United States entered World Was I, Porter moved to Paris. He joined the French Foreign Legion, served in North Africa, transferred to the French Officers' School at Fontainebleau, and taught gunnery to U.S. soldiers. After the war,

Porter leased a luxury apartment in Paris, where he hosted lavish parties known for "much gay and bisexual activity, Italian nobility, cross-dressing, and international musicians."

In 1918, Porter met Linda Lee Thomas, a wealthy divorcee eight years his senior. Linda was beautiful and had many social connections. They had mutual interests, including a love of travel. Linda became Porter's companion and confidant.

They were married in 1919, even though Linda was aware of Porter's homosexuality. Linda was provided with continued social status; Porter was provided with a heterosexual image at a time when homosexuality was not acknowledged in public. They were very devoted to each other and remained married until her death in 1954.

Porter enrolled at the Schola Cantorum in Paris to study orchestration and counterpoint with Vincent d'Indy. In 1919, Porter had his first big hit, "Old Fashioned Garden." The following year he contributed several songs to *A Night Out*. Porter had little success with his songwriting in the 1920s. The poor public response to his work hurt him. He came very close to giving up songwriting as a career.

In 1928, at the age of thirty-six, Porter reentered the Broadway scene with his first real hit musical, *Paris,* which included the songs "Let's Misbehave" and "Let's Do It." His revue *Wake Up and Dream* ran for 263 performances in London and then moved to New York, where it ran for 136 performances, being shortened by the Wall Street crash of 1929. Nevertheless, its song "What Is This Thing Called Love?" became extremely popular.

In 1929, Porter wrote the music for *Fifty Million Frenchmen,* which included "You Do Something To Me" and "You've Got That Thing." It was doing poorly at the box office until Irving Berlin placed an advertisement in the newspaper observing: "The best musical comedy I've heard in years . . . One of the best collections of song numbers that I have ever listened to."

In 1930, Porter's *The New Yorker* was popular, particularly the song "Love for Sale." Porter's next success was Fred Astaire's last stage show, *Gay Divorce* in 1932, with Porter's best-known song, "Night and Day."

Anything Goes was an instant hit in 1934 with its "I Get a Kick Out of You," "All Through the Night," "You're the Top," and

"Blow, Gabriel, Blow." It was the first of five Porter shows starring Ethel Merman. In 1935 came *Jubilee,* with "Begin the Beguine" and "Just One of Those Things."

On October 24, 1937, Porter was riding at Piping Rock Club at Locust Valley, when his horse rolled on him and crushed his legs. He became a cripple and was in constant pain for the rest of his life. Linda hurried home from Paris to be with him at the hospital for seven months and afterwards, when he was allowed to return home to the Waldorf Towers.

In 1939, with increased unrest in Europe, Linda closed their house in Paris and purchased a home in the Berkshire Mountains, near Williamstown, Massachusetts. Porter spent time in Hollywood, New York, and their home in Williamstown. Porter continued to write songs for Hollywood movies, including *You'll Never Get Rich* with Fred Astaire and Rita Hayworth. He cooperated with the production of *Night and Day,* the somewhat fictional biography of Cole Porter starring Cary Grant. It was popular principally due to Porter's songs.

In 1948, *Kiss Me, Kate,* Porter's most successful show, was staged, running 1,077 performances in New York and 400 in London. It included "So In Love," "Too Darn Hot," and "Always True to You (In My Fashion)." His *Can-Can* in 1952 was a hit, followed by another success, *Silk Stockings,* his last original Broadway production, in 1955. He wrote the score for *High Society,* including "True Love," in 1956 and some of the songs for *Les Girls* in 1957.

Porter's mother died in 1952, and Linda died in 1954 from emphysema. In 1958, after thirty-four operations, Porter's right leg had to be amputated and replaced with an artificial leg. He never wrote another song. He spent the remaining six years of his life in seclusion. Cole Porter died on October 15, 1964, of kidney failure in Santa Monica, California, at the age of seventy-three.

GEORGE GERSHWIN (1898-1937) *Popular Songwriter and Composer*

"Just seven years tomorrow since George wrote 'Plenty O' Nuttin' and I took it down as he played it. My 'Porgy' lecture honestly wowed the people last night—the music is absolutely sure-fire in *any* group whatsoever. The whole audience left feeling proud that so important a work has been done in this country. And I left with a ghastly sense of the grayness of a world without George, a profound personal and universal sense of loss. For I believe his music is a force for strong Americanism, in the best sense, that it strikes a powerful blow against the evils that besiege us by giving people a magic lift and a strengthening touch . . . It's so positive and confident."

Kay Swift in a letter to Mary Lasker, 1942

George Gershwin composed popular and classical music. His works in both genres are well-known. His best-known orchestral compositions include *Rhapsody in Blue* (1924), *An American in Paris* (1928), and the opera *Porgy and Bess* (1935).

Gershwin studied piano with Rubin Goldmark and composition with Henry Cowell. He began his career as a song plugger in Tin Pan Alley. Then he began to compose Broadway theater works with his brother, Ira, and Buddy DeSylva. He moved to Paris to study.

When Gershwin returned to New York City, he composed *Porgy and Bess*, working with Ira and DuBose Heyward. Initially a commercial failure, it is now one of the most important American operas of the twentieth century. Gershwin moved to Hollywood and composed many film scores until his death of a brain tumor in 1937.

George Gershwin was born Jacob Gershowitz, in Brooklyn, New York, on September 26, 1898, of Russian and Jewish heritage. George's father, Moishe Gershowitz, had worked as a leather cutter in St. Petersburg, Russia. Moishe fell in love with Roza Bruskins, daughter of a furrier. Born in Vilnius, Lithuania, Roza moved with her family to New York because of increasing anti-semitism in Russia. She changed her first name to Rose.

Moishe, faced with compulsory military service in Russia, followed Rose to New York. When he arrived in New York, Moishe Gershowitz changed his first name to Morris. He took a job as a foreman in a workshop. Morris and Rose were married on July 21, 1895. Gershowitz changed his name to Gershwin sometime between 1893 and 1895, perhaps when they were married.

The Gershwin's first child, Ira, was born on December 6, 1896. George Gershwin was born on September 26, 1898. Two more children were born to the family, Arthur in 1900 and Frances in 1906.

George's interest in music began at the age of ten when he heard a friend's violin recital. George's parents bought a piano so Ira could take piano lessons. However, to Ira's relief, it was brother George who took the lessons.

Charles Hambitzer taught Gershwin conventional piano techniques and acquainted him with the music of the European classical tradition. He encouraged Gershwin to attend orchestra concerts and, in effect, became his mentor. Later, Gershwin studied with the classical composer Rubin Goldmark and avant-garde composer-theorist Henry Cowell.

Gershwin left school at the age of fifteen and became a "song plugger" for a publishing firm in Tin Pan Alley. He published his first song at the age of seventeen and another one year later. He had his first national hit in 1919 with his song "Swanee," with lyrics by Irving Caesar. Performances by Al Jolson contributed to the popularity of the song.

In 1916, Gershwin began to work for the Aeolian Company, recording and arranging piano rolls. He produced hundreds of rolls under his name and assumed names. He also performed in vaudeville, providing piano accompaniment.

In the early 1920s, Gershwin collaborated with songwriter and music director William Daly on the Broadway musicals *Piccadilly to Broadway* (1920), *For Goodness' Sake* (1922), and *Our Nell* (1923). Gershwin also worked with Buddy DeSylva frequently. They wrote the one-act jazz opera *Blue Monday,* set in Harlem.

In 1924, Gershwin and his brother, Ira, collaborated on the musical comedy *Lady Be Good,* which included "Fascinating Rhythm" and "Oh, Lady, Be Good." They followed it with *Oh, Kay!* (1926), *Funny Face* (1927), and *Strike Up the Band* (1927). Next came *Show Girl* (1929), *Girl Crazy* (1930), which introduced

"Embraceable You" and "I Got Rhythm," and *Of Thee I Sing* (1931). *Of Thee I Sing* was the first musical comedy to win the Pulitzer Prize for drama.

In 1924, Gershwin composed *Rhapsody in Blue* for orchestra and piano, his first classical work. It was orchestrated by Ferde Grofe and introduced by Paul Whiteman's band in New York. In the mid-1920s, Gershwin moved to Paris, hoping to study with Nadia Boulanger and Maurice Ravel. Both turned him down, thinking that rigorous musical study would ruin his jazz-influenced style. In his rejection letter, Ravel asked, "Why become a second-rate Ravel when you're already a first-rate Gershwin?"

While in Paris, Gershwin wrote *An American in Paris,* which received mixed reviews at its premiere at Carnegie Hall on December 13, 1928. He returned to the United States and wrote his first opera, *Blue Monday,* a short one-act opera that was not a financial success.

In 1935, Gershwin wrote *Porgy and Bess,* based on the novel *Porgy* by DuBose Heyward, which he called a "folk opera." It received mixed reviews from music and drama critics. They had difficulty with it because it wasn't really an opera and it really wasn't a musical. It included "Summertime," "I Got Plenty o' Nuttin'," and "It Ain't Necessarily So."

Gershwin moved to Hollywood in 1936, where he wrote the music for the film *Shall We Dance,* starring Fred Astaire and Ginger Rodgers. His score, which combined ballet with jazz, was very popular.

Gershwin had a ten-year relationship with composer Kay Swift, whom he frequently consulted about his music. They never married. After Gershwin's death, Swift arranged some of his music, transcribed several of his recordings, and collaborated with his brother, Ira, on several songs.

Early in 1937, Gershwin began to complain of blinding headaches. On February 11, 1937, he performed his *Concerto in F* in a concert with the San Francisco Symphony Orchestra under the direction of Pierre Monteux. He suffered coordination problems and blackouts during the performance. He had been experiencing mood swings and could not eat without spilling his food. On July 9, he collapsed and was rushed to Cedars of Lebanon hospital, where he went into a coma.

It was determined that Gershwin had a brain tumor and that the need for surgery was immediate. He was operated on in the early hours of February 11th, but the operation was not successful. George Gershwin died on the morning of July 11, 1937, at the age of thirty-eight. He was buried at Westchester Hills Cemetery in Hastings-on-Hudson, New York.

One of the observations Gershwin made about his music was: "True music must reflect the thought and aspirations of the people and time. My people are Americans. My time is today."

HOAGY CARMICHAEL (1899-1981) *Composer of Popular Music*

"Hoagy Carmichael was the most talented, inventive, sophisticated and jazz-oriented' of the hundreds of writers composing pop songs in the first half of the 20th century."

Alec Wilder, *American Popular Song: The Great Innovators, 1900-1950*

Hoagy Carmichael, in addition to being a composer, was also a pianist, an actor in thirteen films, a singer, and a bandleader. He composed thirty-eight songs from 1924 to 1953. Four of his most well known songs are:

"Stardust" with lyrics by Mitchel Parish
"Heart and Soul" with lyrics by Frank Loesser
"The Nearness of You" with lyrics by Ned Washington
"Skylark" with lyrics by Johnny Mercer

Carmichael was the son of Howard Carmichael, an electrician, and Linda Robinson Carmichael, a pianist who had played accompaniment for silent movies. He was named Hoagland after a circus troupe "The Hoaglands" who stayed at the Carmichael house when they visited Bloomington, Indiana. Carmichael began to sing and play the piano, learning from his mother. He never had formal piano lessons. In high school, his spare time was spent on the piano. He listened to ragtime pianists Hube Hanna and Hank Wells.

Living in Indianapolis at the age of eighteen, Carmichael worked at part-time jobs to help support the family. He had a close friendship with Reg Duvalle, a black pianist and bandleader known as "the elder statesman of Indiana jazz" and "the Rhythm King," who taught him jazz piano improvisation.

Carmichael attended the University of Indiana and the University of Indiana Law School. He received a bachelors degree in 1925 and a law degree in 1926. He played the piano for his "Collegians" all around Indiana to help to pay for his college costs.

Carmichael met and became a friend of cornetist Bix Beiderbecke and was influenced by his classical and impressionistic musical themes. Beiderbecke introduced Carmichael to Louis Armstrong, who was playing with King Oliver's Creole Jazz Band in Chicago.

The first songs that Carmichael composed were "Washboard Blues," "Boneyard Shuffle," and "Riverboat Shuffle," which was recorded by Beiderbecke. According to Richard M. Sudhater in *Stardust Melody,* Carmichael had discovered his method of songwriting: *"You don't write melodies, you find them ... If you find the beginning of a good song, and your fingers do not stray, the melody should come out of hiding in a short time."* In 1927, his career began to take off when he wrote "Stardust," which was recorded by Gennett Records in Richmond, Indiana, with Carmichael at the piano.

Paul Whiteman recorded "Washboard Blues," with Carmichael playing and singing. The Dorsey brothers and Bix Beiderbecke played in the orchestra. His first song with his own lyrics was "Rockin' Chair," which was recorded by Louis Armstrong and Mildred Bailey. Despite this early success, he was at a disadvantage because of his inability to sight-read and to notate music correctly. He signed up for coaching and improved his ability to arrange his own music.

In 1929, Carmichael moved to New York City and met Duke Ellington's agent and publisher Irving Mills, whom he hired to record his music. The stock market crash hurt him financially. He had to take a job in an investment house and he seriously considered changing his profession. Fortunately, Louis Armstrong's recording of "Rockin' Chair" and the success of "Georgia on My Mind" gave him some needed income.

During the Depression, people were no longer paying to attend clubs or buying sheet music. The demand for jazz appeared to be fading. However, the time of the big bands, with bandleaders such as Benny Goodman and Tommy Dorsey, was coming. In 1933, his "Lazybones" with lyrics by Johnny Mercer was a financial success.

In 1935, Carmichael married Ruth Menardi, a preacher's daughter. They moved to California, where he accepted a contract with Paramount. Other songwriters working for Hollywood studios included E. Y. Harburg at MGM and Harry Warren at Warner Brothers. In 1937, Carmichael appeared in his first movie, *Topper.*

In 1938, Carmichael wrote "Two Sleepy People" and "Heart and

Soul." During the 1940s, he performed in many USO shows. He maintained a close professional relationship with Johnny Mercer. He worked on a song steadily for days or weeks until he thought it was perfect.

In 1943, Carmichael returned to the movies in Ernest Hemingway's *To Have and Have Not* with Humphrey Bogart and Lauren Bacall. He was in *Young Man with a Horn,* based on Bix Beiderbecke's life, with Myrna Loy and Fredric March.

In the early 1950s, Carmichael composed "In the Cool, Cool, Cool of the Evening," with lyrics by Johnny Mercer, which won his first Academy Award for Best Original Song. The coming of rock and roll in the mid-1950s negatively affected the careers of older songwriters like Carmichael. He and his wife divorced. Fortunately, his royalties kept him solvent.

In 1971, Carmichael was inducted into the Songwriters Hall of Fame along with Duke Ellington. His composer's fame continued to fade because of the popularity of rock music. In 1972, the University of Indiana awarded him an honorary doctorate in music.

In 1977, Carmichael married Wanda McKay. On June 27, 1979, he was honored on his 80th birthday by the Newport Jazz Festival with a concert "The Stardust Road: A Hoagy Carmichael Jubilee" in Carnegie Hall, hosted by Bob Crosby and including singers like Kay Starr and musicians such as Billy Butterfield.

On his 80th birthday, Carmichael observed: "I'm a bit disappointed in myself. I know I could have accomplished a hell of a lot more ... I could write anything anytime I wanted to. But I let a lot of other things get in the way ... I've been floating around in the breeze."

Carmichael died of heart failure at the Eisenhower Medical Center in Rancho Mirage, California, on December 27, 1981. In 1986, the Carmichael family donated his piano, memorabilia, and archives to his alma mater, the University of Indiana.

RICHARD RODGERS (1902-1979) *Composer of Popular Music*

"Of all the writers whose songs are considered and examined . . . those of Rodgers show the highest degree of consistent excellence, inventiveness and sophistication . . . After spending weeks playing his songs, I am more than impressed and respectful; I am astonished."

Composer Alec Wilder

Richard Rodgers composed the music for over 1,000 popular songs, of which over 200 were notable hits, and about 100 have become popular classics. He also wrote thirty-five stage productions, including sixteen that were major successes. Two of them established box-office records. The musicals for which he is best known include *A Connecticut Yankee, On Your Toes, The Boys from Syracuse, Pal Joey, Oklahoma, Carousel, South Pacific,* and *The King and I.* His most popular songs include "Some Enchanted Evening," and "You'll Never Walk Alone." Also, he composed music for television and Hollywood films. Rodgers was influenced by composers Victor Herbert and Jerome Kern.

Of Rodgers, Ira Gershwin observed: "I am sure that musicologists, present and future, will have to agree that Rodgers is not only one of our most successful composers of theater music but also one of exquisite taste and resourcefulness, and as a composer-showman, one of integrity and courage." Leonard Bernstein considered Rodgers the most imitated songwriter of our time, and noted: "He has established new levels of taste, distinction, simplicity in the best sense, and inventiveness."

Rodgers's first lyricist partner was Lorenz (Larry) Hart, whom he knew from his years at Columbia University. Later, Oscar Hammerstein II wrote the lyrics for his music. In working with Hart, Rodgers usually composed the music first and then Hart wrote the lyrics. It was the reverse with Hammerstein, who usually wrote the lyrics and then Rodgers composed the music. Occasionally, the composer and the lyricist worked together in an ongoing joint effort.

Rodgers was born on June 28, 1902, into a prosperous German Jewish family in Queens, New York City. He was the son of Mamie

141

Levy Rodgers and Dr. William Abrahams Rodgers, a prominent physician. Rodgers began playing the piano by ear at the age of six and was influenced in his early years by the Broadway operettas his parents took him to see. He attended summer camp at Camp Wigwam in Harrison, Maine, where he composed his first songs at the age of fourteen.

Rodgers was introduced to Hart by mutual friend Philip Leavitt when Rodgers was in high school and Hart had dropped out of Columbia College at the age of twenty-three. Rodgers decided to work with Hart even though he was known to be difficult and unreliable. Later, Rodgers noted that "In one afternoon, I acquired a career, a partner, a best friend, and a source of permanent irritation."

In 1919, Rodgers decided to attend Columbia College, mainly because it put on varsity shows with student talent. Hart had participated in these shows and had maintained his contacts at the college. Rodgers and Hart worked together on two plays at Columbia.

Rodgers's and Hart's first play on Broadway was *Poor Little Rich Girl*, which opened on July 28, 1920, and ran for 119 performances. Only half the score was by Rodgers, the other half was by Sigmund Romberg. After this modest success, it was five years before their work appeared in the professional theatre. They took any small music job that was available.

Rodgers was discouraged with his lack of success and with the courses at Columbia in which he had no interest, such as history and mathematics. He wanted to concentrate on music and considered transferring to the Institute of Musical Art, which is now Juilliard. He spoke with his father about his plans and his father was beginning to question his son's choice of music as a career, a field in which he did not seem to be experiencing much success. His two years at the Institute opened new opportunities for Rodgers.

William Rodgers was concerned about his son, who was now twenty-two years old and living on an allowance provided by his father. He could see no possibility of his son earning a living from music. William consulted a lawyer friend who suggested that he give Richard a little more time. What William did not know was that Richard himself was beginning to question his preparation for the future.

Rodgers decided to find a job in business. A friend referred him to a manufacturer of children's underwear. Rodgers was offered $50 a week to sell its products and promised a more responsible position if he proved to be successful. Rodgers discussed the position with his father and told him he was tired of living on an allowance and that he wanted to begin to earn his own living.

Fortunately, before Rodgers could accept the job, he received a call from the lawyer friend of his father who had met with some young actors from the Theatre Guild planning a sophisticated revue. They were looking for a composer and a lyricist. The revue, *The Garrick Gaieties,* was scheduled for only two performances — a matinee and an evening at the Garrick Theatre on May 17, 1925. Rodgers and Hart were chosen for the job.

The revue was a series of parodies and comedy sketches that included two very popular Rodgers and Hart tunes: "Manhattan" and "Sentimental Me." The critics were enthralled. Alexander Woollcott called it "fresh and spirited and engaging." Robert Benchley described it as "the most civilized play in town." Four additional performances were scheduled in early June. The revue began regular performances on June 8 and ran for twenty-five weeks. For the first time, Rodgers and Hart earned a regular income.

The next success of Rogers and Hart was *Dearest Enemy,* which included the hit song "Here in My Arms." It ran for just under a year and helped to bring attention to the composer and lyricist. They were much in demand, and in 1926, they had five shows on Broadway, including *The Girl Friend,* which ran for over 400 performances, and *The Melody Man.*

Rodgers and Hart followed with *Peggy-Ann,* an unorthodox play that nevertheless was popular with the critics — Robert Benchley and Dorothy Parker thought that it was the best musical they had seen. It ran for almost a year before moving to London.

Their next musical, *A Connecticut Yankee,* was their most successful to date. It included a song they had written earlier, "My Heart Stood Still," a song popularized in England by the Prince of Wales, who sang it in public." Thou Swell" also gained popularity. In 1925, Rodgers was ready to give up song writing and accept a job in business. One year later, he was the fair-haired boy of Broadway.

Larry Hart continued to be difficult to work with. He was undisciplined and irresponsible. Although Rodgers was younger than Hart, he functioned as his older brother. Rodgers referred to Hart as "the sweetest little guy in the world." Rodgers observed of Hart's writing of lyrics: "He hated doing it and loved it when it was done." In 1929, Rodgers and Hart wrote *Spring Is Here*, which introduced the hit "With a Song in My Heart."

On March 5, 1930, Richard Rodgers married Dorothy Feiner, whom he had known since she was seven years old. Their fathers were friends, and Rodgers and Dorothy's brother, Ben, were also friends. They knew that they were meant for each other from the time she was sixteen. They honeymooned in Europe. In London, they were honored guests at a dinner party given by Lord and Lady Louis Mountbatten.

In the early 1930s, Rodgers and Hart spent four years in Hollywood making movies. *State Fair* was one of the best scores that Rodgers wrote for motion pictures. "It Might As Well Be Spring" won the Academy Award for best song. When they returned to New York, they found that they had almost been forgotten. Their musical *On Your Toes* was one of their early successes on their return to Broadway. This was the first musical in which Rodgers and Hart wrote the book, in addition to the music and lyrics. They began to fully integrate the text and the music, and, to some extent, to tell a story. The ballet "Slaughter on Tenth Avenue" was an important element of *On Your Toes*.

Babes in Arms, which opened in 1937, was the first musical in which Rogers and Hart wrote the entire book without any outside assistance. It contained "Where or When," "My Funny Valentine," "Johnny One Note," and "I Wish I were in Love Again." Its sophisticated "The Lady Is a Tramp" had a new rhythmic energy. One of the last musicals in which Rodgers and Hart collaborated was *Pal Joey*, which opened to mixed reviews from the critics. It was rereleased in 1952 for a 542-performance run on Broadway. It became a very popular musical.

The gulf between Rodgers and Hart widened. The disciplined Rodgers had more difficulty dealing with Hart's drinking. Hart had always been concerned with his short stature and his lack of success with women. Toward the end, he paid no attention to his appearance and people would cross the street to avoid speaking with him. When the end came, it came suddenly, surprising many of his friends. He died in 1943.

Two of Hammerstein's earliest successes were *Rose Marie* and *The Desert Song,* both of which he wrote for Rudolf Friml. The greatest of his early works were the lyrics for *Showboat,* which he wrote with Jerome Kern. It was produced by Florenz Ziegfeld in 1927.

Rodgers began to collaborate with Oscar Hammerstein II as his lyricist. Rodgers and Hammerstein had both attended Columbia College and worked on variety shows. Hammerstein was older than Rodgers; he was Hart's age. Hammerstein, like Rodgers, had an inauspicious start—four failures in three years before he collaborated on a successful Broadway show.

Rodgers's and Hammerstein's first collaboration was the immensely successful *Oklahoma* in 1943. In the opinion of Cole Porter: "The most profound change in forty years of musical comedy has been Rodgers and Hammerstein." The songs,"Oklahoma" and "Oh, What a Beautiful Morning," were two of the most popular songs in a musical rich in good songs. *Oklahoma!* ran for 2,248 performances over five years and nine weeks, the longest run of any Broadway play to date.

The next big Rodgers and Hammerstein hit was *Carousel,* which featured "June Is Bustin' Out All Over," "If I Loved You," and "You'll Never Walk Alone." Subsequent Rodgers and Hammerstein successes included *South Pacific* and *The King and I,* which had 1,246 performances on Broadway over three years.

Rodgers and Hammerstein won a special Pulitzer Prize for *Oklahoma!* in 1944. Their musicals earned them 35 Tony Awards, 15 Academy Awards, two Pulitzer Prizes, two Grammy Awards and two Emmy Awards. Rodgers is a member of the American Theatre Hall of Fame. He died of a heart attack at the age of 77 in 1979. He had survived cancer of the jaw, a laryngectomy, and an earlier heart attack.

ALEC WILDER (1907-1980) *Popular Songwriter and Composer*

"Alec Wilder's music is a unique blend of American musical traditions—among them jazz and the American popular song—and basic 'classical' European forms and techniques. As such, it fiercely resists all labeling. Although it pained Alec that his music was not more widely accepted by either jazz or classical performers, undeterred he wrote a great deal of music of remarkable originality in many forms: sonatas, suites, concertos, operas, ballets, art songs, woodwind quartets, brass quintets, jazz suites—and hundreds of popular songs.

"Many times his music wasn't jazz enough for the 'jazzers,' or 'highbrow,' 'classical,' or 'avant-garde' enough for the classical establishment. In essence, Wilder's music was so unique in its originality that it didn't fit in any of the preordained musical slots and stylistic pigeon-holes. His music was never out of vogue because, in effect, it was never in vogue; its non-stereotypical specialness virtually precluding widespread acceptance."

> Gunther Schuller, Loonis McGlohon, and Robert Levy, "A Short Biography"

Alec Wilder's grandfather, Samuel Wilder, made the family fortune in banking and real estate in Rochester, New York. He was the principal owner of Corinthian Hall, where the Swedish nightingale, Jenny Lind, gave her first Rochester performance. Alec's father, George, Samuel's second son, was also a successful Rochester banker. Alec's mother was Lillian Chew Wilder, daughter of Alexander Lafayette Chew and Sarah Prouty Chew of Geneva, New York. The Marquis de Lafayette was Alexander Chew's godfather.

Alec Wilder was born on February 16, 1907. He had an older brother, George, and an older sister, Helen, with whom he was close. Helen introduced him to music by singing the music of Jerome Kern to him. When Wilder was three years old, his father died. By the time he was a teenager, he knew that he did not want to be a banker like his grandfather and his father: "I wanted no part of it . . . for my family was virtually littered with bankers, nor was I inclined to be friendly with the sons and daughters of the conventional families of my family's world."

The Wilder family moved frequently. Wilder attended three private schools: Saint Paul's in Garden City, Long Island, Lawrenceville in New Jersey, and the Collegiate School in Manhattan, where they lived from 1921 until 1924. His first visit to the theater was to see *Shuffle Along*, Eubie Blake's all-black show.

In his late teens, Wilder toured Europe and became interested by music in Venice and Florence. He composed his first piano piece while in Italy and wrote to a friend:

> Something keeps shouting at me to look deeper and deeper into music. I've heard no music but that of countless people singing in the streets. Yet, I've started buying stacks of music; in fact I've even rented a piano. I don't know about music, don't play worth a damn nor read well, but ever since you took me to that concert at Carnegie Hall and I heard "L'Apres-Midi d'un Faune" I've got the bug. I've even written a piece of music that's not just a tune. I don't think it's good, but it is something which I wrote. And it's the first one.

When Wilder returned to New York, he wrote some popular tunes and then, at the suggestion of his friend, tried a cantata based on one of Kipling's poems.

In 1926, Wilder returned to Rochester for the first time since his family had moved to Garden City during World War I. He had decided on a career in music; however, he did not enroll at the Eastman School of Music. Instead, he took private lessons from two faculty members. He studied counterpoint with Herbert Inch, who later won the Prix de Rome, and composition with Edward Royce, son of Harvard University logician Josiah Royce.

Wilder was impressed with the Eastman School. He noted: "It's the wild, free, searching, roaring world of young people who know what they want . . . and my God, how they love music." He met French horn player John Barrows, oboist Mitch Miller, violist Joe Schiff, and tenor Frank Baker. Wilder was becoming immersed in music: "Music, its sounds, rhythms, patterns and unverbal implications, directions and secret affirmations had always fascinated me. The more I heard, the more I learned, the more dedicated I became to trying to speak its language."

Wilder's favorite composer was Bach. He was also influenced by Mussorgsky, Debussy, and Ravel. Although Howard Hanson was the director of the Eastman School at the time, he and Wilder were too dissimilar to become close. Hanson composed large works in the romantic tradition. His favorite composers were Beethoven, Handel, and Scriabin. Hanson was an autocratic leader; Wilder had little respect for authority. Nevertheless, Hanson said of Wilder's compositions, "His music—intimate, appealing, and very well done—had great charm."

In 1928, Wilder composed eight songs for voice and orchestra based on poems by James Stephens and the song "Annabelle Lee," using text from Edgar Allan Poe. The following year, he composed one of his first works for orchestra, "Symphonic Piece." Also, in his student days, he composed popular songs with a particular singer in mind, e.g. Mildred Bailey, Ethel Waters, and Bing Crosby. "Mildred wound up singing some, Ethel Waters none, and, at the end of his career, Crosby a few."

During his time at the Eastman School, Wilder wrote the revue *Haywire*. His friend, Eastman student Mitch Miller, commented: "He was a very complicated man. I forced him to face his own talent. I got him to write *Haywire*." Although two other students wrote some of the lyrics and one or two of the musical numbers were interpolated, it was loaded with his wit and essentially a Wilder show.

While in Rochester, Wilder became close with his mentor and father figure, James Sibley Watson, Jr., grandson of Western Union co-founder Hiram Sibley. According to Desmond Stone in *Alec Wilder in Spite of Himself,* Watson was "a true Renaissance figure: physician, major influence in American literature in the 1920s, translator of French poetry [such as Rimbaud], pioneer in radiology and in amateur filmmaking, artist, flyer, expert marksman, inventor, millionaire philanthropist."

In association with Melville Webber, Watson produced two American cinematic landmarks: *The Fall of the House of Usher* in 1929 and *Lot in Sodom* in 1932. In the opinion of James Card, previously film archivist at the International Museum of Photography."Watson produced avant-garde films long before there were avant-garde films." Watson provided Wilder with an introduction to filmmaking and film scoring. Another of Wilder's close friends in Rochester was photographer Louis Ouzer. Later, Ouzer was known for his portraits of Marian Anderson, Louis Armstrong, Vladimir Horowitz, Isaac Stern, and other musicians who performed at the Eastman Theatre. He also used his talent in photography to document social change. He was particularly sympathetic to the cause of civil rights for African Americans.

In 1930, Wilder had his first success in writing popular songs: "All the King's Men" written with Eddie Brandt for *Three's a Crowd,* a Broadway revue starring Fred Allen, Libby Holman, and Clifton Webb. By the mid-1930s, Wilder's friends from the Eastman School, Mitch Miller and John Barrows, had moved from Rochester. By this time, Wilder had spent (and given away) his inheritance except for a small quarterly allowance from a family trust fund.

Wilder returned to New York City and lived at the Algonquin Hotel, which would be his home for four decades. As noted by biographer Desmond Stone, in later years Wilder observed:

> I have been coming here since I was a child, and there are still people on the staff who have been here as long as I have. They take care of me. They send out my laundry without my having to fill out a laundry slip, they hang a few suits for me when I'm away, they forward my mail, and they shepherded me through my drinking days . . . I got into a cab to go uptown to a restaurant, and when I got there I simply couldn't move. I told the driver to take me back to the Algonquin, and whoever was on the door sized up the situation immediately. A bellman appeared, and he and the doorman made one of those four-handed seats, got me onto it, and whisked me up to my room.

An anecdote about Wilder's drinking relates that on one occasion while in his cups at the Algonquin's Blue Bar, he asked Benny

Goodman to step outside and take his glasses off. Wilder did not remember the incident the next morning. The story is unlikely. One of Wilder's friends described him as a "great walk-away artist."

Wilder was influenced by the music of Harold Arlen, Jerome Kern, and Vincent Youmans. Wilder's friend, Mitch Miller, obtained a position for him as staff arranger for the *Ford Hour* on radio, but Wilder could not tolerate the lack of freedom that he encountered. Miller also encouraged Wilder to write the woodwind octets that were recorded by the Alec Wilder Octet and introduced him to people in musical circles.

In 1939, Wilder met William Engvick, who became one of his lyricists. Their first collaboration was in revising *Ladies and Gents,* on which Engvick had worked previously.

Wilder met Frank Sinatra when the young singer performed at the Paramount Theatre in New York in the 1940s. In 1945, Mitch Miller talked with Sinatra about performing some of Wilder's orchestral pieces. Sinatra, who had not conducted before, recorded a suite of six numbers mixing classical music, jazz, and pop, *Frank Sinatra Conducts the Music of Alec Wilder,* for Columbia Records. Sinatra observed that Wilder's music "helped my own musical conceptions to reach a higher plane than would have been possible without him."

During the 1940s, Wilder composed many of his best-known popular songs, including "Who Can I Turn To?" (1940); "It's So Peaceful in the Country" (1941), which he wrote for Mildred Bailey; "I'll Be Around" (1942); "While We're Young" (1943); "Trouble Is a Man" (1944); and "Where Is the One?" (1948).

Wilder had the highest regard for cabaret singer Mabel Mercer, whom he considered "the guardian of the tenuous dreams created by the writers of songs." Wilder wrote many songs for her, including "Did You Ever Cross Over to Snedden's?," "Goodbye, John," and "Is It Always Like This?" Mercer and Wilder were friends for forty years.

Wilder had successes but never the big one. His lyricist, William Engvick, identified the problem: "Wilder's unusual and, for the time, difficult arrangements and his oddly shaped, understated and unpredictable melodies caused much antagonism (as they still do) and his progress was difficult. This was complicated by a totally uncommercial dignity and a trenchant wit which left his antagonists sneering, unaware that they were bleeding internally."

Wilder hurt himself by refusing to promote his own works. At times, he was stubborn; he lost the opportunity to write the score for *Peter Pan* for Mary Martin because he did not want to work with Martin's lyricist. He turned down a man who called him to ask if he would do the score for a ballet because "I didn't like the sound of his voice." The ballet was *Fancy Free,* which established Leonard Bernstein's stage reputation. Wilder described this behavior: "I blame no one but myself for the minimal success I have known. I have had to pay this price for keeping myself whole."

In the late 1940s, Wilder wrote his first opera, *The Impossible Forest.* Dancer Gene Kelly had recommended that Wilder compose the music. The libretto was written by Marshall Barer, who wrote *Once Upon a Mattress* with Mary Rodgers. Scenery and costume designer Lemuel Ayers, who had done *Kiss Me Kate,* was signed up, and Jerome Robbins was interested in staging the opera and doing the choreography. Henry Fonda considered starring in it. Unfortunately, sufficient funding could not be raised.

Wilder composed a second opera, *The Wind Blows Free,* with playwright and lyricist Arnold Sundgaard, which suffered the same fate, insufficient funding. In Sundgaard's opinion, "The songs worked fine, but not the play itself." Two of Wilder's songs survived on their own. He went back to writing popular songs, some of which, such as "While We're Young," were sung by Peggy Lee.

Wilder and Engvick were invited to Hollywood by Twentieth Century Fox to write the songs for *Daddy Long Legs.* After writing fifteen songs, they were told that the script was not ready and that they would have to wait until it was. Even though he would be retained on salary, Wilder decided to return to New York. Fox sold the rights to the movie and when *Daddy Long Legs* was finally filmed with Fred Astaire and Leslie Caron, the music of Johnny Mercer (who later wrote lyrics for Wilder) was used instead. The original songs remained out of the public domain.

Wilder developed a friendship with Judy Holliday. Her reputation had been made when she was asked, on short notice, to fill in for Jean Arthur, who had become ill while starring in Garson Kanin's hit comedy, *Born Yesterday.* In 1958, Holliday made a record album for Columbia Records, *Trouble Is a Man.* She chose songs by Berlin, Bernstein, Wilder, and others. She opened the

151

album with the title song by Wilder. It was thought that Wilder had an idealized love for Holliday, whose personality he considered a "sometime, someplace woman, girl, female."

With the introduction of rock and roll in the 1950s and 1960s, interest in popular music waned. Wilder's old friend from the Eastman School, John Barrows, turned him toward concert music and introduced him to many musicians. Wilder's first efforts were two sonatas for horn and piano and *Suite for French Horn and Piano*. He composed for instruments that had been ignored by composers over the years, including the tuba, marimba, guitar, baritone saxophone, and harp.

In 1959, Wilder wrote *Sonata No. 1 for Tuba and Piano*. Only two solos had been written for tuba previously, one by Vaughan Williams and the other by Paul Hindemith. Next he composed *Effie Suite* for tuba, about the experiences of an elephant named Effie. These were followed by *Sonata for Bass Trombone and Piano; Concerto for Oboe, String Orchestra, and Percussion; Jazz Suite for Four Horns; Concerto No. 1 for Horn and Chamber Orchestra;* and *Suite No. 1 for Horn, Tuba, and Piano.*

Wilder also wrote many children's pieces, some by himself and some with Engvick or Sundgaard. In 1954, Wilder wrote, with lyrics by Marshall Barer, *A Child's Introduction to the Orchestra,* which Mitch Miller conducted with the Golden Symphony and the Sandpiper Chorus. In 1965, *Lullabies and Night Songs,* an illustrated collection of children's songs by Wilder and Engvick, was published by Harper & Row.

Wilder teamed with his third lyricist, Loonis McGlohon, on *Land of Oz,* an outdoor version of *The Wizard of Oz* staged on top of Beech Mountain in western North Carolina. It was the first of many successful collaborations with McGlohon. One of the finest was "Blackberry Winter." McGlohon was a composer as well as a lyricist. As a pianist, he had accompanied Eileen Farrell, Judy Garland, Maxine Sullivan, and Maxine VerPlanck. Buffalo native Harold Arlen gave them permission to use "Over the Rainbow" for *Land of Oz,* and Wilder composed many new numbers.

In 1968, Wilder began to work on *American Popular Song: The Great Innovators, 1900-1950,* edited by James Maher, who also wrote the Introduction. The book, a distillation of a half-century of popular songwriting, was published by Oxford University Press in

1972 to critical acclaim. None of Wilder's works are included in the book, but 800 others are examined. In 1973, the book won the Deems Taylor ASCAP Award and a National Book Award nomination.

When Maher visited Wilder in Manhattan to begin their collaboration, Wilder invited him up to his room at the Algonquin Hotel. Maher, who assumed that he was being invited to a suite of rooms, observed: "This was the suite of Alec Wilder! No books, no records — no room, for that matter. There was a second chair, a side chair, but I couldn't see it because there was an opened suitcase on it. Tobacco, some shirts, a bobble bird, a jar of special honey, some airmail writing pads, and similar odds and ends lay on top of the dresser." Nevertheless, as soon as he and Maher began to discuss the book, Wilder knew that he had found the organized collaborator that he needed.

It was important to Wilder that he could be packed and out of his room in twenty minutes. One of his pastimes was riding the railroad — not to any particular destination. Biographer Desmond Stone quoted Wilder:

> Years ago, I'd check out when I had a little money and get on a train, and I'd stay on trains for weeks at a time. I'd travel the main trunks, and I'd transfer and take all the spurs. I loved sitting in a junction in the back of the beyond on a hot day and reading a long novel and listening to the chatter between the baggage man and the conductor. I loved talking with the engineer when he oiled his engine. Can you imagine nattering with a man fueling a jet?

Wilder's persona evolved to resemble a rumpled professor of English Literature. In 1974, Whitney Balliett described Wilder in his *New Yorker* profile, "The President of the Derriére-garde":

> Wilder is is a tall man with a big head and small feet. He was wearing a sports jacket, gray slacks, and loafers, and they had a resigned look of functional clothes. He has a long, handsome face and

receding gray hair that flows out the back of his head, giving the impression that he is in constant motion. His eyebrows are heavy and curved, and when he has finished making a point—often punctuated by his slamming his fist down on the nearest piece of furniture—they shoot up and the corners of his mouth shoot down.

He has piercing, deep-set eyes cushioned by dark, doomsday pouches—diamonds resting on velvet. His face is heavily wrinkled—not with the soft, oh-I-am-growing-old lines but with strong, heavy weather ones. He has a loud baritone voice, and he talks rapidly. When he is agitated, his words roll like cannonballs around the room. He laughs a lot and he swears a lot, in an old-fashioned, Mark Twain manner, and when he is seated, he leans forward, like a figurehead breasting a flood tide. A small, serene mustache marks the eye of the hurricane.

On one occasion, a visitor to the Algonquin Hotel asked the doorman if he had seen Wilder. The doorman replied that you don't see Mr. Wilder, you hear him.

In 1975, Wilder was commissioned by the New York State Arts Council to compose an orchestral piece. *Entertainment No. 6* was first performed in 1977 by the Rochester Philharmonic Orchestra. That year and the following year, he completed many more instrumental compositions, including *Brass Quintet No. 6, Concerto for Flute and Chamber Orchestra, Sextet for Marimba and Wind Quintet, Suite for Flute and Marimba, Woodwind Quintet No. 13, Brass Quintet No. 7, Suite for Flute and Strings, Suite for Horn and Tuba,* and *Suite for Trumpet and Marimba.* Interest in these pieces was limited, but they pleased the musicians for whom they were written.

By 1978, Wilder knew that his health was slipping. In November that year in Gainesville, Florida, the life-long smoker had a cancerous lung removed. He recovered slowly, but eventually he began to compose again. Two of his last collaborations with

McGlohon were "A Long Night" and "South to a Warmer Place," which subsequently were recorded by Sinatra. By December 1980, Wilder was short of breath and hallucinating.

Wilder's friend Louis Ouzer told another Rochester friend, lawyer and jazz program host Thomas Hampson, about their mutual friend's condition. Hampson flew to Gainesville to find that Wilder's condition was deteriorating rapidly. Hampson updated his friend's will and was appointed executor. Wilder died early in the morning of December 24.

Wilder was buried in St. Agnes Cemetery in Avon, New York, near the plot where his friend, Father Henry Atwell, previously pastor of St. Agnes Church, had been buried. Wilder had requested that there be no funeral, no religious service, and no notice in the newspapers of his death. Hampson notified friends that he had arranged for a modest gravestone and a short burial ceremony: "I intend to honor Alec's request that there be no religious service, but a number of his friends said that they wanted to be present, and I certainly think that they should be permitted to do so."

Mitch Miller and longtime friend jazz pianist Marian McPartland, for whom Wilder had written a dozen pieces, were among those who attended the burial ceremony. Loonis McGlohon paid tribute to his collaborator: "Letters from strangers never went unanswered, even when they came from, in your words, people who lived in old soldiers' homes who thought that you were Thornton's brother . . . You were a soft touch, Alec. As long as people believed in something, you couldn't say no." The ceremony was concluded by a trumpet playing "It's So Peaceful in the Country" and by old friend Louis Ouzer blowing a string of bubbles, something that Wilder and his friends, including Marian McPartland, had enjoyed doing, over the grave.

Wilder's own observation on his music was: "My life's work is accepted in large measure only by the old and the young. The middle-aged self-proclaimed musical elite dismiss it as traditional, and therefore suspect." In 1983, Alec Wilder was inducted into the Songwriters' Hall of Fame, and, in 1991, the Alec Wilder Reading Room in the Sibley Music Library was dedicated at the Eastman School of Music.

CHAPTER 5

Late or Unrecognized Success

"If you wish success in life, make perseverance your bosom friend, experience your wise counselor, caution your older brother, and hope your guardian angel."

Joseph Addison

HERMAN MELVILLE (1819-1891) *Author Unappreciated in His Lifetime*

"Melville's values were not the values of his generation. He never strove for fame, 'the triumph of insincere mediocrity.' He was not sure of anything, including mankind, never unreservedly affirmative. Unable to accept the the sweeping optimism of Longfellow, Emerson, and Whitman, he adds his skepticism to that of Hawthorne and Poe. Against the happy yea-sayers he pits his tragic and challenging "no." Instead of Emerson's peaceful rainbow, he presents thunderheads; instead of Whitman's splendid sun, he calls up heroic blackness. His stature constantly increasing, Melville not only measures up to the American giants but towers darkly above them."

Louis Untermeyer, *Makers of the Modern World*

During his lifetime, Herman Melville was considered only a moderately successful author. He did most of the writing for which he is known from 1846 until 1852, between the ages of twenty-seven and thirty-two. During that span of time, his work was considered obscure; a later generation interpreted his work more fully and established his reputation as a leading author of romantic fiction. Rarely has an author faded from popularity and experienced an almost total obliteration of his reputation as Melville did. From 1860 until 1921, Melville was an almost totally forgotten author.

Melville's renaissance began in 1921 when Raymond M. Weaver published *Herman Melville: Mariner and Mystic*. In 1922, a comprehensive edition of Melville's work was compiled in London and published as a sixteen-volume set in 1924. Many biographies and essays were written about Melville and his work from the 1920s through the 1950s. He became one of America's most widely read and analyzed and highly regarded authors.

Herman Melville was born on August 1, 1819, in New York City. His paternal grandfather was Major Thomas Melville, a participant in the Boston Tea Party; his maternal grandfather was General Peter Gansevoort, who had successfully defended Ft. Stanwix against General Burgoyne and his Indian allies.

Melville's father, Allen Melville, was a successful importer and commission merchant until 1830, when he was forced into bankruptcy during a general business depression. He moved his family to Albany to be near his wife's relatives. Weighed down by his financial failure, he was a defeated man. He became physically ill and died of a stroke in his forties.

Herman Melville's oldest brother, Gansevoort, undertook the responsibility of supporting the family by attempting to maintain what was left of their father's business. Herman attended the Albany Academy and the Albany Classical School; however, Gansevoort's business did not prosper, and Herman had to drop out of school. He worked in a bank for a while, and then taught school in Pittsfield, Massachusetts.

Melville's introduction to the sea, which is the principal subject of his books, was in 1829 at age twenty, when he signed on as cabin boy on the *St. Lawrence* bound for Liverpool. He made an entry in his diary:

> I was conscious of a wonderful thing in me, that responded to all the wild commotion of the outer world and went reeling on and on with the planets in their orbits and was lost in one delirious throb at the center of the All. A wild bubbling and bursting at my heart, as if a hidden spring gushed out there.... But how soon these raptures abated, when after a brief interval, we were again set to work, and I had a vile commission to clean out the chicken coops and make up the beds of the pigs in the long boats. Miserable dog's life is this of the sea: commanded like a slave and set to work like an ass; vulgar and brutal men lording it over me, as if I were an African in Alabama.

However, his reservations about life at sea during his first voyage were not enough to prevent him from signing on for another voyage of three years' duration. He sailed on the whaler *Acushnet* from New Bedford on January 3, 1841, with a tyrannical captain and a near-mutinous crew. They sailed around Cape Horn and up the west coast of South America to the Galapagos Islands and continued westward. Conditions eventually became unbearable, and he and a friend, Richard Tobias Greene, jumped ship when they reached the Marquesas.

Nevertheless, Melville was aware of the wealth of knowledge and experience he had accumulated on the whaler. He made the following diary entry:

> If I ever deserve any real repute in that small but high-bushed world which I might not unreasonably be ambitious of; if hereafter I shall do anything that, upon the whole, a man might rather have done than left undone; if at my death, my executors or more properly my creditors find any precious manuscripts in my desk, then I prospectively ascribe all the honor and glory to whaling; for a whaleship was my Yale College and my Harvard.

The island of Nuku Hiva in the Marquesas, where Melville and Toby Greene escaped from the *Acushnet*, was inhabited by a tribe of cannibals called Typees (Taipis). He and his friend were treated simultaneously as prisoners and honored guests. However, despite the peaceful life and the attention of the native girls, Melville and Greene were not ready to turn their back on civilization forever.

Greene returned to Anna Maria Bay to look over a French warship and did not return. Melville escaped later and made his way out to an anchored Australian whaler, the bark *Lucy Ann*. The combination of a captain who was ill and a drunken first mate made conditions on the *Lucy Ann* no more tolerable than the *Acushnet*. When the *Lucy Ann* put into Papeete, Melville refused to go any further with the ship and was put into prison on shore. The natives allowed him to escape.

Melville signed up as harpooner on the *Charles and Henry* out of Nantucket for the voyage to the next port. In May 1843, he was discharged from the *Charles and Henry* in Lahaina, Hawaiian Islands. He went to Honolulu, where he worked as a storekeeper and a pinsetter in a bowling alley while awaiting passage home. In August, he signed on the frigate *USS United States;* he was discharged when the ship reached Boston in October 1844.

Melville joined his family at Lansingburgh, near Albany. At the age of twenty-five, he was glad to be home; he was welcomed by a family who were spellbound by his storytelling of his adventures at sea. He began to write shortly after his return home. The narrative of his adventures on Nuku Hiva became *Typee*. His storytelling is so elevated that it is difficult for the reader to determine where fact leaves off and imagination begins.

Melville's older brother was appointed to a diplomatic post in London and took the *Typee* manuscript with him to submit to John Murray, the English publisher, who accepted it for his Home and Colonial Library. Since Murray claimed in his advertising that his books were true but were as exciting as fiction, he asked for proof of the story's authenticity. Toby Greene came forward and verified Melville's story. He told Melville that he had been pressed aboard the French warship at Nuku Hiva and had left against his will. Greene became a journalist and editor and served at the headquarters of General Grant during the Civil War.

Typee was a moderate success, and, although some critics objected to Melville's description of native customs, this success encouraged him to continue to write. Next, he wrote *Omoo* (beachcomber), a narrative of the events after he escaped from the Typees and made his way to Tahiti. He learned from his experiences with publishers on *Typee; Omoo* was essentially a sequel to *Typee* but Melville wrote it in a more straightforward and believable style. As with *Typee, Omoo* was a blending of Melville's actual experiences and his imagination, in which he built upon his memory and extrapolated what might have happened to enhance his story. *Omoo* was also a minor success; Melville was optimistic about his future prospects.

Melville courted Elizabeth Shaw, daughter of Lemuel Shaw, Chief Justice of Massachusetts, who had been a friend of Melville's father. Melville had known Elizabeth since childhood; she was one of his sister's friends. They were married on August 4, 1847, and bought a house in New York, where his editor, Evert Duychinch, was located. Melville considered himself a professional writer, and, in addition to beginning a third novel, he wrote reviews for *Literary World*.

After settling in New York, Melville read more widely, including the works of Dante, Rabelais, Spenser, Robert Burton, Coleridge, and Sir Thomas Browne. In particular, he was moved by Shakespeare; he found it hard to believe that he had not encountered Shakespeare previously in his twenty-nine years.

Melville's third book, *Mardi*, was a departure from his earlier works. He attempted a different style of writing in which he was influenced by his recent reading. *Mardi* confused critics as well as readers; it did not sell. It was his first unsuccessful book, and it caused him to return to telling stories about the sea.

Melville's next book was *Redburn*, the story of his first voyage as a cabin boy aboard the *St. Lawrence*. He relates his experiences aboard ship and in Liverpool. In this book, he became more of a novelist. The plot is fiction; nevertheless, some of the characters are the actual people who sailed with him. It was not one of his better books; however, he was now writing for income.

After *Redburn*, Melville wrote *White Jacket,* based on his experiences aboard the frigate *USS United States*. *White Jacket* was an indication that he was maturing as an author, and it was a book with a purpose. In it, Melville documented a cruel shipboard practice, flogging. As a result of his description and the public outcry at the time, flogging was abolished by the U.S. Navy.

By this time, Melville had written five books in five years and was in need of a change of pace. He borrowed money from his father-in-law to buy Arrowhead, the Melville farm in western Massachusetts, where he had worked as a boy to help his uncle. If he were looking for a change to inspire him, he was successful. At Arrowhead, he planned and wrote *Moby Dick*, his greatest achievement.

In August 1850, while writing *Moby Dick*, Melville invited some of his New York friends to Arrowhead, including Evert Duychinch, his editor; Cornelius Mathews, the critic; and James Fields, the publisher. While they were there, he invited Nathaniel Hawthorne and Dr. Oliver Wendell Holmes, who had summer homes in the Berkshires, to Arrowhead for a house party.

They picnicked at Monument Mountain near Stockbridge, where they read a poem by William Cullen Bryant and speculated on the influence of geography on creativity and intelligence. Melville, who was thirty-one at the time, was impressed by being in company with authors of the caliber of Hawthorne and Holmes. Hawthorne had just published *The Scarlet Letter* and was working on *The House of the Seven Gables*. Melville sought the counsel and companionship of Hawthorne, whose summer home was only six miles away. For a time, Nathaniel and Sophia Hawthorne socialized with the Melvilles.

Sophia Hawthorne had formed a comprehensive impression of Melville:

> I am not quite sure that I do not think him a very great man.... A man with a true, warm heart, and a soul and an intellect—with life at his finger tips; earnest, sincere, and reverent; very tender and modest. He has a very keen perceptive power; but what astonishes me is that his eyes are not large and deep. He seems to me to see everything accurately; and how can he do so with his small eyes, I cannot tell. His nose is straight and handsome, his mouth expressive of sensibility and emotion. He is tall and erect, with an air free, brave and manly.
>
> When conversing, he is full of gesture and force, and loses himself in his subject.... Once in a while, his animation gives place to a singularly quiet expression out of those eyes to which I have objected: an indrawn, dim look, but what at the same time makes you feel that he is at that moment taking deepest note of what is before him. It is a strange, lazy glance, but with a power in it quite unique. It does not seem to penetrate through, but to take you into itself.

Moby Dick begins as a story about whale fisheries and becomes a complex narrative that can be interpreted in many ways. Melville's story of Captain Ahab of the whaling ship *Pequod* pursuing the malicious great white whale that had taken off his leg in a previous encounter draws upon whaling lore. It includes folklore, descriptions of shipwrecks, legends, and as many details of the whaling trade as Melville could incorporate. It combines the strengths of all of his earlier books and adds something uniquely its own. Included in *Moby Dick* are the descriptions of the tropics in *Typee* and *Omoo*, the allegory and satire of *Mardi*, the narrative quality of *Redburn*, and the well-drawn characters of *White Jacket*. Melville stated that he did not consciously write *Moby Dick* with the idea of an allegory in mind. However, over time, the complexity of the book and its different meaning to different people are factors that promoted its later popularity.

In explaining his contention that he did not intend *Moby Dick* to be an allegorical work, Melville said, "I had some vague idea while writing it, that the whole book was susceptible to an allegorical construction, and that parts of it were—but the specialty of many of the particular subordinate allegories were first revealed to me after reading Mr. Hawthorne's letter." Hawthorne had exclaimed, "What a book!" when he wrote Melville that he understood the book and the allegorical references made by Melville.

The view of *Moby Dick* as an allegory has persisted with a wide range of meanings generated from the story. A French critic noted that Captain Ahab wanted to harpoon Moby Dick because he could not harpoon God. Richard Chase viewed it similarly, "Ahab is the American cultural image: the captain of industry and his soul.... Moby Dick is God incarnate in the whale." In *Great Novelists and Their Novels*, W. Somerset Maugham observes that:

> According to Ellery Sedgwick, Ahab is Man—man sentient, speculative, religious, standing his full stature against the immense mystery of creation. I find this hard to believe. A more plausible interpretation is Mumford's. He takes Moby Dick as a symbol of Evil, and Ahab's conflict with him as the conflict of Good and Evil in which Good is finally vanquished.... Why have all the commentators assumed that Moby Dick is a symbol of evil?

> Why should the White Whale not represent goodness rather than evil? Splendid in beauty, vast in size, greater in strength! Captain Ahab with his insane pride is pitiless, harsh, cruel and revengeful; he is evil.... Or, if you want another interpretation, you might take Ahab with his dark wickedness for Satan and the White Whale for his Creator.... Fortunately, *Moby Dick* may be read, and read with passionate interest, without a thought of what allegorical significance it may or may not have.

Unfortunately, when *Moby Dick* was published, it was not a success. It failed to impress either the critics or the reading public. A critic wrote in *The New Monthly Magazine* that the book was "mad as a March hare; gibbering, screaming, like an incurable Bedlamite, reckless of keeper or straitjacket." Writing *Moby Dick* seemed to have sapped Melville's energy, and yet the economics of raising a family—his second son had just been born—and of running a farm motivated him to write. The poor response to *Moby Dick* seemed to have taken the spirit out of him.

Melville wrote Hawthorne, to whom he had dedicated *Moby Dick*, in 1851:

> I am so pulled hither and thither by circumstances. The calm, the coolness, the silent grass-growing mood in which a man ought always to compose— that I fear can seldom be mine. Dollars damn me; and the malicious Devil is forever grinning in upon me, holding the door ajar.... What I feel most moved to write, that is banned—it will not pay. Yet write another way, I cannot. So the product is a final hash, and all my books are botches.... What's the use of elaborating! Though I write the Gospels in this century, I should die in the gutter. What reputation H. M. has is horrible. Think of it! To go down in history as the man who lived among the cannibals!

Melville continued to write but his remaining years were not happy ones, at least not in terms of literary success. In a sense, he had peaked before he was thirty-two. He attempted a novel without any reference to the sea, *Pierre*, and it did not sell. In 1853, Melville became a contributor to *Putnam's Monthly Magazine*. In December of that year, one of his first short stories was published, *Bartleby the Scrivener: A Story of Wall Street*. In this story, Melville describes a passive hero who is defiant and refuses to crawl in the dirt and to conform to all of his environment's expectations of him.

In his late thirties, Melville published a long short story, *Benito Cereno*; a novel, *The Confidence Man*; and a collection of short fiction pieces, *The Piazza Tales*. He began to lose the motivation to write. Also, he suffered from neurasthenia, rheumatism, and sciatica; he had the appearance of a much older man. His health deteriorated to the point that his family was concerned that he would have a breakdown. His father-in-law advised him to give up his writing and paid for a trip abroad for him. He visited Greece, Turkey, and Egypt as well as Italy and England. Upon his return, he went on the lecture circuit, but he found that it was neither financially rewarding nor to his liking.

Over the years that his books were not selling, Melville had on several occasions attempted to obtain a government appointment, including applying to Hawthorne's friend, Franklin Pierce, for a diplomatic post abroad. He did not obtain one, but he persisted in pursuing a job that would give him financial security.

At age forty-seven, Melville was appointed Inspector of Customs for the Port of New York, requiring that he move his family from Pittsfield to New York. His post was in the Surveyor's Department, and, although it was not challenging, it provided him with the security that he had been seeking. He worked in this post for almost twenty years, until a legacy from Mrs. Ellen Marett Gifford allowed him to retire on December 3, 1885. Mrs. Gifford was the daughter of an associate of Melville's father who had been at least partly responsible for his bankruptcy. This action had been on her father's conscience, so she did what she could to compensate the Melville family.

At age fifty, Melville turned from writing novels to writing poetry. Two of his most notable efforts were a book of short poems about the Civil War, *Battle Pieces*, and a narrative poem about the Holy Land, *Clarel*. His story of a young man's search for religious faith was not a popular work; the cost of its publication was paid by his uncle, Peter Gansevoort.

Melville's last work was *Billy Budd, Foretopman*, the story of a young sailor who was falsely accused of treason by the Master-at-Arms. Since Billy stammered when he was excited, he was unable to respond to the accusation. Instead, he struck his libeler on the temple, killing him. Since this happened in front of the Captain, Budd was sentenced to death by hanging.

In 1842, a similar incident had occurred on the frigate *USS Somers* involving Philip Spencer, the son of the Secretary of War.

Melville's cousin, Guert Gansevoort, the first lieutenant on the *Somers*, presided over the court martial that handed down the sentence. Lieutenant Gansevoort became a target of congressional investigations and was threatened with arrest. This incident formed the plot for Melville's last book.

Herman Melville died on September 28, 1891 of "cardiac dilation." Attacks of erysipelas had enlarged his heart. Most New York newspapers carried no notice of his death; the New York *Press* was an exception: "There died yesterday at his quiet home in this city a man who although he had done almost no literary work during the past sixteen years, was once one of the most popular authors in the United States. Herman Melville probably reached the height of his fame about 1852, his first novel having been printed about 1847 [1846]." The New York *Daily Tribune* printed a brief paragraph in which the observation was made that *Typee* was Melville's best work.

Melville's principal achievements during his lifetime were his successful early efforts: *Typee, Omoo*, and *Redburn*. His master work, *Moby Dick*, was considered too difficult to understand. A narrative that concluded with the destruction of the captain, crew, and ship, with the narrator the only one left to tell the story, was not to the public's liking. Melville was a twentieth-century author writing in the nineteenth century. His masterpiece and some of his other works were not appreciated until twenty-one years into the twentieth century, thirty years after his death.

EMILY DICKINSON (1830-1886) *Poet Unknown In Her Lifetime*

> "I'm nobody! Who are you?
> Are you nobody, too?
> Then there's a pair of us—don't tell!
> They'd banish us, you know!
>
> How dreary to be somebody!
> How public, like a frog,
> To tell your name the livelong day
> To an admiring bog!"
>
> Emily Dickinson

Emily Dickinson spent her days as a recluse in her parents' home writing poetry. By the late 1860s, she had discontinued virtually all contact with the outside world, except for a small group of relatives and friends. Her mentor, Thomas Wentworth Higginson, observed upon meeting her, "She was much too enigmatical a being for me to solve in an hour's interview, and an instinct told me that the slightest attempt at cross-examination would make her withdraw into her shell; I could only sit still and watch, as one does in the woods."

During her lifetime, Dickinson published only seven poems, all anonymously. After her death in 1886, Lavinia Dickinson found 900 of her sister's poems in a locked trunk in her bedroom. Later, 875 additional poems were discovered. Dickinson's highly crafted and usually short poems were written in a conversational idiom about a wide variety of topics. She was a pioneer in the use of rhyme and measured poetic patterns; she was an original and is considered a founder of modern American poetry.

Louis Untermeyer summarized Dickinson's poetry in *Makers of the Modern World:*

> She wrote both as a bereaved woman and a happy, irresponsible child. Often, indeed, her writing is almost too coy for comfort. There is, at times, an embarrassing affectation, a willing naiveté, as though she were determined to be not only a child but a spoiled child—a child who patronizes the

universe and is arch with its Creator. But the pertness suddenly turns to pure perception, and the teasing is forgotten in revelation.

There is no way of analyzing her unique blend of whimsicality and wisdom, of solving her trick of turning what seems to be cryptic *non sequiturs* into crystal epigrams, no way of measuring her deceptive simplicity and her startling depths. The mystery of Emily Dickinson is not the way she lived but the way she wrote, a mystery which enabled a New England recluse to charge the literature of her country with poems she never cared to publish.

Emily Dickinson was born to Edward and Emily Norcross Dickinson on December 10, 1830, in Amherst, Massachusetts. She was a middle child; her brother Austin was two years older, and her sister Lavinia was two years younger. Emily was born in a large, brick house called the Homestead, built by her grandfather, Samuel Dickinson, a founder of Amherst College. Samuel, a successful lawyer, was such a strong supporter of the College that he spent his savings on the struggling school in its early days. After finishing college and entering law practice, Emily's father supported his parents and his siblings.

Edward was a strict disciplinarian with his children. Emily's view of him was that his "heart was pure and terrible, and I think no other like it exists." Nevertheless, he believed in education and ensured that his daughters were well educated. Emily's mother was a literate woman; however, Emily once said of her: "Mother does not care for thought." Later in life, Emily told her mentor that she "never had a mother." Like his father, Edward was the treasurer of Amherst College. He also served as a member of the Massachusetts General Court and as U.S. Congressman for two terms.

As a member of a religious Congregationalist family, Emily was discouraged from reading fiction in her adolescent years; nevertheless, she was allowed to read the novels of Nathaniel Hawthorne, Charles Dickens, and Sir Walter Scott. She also read the works of Ralph Waldo Emerson, Henry Wadsworth Longfellow, Henry David Thoreau, and British writers, including the Brontë sisters, Elizabeth Barrett Browning, and George Eliot.

After attending Amherst Academy, Emily enrolled at the Mt. Holyoke Female Seminary established by Mary Lyon, who had been a student of Edward Hitchcock, the President of Amherst College. The program at Mt. Holyoke was a combination of academic courses and religious services. Students were encouraged to "convert" to become committed Christians. Emily's religious beliefs were continually questioned, and she was admonished daily to save her soul. She hesitated to convert because "it is hard for me to give up the world." She left Mt. Holyoke after one year because of the religious pressures and homesickness.

When she returned home, Dickinson found that many of her friends had left Amherst. She became a good friend of Susan Gilbert, who later became her sister-in-law. Dickinson was close with her sister, Lavinia, throughout their lifetimes. In 1850, following a religious revival near Amherst, Susan Gilbert as well as Dickinson's brother, Austin, and sister, Lavinia, converted. Dickinson's hesitancy about religion remained; she did not convert. She expressed her feeling in verse:

> I shall know why—when Time is over—
> And I have ceased to wonder why—
> Christ will explain each separate anguish
> In the fair schoolroom in the sky—
> He will tell me what "Peter" promised—
> And I—for wonder at his woe—
> I shall forget the drop of anguish
> That scalds me now—that scalds me now.

In 1850, Austin went to Cambridge for four years to attend Harvard Law School. Dickinson wrote to him almost every day. She wrote poetry throughout the decade of the 1850s. Her first two published poems were valentines, printed in the *Amherst College Indicator* and the Springfield *Republican*. Both poems were published anonymously.

Dickinson was encouraged in her writing by Benjamin Newton, a clerk in her father's law office from 1847 to 1849. He was a prolific reader nine years her senior, who helped her with her evolving style. She wrote to Susan, "I have found a beautiful new friend." It is probable that they were just friends; however, some biographers consider Newton Dickinson's first love interest. Three years after meeting Dickinson, Newton married a woman twelve years older than he. He died of tuberculosis in 1853.

Dickinson's friendship with Susan Gilbert was enhanced by their mutual interest in literature. Susan was also well educated. She and Dickinson were a good intellectual match; however, their relationship was sometimes strained. In 1856, Susan and Austin Dickinson were married and moved into their home, Evergreen, next door to the Homestead. Susan was loved by the Dickinson family; nevertheless, the relationship between Susan and Lavinia was occasionally tense.

Emily Dickinson rarely left Amherst, but in 1855 she visited Philadelphia and Washington, D.C. with her father. In Philadelphia, she met Charles Wadsworth, a young minister with personal magnetism. Many of Dickinson's biographers think that she had a romantic relationship with Wadsworth, a married man. In 1862, Wadsworth received a call from Calvary Church in San Francisco and moved there. Dickinson expressed her feelings in a sad poem:

> I cannot live with You—
> It would be Life—
> And Life is over there—
> Behind the Shelf
>
> ....
> So we must keep apart—
> You there—I—here—
> With just the Door ajar
> That Oceans are—and Prayer—
> And that White Sustenance—
> Despair—

Wadsworth visited Amherst twice, in 1860 and 1880; he and Dickinson corresponded regularly.

In 1860-61, Dickinson wrote moving letters to her "Master":

> I am older—tonight, Master—but the love is the
> same—so are the moon and the crescent. If it had
> been God's will that I might breathe where you

breathed—and find the place—myself—at night—
if I [can] never forget that I am not with you—and
that sorrow and frost are nearer than I.... I want to
see you more—Sir—than all I wish in this world—
and the wish—altered a little—will be my only
one—for the skies.

Dickinson wrote one of her more passionate love poems in
1861:

Wild Nights—Wild Nights!
Were I with thee
Wild Nights should be
Our luxury!
Futile—the Winds—
To a Heart in port
Done with the Compass—
Done with the Chart!
Rowing in Eden—
Ah, the Sea!
Might I but moor—Tonight
In Thee

She did not date her poems. Thankfully, her handwriting changed
over the years; handwriting analysis was helpful in assigning an
approximate date to her work.

Martha Dickinson Bianchi, Dickinson's niece, thought that
Wadsworth was her aunt's "fate," and that they had fallen in love at
first sight. Dickinson destroyed most of her correspondence before
she died; however, three letters addressed to her "Master" were
found among her papers, which caused much speculation.
Wadsworth died in 1882. Dickinson wrote a poem that biographers
speculate refers to the deaths of Newton and Wadsworth:

My life closed twice before its close;
It yet remains to see
If immortality unveil
A third event to me,
So huge, so hopeless to conceive,
As these that twice befell.

> Parting is all we know of heaven,
> And all we need of hell.

Late in the decade of the 1850s, Dickinson began to withdraw increasingly from society. As she retreated from society, her output of poetry increased significantly. However, her brother and sister-in-law were very active socially, and Dickinson met many famous people at Evergreen, the house next door. In 1857, Ralph Waldo Emerson stayed at Evergreen during a series of lectures at Amherst College, and Austin and Susan also hosted Harriet Beecher Stowe, author of *Uncle Tom's Cabin*, and Samuel Bowles, editor of the Springfield *Republican*. Bowles, an ambitious, charismatic man, published several of Dickinson's poems in the 1850s.

In 1860, Dickinson stopped attending church. She commented that some people kept the Sabbath by going to church, but that she kept it by staying at home.

In the early 1860s, Dickinson's eyesight began to fail. Her vision was blurred, and her eyes were extremely sensitive to light. She visited ophthalmologists in Boston and was advised to use her eyes less, a heart-rending prescription for a person like her. Worried that her ailment might be progressive, she stepped up her production of poems. Fortunately, her eyesight improved during the late 1860s.

Dickinson had a high regard for the literary opinions of her sister-in-law, Susan. She sent 267 poems over the years to her, soliciting suggestions for improvement. Susan did not always respond, causing some friction between the two women. In 1861, Susan had her first child, Edward; raising a family put increased demands on her time.

Dickinson responded to an essay in the newspaper, "Letter to a Young Contributor," by Thomas Wentworth Higginson, who became her mentor. She sent four poems to him and asked for his advice, and then didn't take it. He asked her to visit him in Boston so that he could introduce her to his literary friends. She didn't make the trip to Boston, but she invited him to Amherst. After corresponding for eight years, he finally visited her at her home.

When Higginson entered the house, Dickinson presented him with two lilies and said, "These are my introduction. Forgive me if I am frightened; I never see strangers and hardly know what to say." He remembered that, "She talked soon and henceforward continuously for her own relief, and wholly without watching its effect on her hearer." She told Higginson, "If I read a book [and] it makes my whole body so cold no fire can ever warm me, I know that is poetry. If I feel physically as if the top of my head were taken off, I know that is poetry. These are the only ways I know it." Higginson admitted, "I never was with anyone who drained my nerve power so much. Without touching her, she drew from me.... I am glad not to live near her."

Initially, Dickinson was too obscure for him to understand her well. She experimented with meter and rhyme, including eye rhymes: words that are spelled similarly but do not rhyme, such as sword and word. However, she was meticulous in her choice of words. Although Higginson encouraged her, she never sought publication of her poems.

As Dickinson's poetry became more profound, she socialized less and less. During the 1860s, she was a prolific writer of poetry. She wrote her poems on large sheets of paper and organized them into small bundles by folding the sheets and sewing the pages together. Thirty-nine of these packets, containing a total of 811 poems, were found after her death.

By 1869, Dickinson rarely ventured out of the house. She said, "I do not cross my father's ground to any house or town." Lavinia commented on the family's spheres of activity: "Emily had to think—she was the only one of us who had that to do.... Father believed; and mother loved; and Austin had Amherst; and I had the family to keep track of."

Friends admired Dickinson's work and suggested that she publish her poems; she resisted. One was her childhood friend, Helen Fiske, who married E. B. Hunt and was widowed during the Civil War. She then married W. S. Jackson, and as Helen Hunt Jackson became the best-known woman poet in America at the time. In particular, she wanted Dickinson to publish the following poem:

> Success is counted sweetest
> By those who ne'er succeed.
> To comprehend a nectar
> Requires sorest need.

Not one of all the purple Host
Who took the Flag today
Can tell the definition
So plain of Victory

As he defeated—dying
On whose forbidden ear
The distant strains of triumph
Break, agonizing clear!

The poem was published with the title "Success" in *A Masque of Poets* anthology in 1878.

Dickinson's third romance was with Judge Otis Phillips Lord, a friend of her father nineteen years her senior. Lord was an Amherst alumnus who returned regularly for reunions and visited the Homestead, even after Edward's death. Friendship evolved into romance. One year after the death of Lord's wife, Dickinson wrote in one surviving letter, "I confess that I love him—I rejoice that I love him—I thank the Maker of Heaven and Earth—that gave him me to love." It is not known whether he ever proposed to her. He passed away in 1884.

Dickinson's reputation as an eccentric grew. Mabel Loomis Todd, who was married to an Amherst professor, moved to town in the fall of 1881 and wrote to her parents about the "nun of Amherst": "I must tell you about the character of Amherst; it is a lady whom the people call the 'Myth.' She is a sister of Mr. Dickinson and seems to be the climax of all the family oddity. She has not been out of her own house in fifteen years, except once to see a new church, when she crept out at night and viewed it by moonlight." Mabel Loomis Todd first listened to Dickinson's poems at Evergreen and thought that they were "full of power."

Dickinson had a reputation for remaining behind half-closed doors instead of mixing with visitors to the Homestead. In her later years, she always wore white. She liked children, but would not go outside to talk with them. She lowered candy and cookies to them in a basket from her bedroom window.

Mabel Loomis Todd and her husband, David Peck Todd, socialized with Austin and Susan Dickinson as well as with Lavinia Dickinson. Shortly after her first visit to Evergreen, Loomis Todd and Austin Dickinson began a love affair that continued until he died in 1895. They made no attempt to hide their emotions.

In the spring of 1884, Dickinson became ill with the kidney disease that ultimately caused her death. On May 13, 1886, she went into a coma; she died two days later. Her obituary appeared in the Springfield *Republican*: "Very few in the village, except among the older inhabitants, knew Miss Emily personally, although the facts of her seclusion and her intellectual brilliancy were familiar Amherst traditions.... As she passed on in life, her sensitive nature shrank from much personal contact with the world, and more and more turned to her own large wealth of individual resources for companionship."

Shortly after Dickinson's death, Lavinia Dickinson discovered her sister's poems. In 1890, the first edition of *Emily Dickinson's Poems* was published. William Dean Howells, America's dean of letters at the time, praised the volume as a "distinctive addition" to the country's literature. During her later years, Dickinson wrote her poems on scraps of paper and the flaps of envelopes as thoughts occurred to her. This made editing her work extremely difficult. In 1891, Loomis Todd and Higginson edited a second volume of Dickinson's poetry, and, in 1893, Loomis Todd published another volume of Dickinson's poetry.

After Austin Dickinson died in 1895, Lavinia Dickinson, who had been working with Loomis Todd editing her sister's poems, decided that she no longer wanted Loomis Todd to edit the remaining poems. Tension had built up over the more than ten-year duration of Loomis Todd's affair with Austin Dickinson. Loomis Todd put the poems that she had been editing in the attic of her house, where they stayed for thirty years.

In 1914, Martha Dickinson Bianchi, Dickinson's niece, published 143 of her aunt's unpublished poems. In 1930, Millicent Todd Bingham, Loomis Todd's daughter, and Alfred Leete Hampson edited and published *Further Poems of Emily Dickinson*. Subsequent collections were published in 1935 and 1945. In 1955, *The Poems of Emily Dickinson*, all 1,775 original poems in three volumes, was published.

The principal insight into Dickinson's inner life is in her poetry, not her biographies. She provided at least a limited view of her thoughts about her verse:

This is my letter to the World
That never wrote to Me—
The simple News that Nature told—
With tender Majesty
Her Message is committed
To Hands I cannot see—
For love of Her—Sweet countrymen—
Judge tenderly—of Me.

CHARLES IVES (1874-1954) *Composer Unrecognized for Thirty Years*

'Tis known by the name of perseverance in a good cause—and obstinacy in a bad one."

Lawrence Sterne, *Sermons*

Charles Ives is an excellent example of an individual who persevered in doing what he had to do. Composing music became a second career that paralleled his career in the insurance business. Most of his compositions were written in the twenty-year period between 1896 and 1916. Public recognition of his music didn't come for another half century, however. He knew that the music he was writing was revolutionary and wasn't liked by his friends or by the listening public. It was too full of dissonance and discord for the average ear. When asked by a friend why he didn't compose what people liked to hear, Ives replied, "I can't do it. I hear something else."

Ives is frequently compared with Bartok, Milhaud, Stravinsky, and Schoenberg. However, his pioneering predates all of theirs. For example, he used discords prior to Bartok; he composed polytonal music (music written in several keys simultaneously) before Milhaud; he utilized polyrhythms (a diverse set of rhythmic forms at the same time) earlier than Stravinsky; and he composed atonal music (music in no fixed key) that predated Schoenberg.

Henry Bellaman, the author of *King's Row,* who became familiar with Ives's work while lecturing in the South, was one of his early promoters. Bellaman arranged for "Concord Sonata" to be performed in New Orleans in October 1920. In January 1939, American pianist John Kirkpatrick played Ives's "Concord Sonata" at Town Hall, New York. It was performed again several weeks later to critical acclaim. Lawrence Gilman of the *Herald Tribune* declared that Ives was "the most original and extraordinary of American composers."

Most American composers were strongly influenced by European composers. Ives wasn't; he drew upon American subjects. His music was influenced by square dances, camp meetings, Fourth of July picnics, religious revival gatherings, rural and small town American settings, and the songs of America. American hymns and marches, and Stephen Foster's tunes are woven into

177

many of Ives's compositions.

Ives asked himself, "Why is it that I like to use these different things and try out other ways . . . which nobody has any pleasure in hearing, seeing and thinking about? Why do I like to do it? Is there some particular defect in me, or something worse that I'm afflicted with?"

During all the years when lack of recognition could have led to self-doubt, Ives persevered in writing the music that he felt he had to write. The support of his wife, Harmony Twitchell Ives, never flagged. In later years, he wrote, "She never once said: 'Now why don't you be good and write something the way they [his friends] like it?'—Never—she urged me on my way—to be myself! She gave me not only hope but a confidence that no one else since my father had given me."

Ives wrote his "First String Quartet" with four movements: "Chorale," "Prelude," "Offertory," and "Postlude," while in his sophomore year at Yale. He chose a technique in the quartet for which he later became known—the insertion of familiar melodies into his works. He incorporated the hymn "From Greenland's Icy Mountains" into the first movement of the quartet. Ives also wrote his "First Symphony," a remarkable accomplishment for an under-graduate, while at Yale. His music professor was highly critical of it and asked him to rewrite it using fewer keys. Ives preferred the less conventional version. Another of Ives's early, serious pieces was the "Prelude and Postlude for a Thanksgiving Service" for the organ, which he composed in 1897. His music professor disliked this work because it contained polytonal passages.

After graduating from Yale, Ives chose not to become a professional musician. In making this career decision, he was heavily influenced by his father's viewpoint on the subject. George Ives said:

> A man could keep his music interest stronger, cleaner, bigger, and freer if he didn't try to make a living out of it. Assuming a man lives by himself with no dependents, he might write music that no one would play prettily, listen to or buy. But—but if he had a nice wife and some nice children, how can he let the children starve on his dissonance? So

he has to weaken (and if he is a man, he SHOULD weaken for his children), but his music more than weakens—it goes "ta-ta" for money! Bad for him, bad for music!

George Ives, a serious musician, had followed his own advice; he worked for the Danbury Bank.

Charles Ives moved to New York City and went into the insurance business. During his early years in New York, he composed evenings, weekends, and during vacations. Occasionally, he attended a concert at Carnegie Hall, but generally he didn't listen to other composers' works. It took time away from the small amount of time he had to compose. Also, he tended to carry the music he was composing in his head rather than write it down immediately. Attending concerts and listening to the music of others confused him in his own work.

In 1902, Ives completed his "Second Symphony" while living in New York. He thought that it expressed the musical feelings around Danbury, Connecticut, in the 1890s, that is, the music of the country folk. It includes melodic strains from "Columbia, the Gem of the Ocean," "America, the Beautiful," "De Camptown Races," and "Old Black Joe." Concurrently, he worked on his score for "Third Symphony," although it wasn't completed until 1904. The inspiration for this work was provided by the camp meetings held in the Danbury area. He drew upon hymns for a portion of this work, including "O for a Thousand Tongues" and "Just as I Am." It was first conducted by Lou Harrison on April 5, 1946, forty-two years after the score was completed.

During the years 1909-15, Ives wrote his "Concord Sonata," which is probably the best known of his works. It is a piano sonata with four movements, each one named for Concord residents: "Emerson," "Hawthorne," "The Alcotts," and "Thoreau." Ives intended to express his emotional bond with the New England Transcendentalists and the primacy of the spiritual and superindividual versus the material and the empirical. Ives wrote a booklet, "Essays before a Sonata" to help explain it. It included a dedication: "These prefatory essays were written by the composer for those who can't stand his music—and the music for those who can't stand his essays; to those who can't stand either, the whole is

179

respectfully dedicated."

From 1903 to 1914, he worked on "Three Places in New England," with its movements, "Boston Common" (influenced by the St. Gaudens statue of Colonel Shaw and his African-American regiment); "Putnam's Camp" in Redding, Connecticut; and "The Housatonic at Stockbridge." This piece was inspired by three geographic settings in New England, rather than by hymns, marches, or folk songs, as were some of his earlier works. On January 10, 1931, it was heard for the first time, with Nicolas Slonimsky conducting the Boston Symphony Orchestra.

Ives's strong feelings for his style of music were demonstrated at this concert. Three American works were performed and all three were loudly hissed and booed, including Ives's "Three Places in New England." Ives remained silent while his work was booed. However, when the audience booed Carl Ruggles's "Men and Mountains," Ives couldn't contain himself any longer. He stood and shouted to the audience in general, "Don't be such a sissy! When you hear strong music like this, get up and try to use your ears like a man!"

In 1914, Ives completed his "Fourth Symphony," the last and most complicated of his symphonies. Its score was written for a huge orchestra with a brass band and a chorus. Twenty-seven different rhythms are played at the same time at one point in the symphony. Occasionally, it has required three conductors to conduct it. It includes portions of many hymns, including "The Sweet Bye and Bye," "Nearer My God to Thee," and "Watchman, Tell Us of the Night," as well as "Yankee Doodle" and "Turkey in the Straw." Its world premiere was on April 26, 1965, by the American Symphony Orchestra conducted by Leopold Stokowski and two assistants.

Ives was a promoter of concert music based on things American, not things European. A friend of Ives was asked by the French composer Vincent D'Indy, "Why don't your American composers inspire themselves by their own landscapes, their own legends and history, instead of leaning on the German walking stick?" That is precisely what Ives did. In referring to his dreams for the future, he said "We would rather believe . . . that the time is coming, but not in our lifetime, when music will develop possibilities inconceivable now—a language so transcendent, that its heights and depths will be common to all mankind. The future may not be with music itself, but rather . . . in the way it makes itself a part of the finer things humanity does and dreams of."

In 1946, Ives was elected to the National Institute of Arts and Letters, and his "Third Symphony," for which he won a Pulitzer Prize, was played for the first time—more than forty years after he wrote it. Leonard Bernstein and the New York Philharmonic performed the premier of Ives's "Second Symphony" in Carnegie Hall in 1951, almost fifty years after he composed it.

When Austrian composer Arnold Schoenberg died in 1951, a note was found among his papers:

> There is a great man living in this country—a
> composer.
> He has solved the problem how to preserve
> oneself and learn.
> He responds to negligence with contempt.
> He is not forced to accept praise or blame.
> His name is Ives.

ROBERT GODDARD (1882-1945) *Rocketry Pioneer*

"As I looked toward the fields in the East I imagined how wonderful it would be to make some device which had even the possibility of ascending to Mars, and how it would look on a small scale if sent up from the meadow at my feet. I was a different boy when I descended the tree from when I ascended, for existence at last seemed very purposive."

Robert Goddard

On October 19, 1899, at age seventeen, Robert Goddard climbed a large cherry tree in the backyard of his home to prune dead branches. He had recently read H. G. Well's *War of the Worlds*, which at least partially explains the significant emotional event that occurred.

He climbed down from the tree and made the following entry in his diary: "As I looked toward the fields at the east, I imagined how wonderful it would be to make some device which has even the possibility of ascending to Mars, and how it would look on a small scale, if sent up from the meadow at my feet . . . I was a different boy when I descended the tree from when I ascended, for existence at last seemed very purposive."

That phrase, "for existence at last seemed very purposive," was a great motivator for Goddard's subsequent endeavors. He felt that he now had a purpose in life and a goal to develop something that would go higher than anything had gone previously. Every year for the remainder of his life, he viewed October 19 as his "Anniversary Day."

Goddard began his research with rockets as an undergraduate at Worcester Polytechnic Institute and as a graduate student at Clark University. While recovering from an illness in 1913, he developed rocket designs. During this time, he applied to the U.S. Patent Office for the first two of approximately 200 patents he was granted in his lifetime. His first patent described the characteristics required by all modern rockets: a combustion chamber with a nozzle, a pump to force fuel into the combustion chamber, and the propellant, either solid or liquid, which burns in the combustion chamber.

Goddard's second patent outlined the concept of the multistage rocket that is the forerunner of all high-altitude rockets in use today. Earlier, Goddard investigated the efficiency of rocket fuel. A simple rocket using gunpowder placed in a cylinder closed at one end and ignited uses only about two or three percent of the energy of the fuel. His two principal goals were to improve the basic design of the rocket and to develop an improved propellant.

By the fall of 1914, Goddard was well enough to resume work on a part-time basis on the faculty of Clark University. Within a year, he had built some of the rockets that he had designed. He developed a nozzle design to improve propellant efficiency and to generate more thrust. By the summer of 1915, working with solid-fuel rockets, he had achieved a fuel efficiency of forty percent and was recording ejection velocities of 6,700 feet per second. After many partial successes, he launched a rocket that reached a height of 486 feet and had an ejection velocity of just under 8,000 feet per second.

Goddard realized that he could not afford to continue his research on his own. He wanted to begin his experiments with liquid fuels, and he knew that the effort would be costly. He wrote a paper to describe his rocket theory, the mathematics that supported it, and his expectations for further development. He forwarded his paper entitled "A Method of Reaching Extreme Altitudes" to several scientific institutions to promote interest in his endeavors.

The Smithsonian Institution, whose stated propose is the increase of knowledge, was one of the institutions to which he sent his paper. In his letter to the Smithsonian, he wrote, "For a number of years, I have been at work on a method of raising recording apparatus to altitudes exceeding the limit of sounding balloons . . . I have reached the limit of the work I can do singlehanded, both because of the expense and also because further work will require more than one man's time." Goddard and the Smithsonian scientists knew that it would be useful for meteorologists to have additional knowledge of the atmosphere hundreds of miles from the earth's surface.

The Smithsonian Institution decided to support Goddard's projects. Goddard provided the status of his development effort to the Smithsonian on a regular basis. In one of his communications, he mentioned the potential usefulness of rockets in wartime. When the United States declared war in 1917, Dr. Abbott of the Smithsonian passed on his suggestions to the U.S. Army Signal Corps.

Goddard left his teaching position at Clark University and began working on a rocket to be used by the U.S. Infantry against enemy tanks. A successful demonstration was conducted in the fall of 1918 at the Aberdeen Proving Grounds in Maryland. It appeared that this weapon, the forerunner of the World War II bazooka, would be put into immediate production. However, with the signing of the armistice on November 11, 1918, the U.S. Army suspended their interest in rockets for over twenty years.

Goddard returned to Clark University and evolved his designs for nose cones, combustion chambers, and nozzles; he also investigated liquid fuels. He realized early that liquid hydrogen and liquid oxygen would be an optimal fuel. However, liquid hydrogen was very difficult to manage, so he searched for a substitute. He chose gasoline since it was inexpensive and relatively dependable. Handling liquid oxygen was also problematical since its boiling point is 298 degrees below zero Fahrenheit, and it had to be kept under pressure.

Goddard conducted tests of his liquid fuel rockets at a farm owned by a family friend. He first launched a liquid-fuel rocket flight on March 16, 1926. The rocket reached a height four times its length and a speed of sixty miles an hour while traveling a distance of 220 feet. He had to redesign the original rocket because the combustion chamber burned through due to the intense heat. Use of sheet steel was a short-term solution to the problem. He experimented with increasingly large rockets, and he added a thermometer and a barometer as well as a small camera to record the instrument readings.

In July 1929, Goddard had his most successful flight so far. The rocket gained an altitude of ninety feet and traveled 171 feet in its eighteen and one-half seconds of flight. As Goddard and his associates picked up the reusable pieces of the rocket, the crash site was visited by an ambulance, several police cars, and cars with signs marked "Press." They had received a report of an airplane crash. This incident gave the rocket experiments bad publicity. The Smithsonian Institution supported Goddard by explaining that he was attempting to collect weather information at high altitudes. Commonwealth officials would not allow any more experimental rocket flights to be conducted in Massachusetts, however.

Goddard and his assistants looked for a more compatible location to resume rocket testing. They considered the amount of rainfall, topological factors, and general climate conditions and chose Roswell, New Mexico, for future tests. In addition to the favorable climate, the area around Roswell was sparsely settled and met their criterion of having few neighbors to become alarmed by the noise of their experiments.

The first major test at the Roswell site was in December 1930. The purpose was to determine if compressed nitrogen gas from an outside tank could be used, when routed through tubes to the fuel and oxidizer tanks, to force gasoline and liquid oxygen into the combustion chambers. In this successful flight, the rocket reached a speed of 500 miles per hour and an altitude of 2,000 feet and traveled 1,000 feet from the launch tower.

Goddard experienced continuing problems with the burning through of the narrow opening between the combustion chamber and the nozzle. He tried different metals but finally concluded that the walls of the combustion chamber needed cooling. He solved this problem by using curtain cooling. He evolved a design in which gasoline was sprayed on the inner wall of the combustion chamber prior to its ignition.

In effect, he placed a layer of burning gas around the inside of the combustion chamber that, because it was cooler than the burning gasoline and oxygen in the center of the chamber, resulted in the necessary cooling. In future tests, the problem of rocket engines burning through was reduced considerably. He also experimented with placing parachutes in the nose cone to lessen damage to the rockets as they returned to earth.

On April 19, 1932, Goddard conducted his first test of a rocket equipped with a gyroscope to control the guidance vanes of the rocket. These adjustable vanes were used to keep the rocket on a vertical course longer than had been possible previously. Also, the gyroscope was used to release the parachute as the rocket approached its maximum altitude.

The Guggenheim Foundation, which supported Goddard's research when the need for funds exceeded the amount provided by the Smithsonian Institution, was unable to provide support for the years 1933 and 1934. Goddard returned to Worcester and resumed teaching at Clark University. Resumption of the support from the

Smithsonian Institution allowed Goddard to continue his design efforts.

The most significant development during Goddard's time back in Worcester was a combustion chamber in which atmospheric air was used as the oxidizer. Obviously, this would not work for a high altitude rocket, but it worked for a rocket that traveled horizontally at low altitudes. This type of rocket could be much lighter than a high altitude rocket since it would not have to carry a tank of liquid oxygen.

Goddard used a funnel as the air intake at the front of the rocket motor. The air passed by a shutter-type intake valve on its way to the combustion chamber. The air came in while the shutters were open, the shutters closed, and combustion occurred, providing the thrust. Then the shutter opened and the process was repeated over again. This concept was used by the Germans on their V-1 rocket of World War II. The air resonance noise of the shutter opening and closing was the unusual sound that gave the "buzz-bomb" its name.

The Guggenheim Foundation resumed its support of Goddard's work in the fall of 1934. By this point, Goddard had concluded that the current design was too complex, and that it must be simplified to increase reliability. He wanted to eliminate the need for nitrogen gas and its associated tank and to use centrifugal pumps to force liquid oxygen and gasoline into the combustion chambers. The size of the tanks and their weight was the main difficulty. Goddard and his associates worked until 1940 to reduce the size and weight of the tanks and pumps.

By 1937, German scientists were performing rocket experiments at a large, liquid-propellant facility at Peenemunde. The Nazi government provided ample financial backing; they had an operational V-2 rocket by 1943.

In May 1940, Harry Guggenheim of the Guggenheim Foundation called a meeting of representatives of the armed forces that provided Goddard an opportunity to present his work and to promote the potential of liquid-propellant rockets in time of war. The Army representative stated that the next war, which had already started in Europe, "will be won by trench mortars." The only interest expressed by Army Air Corps and Navy authorities was for a rocket motor to assist short runway take-off of heavily loaded aircraft.

This joint Army Air Corps and Navy project was the first one assigned to Goddard to aid the war effort. Out of this work came the JATO unit, the jet-assisted take-off device that used solid fuel. His next assignment was to develop a rocket motor with variable thrust that could be controlled by a pilot. This engine design was successful; a version of it was used later on the X-2 and the X-15 experimental aircraft. His last assignment was the development of a small liquid oxygen and gasoline-powered rocket for use in a guided missile.

Goddard laid out the principles underlying rocket flight, and all modern rockets evolved from concepts developed by him; unfortunately, the United States did not take advantage of his work. Documentation of many of Goddard's early rocket designs was provided upon request. Some of it was technical literature available from the Smithsonian Institution. German rocket scientists, including Werner Von Braun, acknowledged openly that their work was based on Goddard's earlier development.

Robert Goddard is example of an individual whose early academic work was not notable, but, once he had a firm goal in mind, he applied himself to achieve that goal. He was motivated to add to his chosen body of knowledge, even though he received little recognition for his efforts.

JOHN ATANASOFF (1903-1995) *Inventor of the Computer*

"One night in the late 1930s, in a bar on the border of Illinois and Iowa, a professor of physics at Iowa State College had an idea. After a frustrating day performing tedious mathematical computations in his lab, John Vincent Atanasoff realized that a combination of the binary number system and electronic switches, together with an array of capacitors on a moving drum to serve as memory, could yield a computing machine that would make his life—and the lives of similarly burdened scientists—easier. Then he went back and built the machine in the basement of the physics building. It worked. The whole world changed."

Jane Smiley, *The Man Who Invented the Computer*

John Vincent Atanasoff was born on October 4, 1903, the son of Bulgarian immigrants. Atanasoff's father, a graduate of Colgate University, worked as an industrial engineer in New York and New Jersey before moving the family to Brewster, Florida. Young John was a precocious student, with practical interests as well, such as repairing his father's Model T Ford. After graduating from high school, he worked for a year and taught math classes to earn money for college.

Atanasoff was creative from his youngest days. In *Explaining Creativity,* R. Keith Sawyer cites the traits of creativity: self-confidence, independence, high energy, willingness to take risks, above-average intelligence, openness to experience, and preference for complexity. Atanasoff displayed all of these qualities in addition to what Sawyer describes as "problem finding"—the ability to productively formulate a problem so that the terms of the problem lead to the solution.

Atanasoff majored in electrical engineering at the University of Florida. When he graduated in 1925, he had the highest grade point average up until that time at the University. He applied for master's programs in physics, his first love. Iowa State was the first to reply with an offer of admission and aid. Later, he was accepted for graduate study at Harvard, but he had already been accepted by Iowa State. In addition to taking graduate courses, Atanasoff also taught undergraduate math courses.

Atanasoff met Lura Meeks, an undergraduate student at Iowa State. She had grown up on a farm in Oklahoma. She was intelligent, energetic, and enterprising. They were married when he received his master's degree in physics in June 1926.

Atanasoff accepted a position teaching mathematics and physics at Iowa State while taking additional graduate physics courses to prepare himself for doctoral studies at the University of Wisconsin, which he began in the winter of 1927. He specialized in quantum mechanics, the science that predicts what happens in systems. His professor of quantum mechanics was John Hasbrouck Van Vleck, who was to win the Nobel Prize in 1977.

Atanasoff's theoretical physics dissertation was "The Dielectric Constant of Helium." Dielectric constant is a practical measurement, the ratio of the electric field in a vacuum to the electric field in a medium. Obtaining solutions to the linear equations that his work required was laborious and time consuming.

Atanasoff got his Ph.D at the University of Wisconsin in July 1930. He accepted a position as assistant professor of mathematics and physics at Iowa State. After committing to the position, he was offered a job at Harvard, which he again turned down. He was a gifted teacher who engaged his students in discussions and questioned them to determine their areas of knowledge and ignorance.

Most calculators in the 1920s were analog, not digital. Atanasoff read about the Differential Analyzer, developed at MIT in 1927-31 by Vannevar Bush. At Harvard, Howard Aiken was looking for a way to improve the 1822 Difference Engine of Charles Babbage, which had never really worked. Babbage later designed an Analytical Engine using gears and shafts, with which he tried to accomplish too much by building a universal machine.

Aiken attempted to update Babbage's ideas with modern techniques. This included using a power supply and electric motor for driving the machine, and master control panels controlled by instructions on punched rolls of paper tape synchronized with the machine along with manual adjustments for controlling the calculation of functions. It used a decimal (base ten) numbering system.

Aiken was driven to develop a calculating machine that could solve differential equations. His doctoral dissertation at Harvard was "Theory of Space Charge Conductions." It was similar to Atanasoff's dissertation in that it considered the properties of vacuum tubes—devices in which electric currents pass through a vacuum between two metal electrodes. The simplest vacuum tube was a diode in which a cathode is heated, releasing negatively charged electrons that flow to a positively charged anode.

Atanasoff wrestled with a number of approaches to building a calculating machine. By the winter of 1937, he knew that whatever design he chose, it had to separate memory from computation. All of his design ideas were unsuccessful, and "I was in such a mental state that no resolution was possible. I was just unhappy to an extreme degree." He knew that he had to get away, at least briefly. He got in his new Ford V8 and drove east, with no destination in mind, until he was across the Mississippi River in Rock Island, Illinois, 189 miles from home.

Atanasoff noticed a tavern sign and went in and ordered a drink. As he waited for his drink, the general design of his computing machine came to him as a logical whole. He began to visualize how the component pieces would come together. For several hours he thought about his design, particularly how the memory would work and how an electronically based on-off (binary) system would calculate. Specifically, he pondered the working of the calculator's "regenerative memory"—the mechanism by which capacitors and vacuum tubes would charge one another in a feedback loop.

In 1938, Atanasoff worked on theoretical and practical aspects of four related ideas that he had thought of in the tavern in Illinois:

1. Electronic logic circuits that performed a calculation by turning on and off
2. A binary numbering system, using only 0 and 1 to indicate off and on
3. Capacitors for regenerative memory, which can store electrical charge while not connected to a source
4. Computing by direct logical action, not by enumeration, that is, by counting rather than measuring; the numbers represented by 1s and 0s, the on-off states of the vacuum tubes, which would directly be added and subtracted

In March 1939, Atanasoff submitted an application for a grant of $650 to attempt to build a calculator. In May, his request was granted: $200 for materials and $450 to pay for a student assistant.

Atanasoff was fortunate in obtaining the services of Clifford Berry as his assistant. Berry was knowledgeable, enthusiastic, and enterprising. He combined an exceptional intelligence and mechanical ability with a strong work ethic. Atanasoff and Berry had a "breadboard" prototype ready to test in October 1939. It incorporated seven innovations:

1. Electronic computing
2. Vacuum tubes as the computing mechanism and operating memory
3. Binary calculation
4. Logical calculation
5. Serial computation
6. Capacitors as storage memory
7. Capacitors attached to a rotating drum that refreshed the power supply of the vacuum tubes to regenerate the operating memory

In January 1940, the construction of the new prototype began. The goal was to focus the design of the machine on the solution of differential equations. The calculator would be able to solve equations containing up to twenty-nine unknowns, three times the number then considered possible with current methods.

Atanasoff and Berry constructed what they called the ABC, the Atanasoff-Berry Computer, in the basement of the physics building. The frame of ABC was seventy-four inches long, thirty-six inches deep, and forty inches tall, including casters. Solving twenty-nine linear equations with twenty-nine unknowns took thirty hours with periodic inputs from the operator, but it could be done and done accurately by the ABC.

In August 1940, Atanasoff completed a thirty-five page manuscript, in which he described the ABC in detail, including a list of nine types of linear algebraic equations a larger machine would be able to solve. He described practical applications in physics, statistics, and technology, ranging from problems of elasticity to quantum physics.

Atanasoff planned to use the manuscript to obtain additional development money—$5,000 was needed for the next phase. Atanasoff made three carbon copies of the original manuscript: one for the research corporation, one for Berry, and one for the patent process that Atanasoff thought the machine was ready for.

In December 1940, Atanasoff attended the annual meeting of the American Association for the Advancement of Science in Philadelphia. He also planned to do some patent research in New York and Washington, D.C. One of the reasons Atanasoff attended this annual meeting was to find out what other inventors were doing.

John Mauchly, a physics professor from Ursinis College in Collegeville, Pennsylvania, gave a talk about correlating weather patterns with solar phenomena. He mentioned that he had developed a calculator, the "Harmonic Analyzer," to do the correlations. He discussed his design and talked about his plans for the future. Although the "Harmonic Analyzer" was an analog machine, he thought the future of computing was electronic (digital).

After Mauchly's talk, he and Atanasoff compared notes on their development efforts. Atanasoff invited Mauchly to Ames to see the ABC. When Atanasoff returned home, he met with college officials to persuade them to hire Richard Trexler, an eminent patent attorney from Chicago to process the patent. Atanasoff sent Trexler a copy of the thirty-five page manuscript describing the ABC.

College president Charles E. Friley and college officials still did not appreciate the value of obtaining a patent, but Atanasoff prevailed. Friley wanted the college to get 90% of the potential profits with nothing for Berry. After six months of negotiations, In July 1941, Friley agreed to giving Atanasoff 50% of the profits, less expenses. Berry would receive 10% of Atanasoff's portion.

Mauchly visited Iowa State for four days in July 1941. Atanasoff was very open with him in discussing the ABC. He was pleased to find someone who was interested in his project. The staff at Iowa State wasn't all that interested. Atanasoff loaned Mauchly a copy of his manuscript on the ABC but would not let Mauchly take a copy back to Philadelphia with him.

Mauchly spent considerable time in the basement of the physics building with the ABC, talking with Berry and others. Mauchly had hands-on access to the ABC and actually helped Berry do a few repairs. He and Atanasoff spent every evening talking about the principles of the ABC. One evening, Mauchly asked Lura for some bond paper and she noticed that Mauchly stayed up late at night with his light on. She suspected that he was copying the thirty-five page manuscript. She was concerned he might be stealing her husband's ideas.

Later, Mauchly claimed that the ABC he viewed in Ames was not a working model. Professor George Snedecor of the Iowa State statistics department noted that he "would send problems over to Atanasoff and the ABC would solve them. Then the secretary would check the results on a desktop calculator. And they would be correct." The ABC was in working order.

In the summer of 1941, Mauchly took a course at the Moore School of Electrical Engineering at the University of Pennsylvania. It was a cram course in electronics sponsored by the War Department for scientists in other fields. There he met his future partner, J. Presper Eckert, who had just graduated from the Moore School. Upon completion of the course, Mauchly was invited to join the staff of the Moore School.

Mauchly wrote to Atanasoff to ask, "Is there any objection from your point of view to my building some sort of computer which incorporates some of the features of your machine? In the event that your present design were to hold the field against all challengers, and I got the Moore School interested in having something of the sort, would the way be open to build an 'Atanasoff Calculator' here?"

In September 1942, Atanasoff left Ames for a war-related position at the Naval Ordnance Laboratory in Washington, D.C. Iowa State told Atanasoff that the patent process was well in hand. He left the ABC in the basement of the physics building. Atanasoff worked for the Naval Ordnance Laboratory for the next seven years, during which time he was out of touch with the patent submission at Iowa State. When he inquired about the patent process, he was not given clear answers.

In the spring of 1943, Mauchly visited Atanasoff at the Naval Ordnance Laboratory. He told Atanasoff about a project at the Moore School calculating trajectories of large artillery pieces. Mauchly described how he and Eckert were devising a machine the army could use to make firing-range calculations. In his paper, "The Use of High-Speed Vacuum Tubes for Calculation," Mauchly described "an electronic device operating solely on the principle of counting." It would do the same tasks as an analog device but would do them faster.

The Moore School began to develop the ENIAC (Electronic Numeric Integrator and Computer). When it was finished, it weighed twenty-seven tons and was eight feet long, eight feet high, and three feet deep. It had 18,000 vacuum tubes, 7,200 diodes, 1,500 relays, and 10,000 capacitors for memory storage. It was not programmable.

Atanasoff met mathematician John von Neumann when he visited the Naval Ordnance Laboratory. Von Neumann wrote a paper describing a second version of ENIAC, "First Draft of a Report of the EDVAC." EDVAC stood for "Electronic Discrete Variable Automatic Computer." The paper described "Von Neumann architecture," in which the computer would contain a set of instructions in its memory, that is, it would be programmable.

In February 1946, Atanasoff attended the unveiling of ENIAC at the University of Pennsylvania. Neither Mauchly nor Eckert were present. He didn't learn much about the principles of the machine. He called Richard Trexler, the Chicago patent attorney, and was told that his patent was never filed because Iowa State had never paid the filing fee.

Another ongoing computer development project at the time was Howard Aiken's Mark I at Harvard, which was built by IBM, the supplier of the punched-card system for ENIAC. In the spring of 1946, Mauchly and Eckert formed their own company. Mauchly's responsibility was to manage the company and to obtain financing and contracts. Eckert was in charge of building the first UNIVAC (Universal Automatic Computer), which became available in March 1951.

The IBM 701 was announced in April 1952, followed by the 702, the 650, and the 705. The 701 and the 650 were designed for business use. Two of IBM's advantages were the punched-card systems in widespread use and the fact that IBM rented their machines.

Filmmaker Kirwin Cox noted that the EDVAC design was closer to the ABC design than the ENIAC configuration and that ENIAC was a hybrid machine—partially ABC, partially Bush Analyzer, and partially ganged calculators. Cox also observed: "John Vincent Atanasoff was a lucky man in many ways. He lived to see his hard work and enterprising intelligence vindicated. He spent a long life trying many things and, because of his energy, organizational skills, and and persistence, mastering everything he tried." Cox called him the "lone inventor" type, who explores and invents and then exhausts his interests in a given idea.

CHAPTER 6

Overcoming Obstacles to Achieve Success

"I have learned that success is to be measured not so much by the position one has reached in life as by the obstacles which he has overcome while trying to succeed."

Booker T. Washington

PAUL WITTGENSTEIN (1887-1961) *One-armed Concert Pianist*

"It [learning to play the piano with one hand] was like attempting to scale a mountain. If you can't climb up from one side, you try another."

Paul Wittgenstein

Paul Wittgenstein was a highly regarded concert pianist prior to World War I. While serving in the Austrian army, he was severely wounded in the right arm, which had to be amputated. For most musicians, loss of an arm would have been a career-ending event. Wittgenstein, however, surveyed the music that could be played with one hand and practiced seven hours a day to learn how to play it. In an article in *The Music Review*, E. Fred Flindell commented on this accomplishment:

> Wittgenstein amazed the post-war generation. In the years following the war, a period of bizarre turmoil and stunting cynicism, Wittgenstein not only attained world-wide fame, his example fostered a unique image in the minds of scholars, concert-goers, and musicians alike. Neither his family, his wealth, his heroic war record, nor his musical talent could alone account for or carve out such an achievement. His was simply a boundless idealism, one embodying devotion, endurance, and temerity in the service of music.

Paul Wittgenstein, who was born on November 5, 1887, in Vienna, Austria, was the seventh of eight children of Karl and Leopoldine Kalmus Wittgenstein. Karl owned several steel factories and became known as the "Iron King" of Austria. Leopoldine Wittgenstein, the daughter of a wealthy merchant, played arrangements for four hands on the organ and piano with young Paul as his skill on the keyboard developed. Paul's younger brother, Ludwig, became a renowned philosopher.

The Wittgenstein family was wealthy. They frequently entertained Brahms, Mahler, and Clara Schumann. Paul was fortunate to have the opportunity to play piano duets with Richard Strauss. Bruno Walter and Pablo Casals also performed in the Wittgenstein home. Karl Wittgenstein provided financial support to Arnold Schöenberg.

Young Wittgenstein took piano lessons from the highly regarded teacher, Malvine Brée. Wittgenstein had an incredible memory for music and was a facile sight-reader. His exposure to masters of music in his home elevated his interest in music. He was not concerned about his own limitations in comparison with them. Next he took lessons from Theodor Leschetizky and the blind Austrian composer, Josef Labor. They helped him search for his own musical identity.

Wittgenstein's friend, Trevor Harvey, said about him at this time, "By all accounts in his early days he built up an astonishing left-hand technique, but when I knew him the nervous intensity that he developed led him often to play insensitively and loudly, and not always with great accuracy." He referred to himself as the "Saitenknicker," the mighty key smasher.

In December 1913, Wittgenstein made his debut as a concert pianist at the Grosser Musikverein Saal in Vienna. Three months later, he gave a solo performance with the Vienna Symphony Verein. In August 1914, he was called to active duty as a second lieutenant in the Austrian Army. He was severely wounded while leading a reconnaissance patrol near Zamosc, Poland.

In his book about Wittgenstein, *The Crown Prince*, John Barchilon described what happened when Wittgenstein's patrol was hit by an artillery shell:

> The ground opened up and hurled them in the air, spinning and twisting. Paul saw earth, fire, and sky. Arms, legs, and black dirt swirled around him, and then he began the endless journey back to earth. He fell and fell and fell, landing on something soft. Where were his legs? His arms, hands, where were they? Where was his foot? He heard nothing. Just silence. Black, black nothing. Was this death?

Wittgenstein was taken to an army hospital at Krasnostov, where his right arm was amputated. He was taken prisoner by the Russian Army at the hospital and moved to hospitals in Minsk and in Orel and Omsk, Siberia, where he had access to a piano. In November 1915, through efforts of the International Red Cross, he was sent from Siberia to Sweden, where he participated in a prisoner exchange sponsored by the Pope.

In March 1916, Wittgenstein was promoted to first lieutenant and retired on a medical disability pension. Leopoldine Wittgenstein received a letter from his commanding officer:

> I wish to express my sincere sympathy with you in connection with the severe wounding of your son. You may be proud of him, because owing to the information obtained by his patrol, the efforts of the Russians to attack us at Famorz were frustrated. He has rendered outstanding services, and I sincerely hope he will get official recognition.

In May 1916, Wittgenstein was awarded the Military Cross Class III and the War Decoration Class III. Five months later, he was awarded the Military Cross Class II by the Grand Duke of Mecklenburg. From the summer of 1917 until August 1918, by his own request, he served as a first lieutenant on the Italian front as a general's aide.

From the time of his return to Vienna until he volunteered for the Italian front, Wittgenstein practiced compositions for the left hand. He performed in five recitals, in which he played Labor's *Concertpiece for Piano and Orchestra, Sonata in E-flat for Piano and Violin,* and *Piano Quartet in C Minor.* In September 1918, he returned to Vienna and the concert stage.

Leschetizky had died in 1915. Wittgenstein did not look for another teacher; he practiced seven hours a day, establishing his own regimen. Initially, he tired easily and had to rest frequently. From 1918 to 1921, Wittgenstein searched libraries, museums, and second-hand retail music shops for compositions for the left hand. He liked Brahms's arrangement of Bach's *Chaconne,* as well as Godowsky's *Suite for the Left Hand Alone,* the *Fugue upon Bach,* and the *Intermezzo and Etude Macabre.* He also admired *Studies for the Left Hand* by Reger, *Etudes for the Left Hand* by Saint-Saëns, and Scriabin's *Prelude and Nocturne for the Left Hand,* which the composer wrote after developing tendonitis in his right hand.

One of the earliest one-armed pianists was the Hungarian Count Geza Zichy, who began playing the piano at the age of five; he decided to be a concert pianist after losing his right arm in a hunting accident in 1864, when he was fifteen. His concert in Berlin in May 1915 was the first known public performance of a one-armed pianist. Count Zichy's friend, Franz Liszt, transcribed a song for him, and Emil Sauer wrote *Etude* for him. Wittgenstein did not like the works that Count Zichy composed for himself.

Wittgenstein wrote his own arrangements of piano compositions and operas using the transcription devices of Liszt and of Godowsky. He also commissioned composers to create new works for the left hand. Wittgenstein observed: "Since it is no particular attainment of mine, I think I may honestly say that I am (perhaps) the pianist for whom the greatest number of special compositions have been written." In 1931, he accepted a teaching position at the New Vienna Conservatory, where he was known for his energy and his optimism.

Wittgenstein didn't hesitate to make extensive changes to other composers' works that he had commissioned, similar to his modifications to Brahms's transcription of Bach's *Chaconne*. He made changes to the compositions of Hindemith and Korngold, as well as to Britten's *Diversions on a Theme*, Prokofiev's *Concerto No. 4*, and *Parergon to the Domestic Symphony* by Richard Strauss. They were twentieth-century composers, and Wittgenstein's style was that of the nineteenth century.

Wittgenstein asked Ravel if he would compose a piano concerto for the left hand. Ravel willingly undertook the project. Initially, Ravel and Wittgenstein did not agree on the finished work. Wittgenstein objected to Ravel's inclusion of jazz rhythms in his composition; however, the differences were resolved. Ravel's *Concerto in D for Left Hand* became one of the most frequently played works for one hand.

Wittgenstein continued to perform on the concert stage. One of his students in the 1930s recalled the first time she had heard him play: "I was about twelve years old when I heard Paul Wittgenstein perform for the first time. I was sitting with my father in our subscription seats in the rear of the Wiener Musikverein Saal. After the concert, my father asked me if I had noticed anything unusual about the pianist. I had not. He told me that the pianist had only played with his left hand. I could not believe it."

In November 1934, Wittgenstein performed the Ravel *Concerto for the Left Hand and Orchestra* with the Boston Symphony. The music critic of the *New York Herald-Tribune* reported:

> Doubtless the greatest tribute one could pay to Paul Wittgenstein, the famous one-armed pianist, is a simple statement of the fact that after the first few moments wondering how the devil he accomplished it, one almost forgot that one was listening to a player whose right sleeve hung empty at his side. One found oneself engrossed by the sensitiveness of the artist's phrasing, the extent to which his incredible technique was subordinated to the delivery of the musical thought.

Wittgenstein taught at the New Vienna Conservatory until he immigrated to the United States in December 1938. From 1938 until 1943, he taught at the Ralph Wolfe Conservatory in New Rochelle, an affiliate of the Mannes Music School; from 1940 until 1945 he was a professor of piano at Manhattanville College of the Sacred Heart. He became a U.S. citizen in 1946. In 1957, Wittgenstein published *School for the Left Hand*. In 1958, he received an honorary Doctor of Music degree from the Philadelphia Musical Academy.

In an interview with Leonard Castle, Wittgenstein described some of the piano techniques that he used in concerts. He did not use the middle or harp pedal on the piano. He used two fingers on one key for increased volume, and difficult leaps over the keys could be avoided by half pedaling that simulated the two-handed technique. His skill was enhanced by the speed with which he used his left hand and his precise control.

On March 3, 1961, Paul Wittgenstein died in Manhasset, New York. In *The Music Review*, E. Fred Flindell wrote what might be considered an epitaph:

It is, however, astonishing how many works [over forty] the artist took an active part in commissioning, determining, and performing. Few knew that Wittgenstein spent years helping others as president of the Society Against Poverty, or of his countless anonymous and gracious deeds of assistance. Perhaps his nineteenth-century ideas and bearing were at times anachronistic, even quixotic. Still, his endeavor and influence, his courage and skill will remain legendary for generations to come.

CHRISTY BROWN (1932-1981) *Overcame Cerebral Palsy to Write Books*

"Seldom, except in the great story of Helen Keller and Annie Sullivan, has a crippled, blind, or deaf person been so gifted that he has been able to lift the curtain that hangs around the lives of so many of our less fortunate brothers and sisters and let us see within. Never, I think, has one read a life so completely different from the normal which has been written with such craftsmanship that one can actually feel what the writer felt himself. For me, the whole experience has been an extraordinary revelation, and a proof of the amazing power of the spirit of the man who overcame the impossible and, perhaps most of all, of the utmost need of the human soul to escape from every sort of prison."

Robert Collis, Foreword, *My Left Foot*

Christy Brown had a severe case of athetosis due to an abnormal birth. In athetosis, the middle part of the brain is affected, causing abnormal writhing when any attempt is made to accomplish coordinated movements. The only muscles that Christy could control were those in the left leg and left foot. He could not speak until he began therapy at the age of seventeen. Christy overcame his ailment to write an autobiography, *My Left Foot*, two novels, *Down All The Days* and *Shadow on Summer*, and two books of poems, *Come Softly to My Wake* and *Background Music*. In achieving success, he was aided by the optimism of his remarkable mother, who worked with him from his early years to deal with his disability.

Christy was born in Rotunda Hospital, Dublin, Ireland, on June 5, 1932. He was the tenth of twenty-two children, four of whom did not survive infancy. His birth was a difficult one, and both he and his mother almost died. He was four months old when his mother began to suspect that he had a physical ailment; his head always fell backwards while he was being fed. She noticed that her son's hands were always clenched, and that he had a difficult time gripping the nipple of the bottle with his jaws. At the age of six months, he had to be surrounded by pillows to sit upright.

When he was a year old, Christy's parents made the rounds of the clinics and hospitals in the area searching for a doctor who could help their son. The doctors were all very negative; they said that his case was hopeless, and that nothing could be done for him. Furthermore, they diagnosed him as mentally retarded, which his mother did not believe.

Mrs. Brown refused to merely feed and wash Christy and then put him in the back room. He was her child, and she was sufficiently optimistic to treat Christy as a full-fledged member of the family. Christy was saved because his mother was driven to help him overcome as many of his obstacles as he could with love. At this time, she had five other children to care for; nevertheless, she spent as much time with Christy as she could. While Mr. Brown, a bricklayer, was at work, Mrs. Brown ensured that the other children treated Christy as an equal member of the family.

At the age of five, Christy showed the first indication of activity. His sister was writing on a piece of slate with a bright yellow piece of chalk. Christy reached over and took the chalk out of his sister's hand—with his left foot. He scribbled on the slate. All other activity in the room stopped. His sister looked at him with wide eyes. His father leaned forward in his chair, looking tense.

Mrs. Brown entered the room, observed the tension, walked over to Christy, and said, "I'll show you what to do with it, Chris." She made an "A" on the slate and told him to copy it. He tried, but he wasn't successful on the first and second attempts. On the third attempt, he began to write the "A," but the chalk broke. Mrs. Brown placed her hand on his shoulder to encourage him. He completed the "A" on the fourth try.

Tears flowed down Mrs. Brown's cheek. Mr. Brown reached down and hoisted his son up to his shoulders. For Christy, writing the letter "A" was the beginning of leading a constructive life. Mrs. Brown taught Christy the entire alphabet. His next projects were to write his initials, "C. B.," and then his full name. Christy surprised his mother one day by calling her over to watch him write a word on the slate. He spelled out "M-O-T-H-E-R." His mother was quiet for some time and then turned, placed her hand on her son's shoulder, and smiled broadly.

When Christy was seven, his brothers took him with them when they played in the streets. All of the neighborhood children accepted Christy; in fact, they treated him with a youthful version of deference and respect. Christy participated in hide-and-seek and blind-man's buff, two of the most popular games.

Eventually, Christy changed. He no longer liked going out and seeing the strange looks that outsiders gave him. Increasingly, he stayed at home. At Christmas, Christy received a box of paints. He was fascinated by the bright colors. Christy began to paint regularly; he had found a reason to be happy again.

When Christy was eleven, his mother became very ill giving birth to the Brown family's twenty-second and last child. She was in the hospital for an extended period, and the family, particularly Christy, missed her. One evening there was a knock on the door, and Mr. Brown opened the door to a slender, eighteen-year-old girl, who was the prettiest girl that Christy had ever seen. She introduced herself as Katriona Delahunt, a social worker from the hospital. Mrs. Brown had told her about Christy. Katriona asked Christy to write a note to his mother, so that she would know that everything was all right at home. Christy wrote: "Dear Mom. Don't worry. All okay. Lots of grub. Get well soon. Christy."

Katriona came into Christy's life at a time when he needed a boost from outside of his own family and neighborhood. He needed someone to make him realize that he could rise above his disability and perhaps accomplish more than his brothers who were beginning to settle into jobs. Katriona brought him many new paints, paintbrushes, and drawing books. Christy still couldn't talk, but they managed to communicate; he always looked forward to her visits.

Just before Christmas, Christy noticed the announcement of a Christmas painting competition for children from twelve to sixteen. He had just turned twelve, and he wanted to enter the competition. Katriona and his mother encouraged him to enter the contest. One day a *Sunday Independent* reporter and photographer knocked on the door. Katriona had told them that one of the entrees in the painting competition was painted by a young boy using his left foot. They wanted to verify what they had been told.

The next copy of the *Sunday Independent* contained a photograph of Christy's painting and announced that he had won the competition. His mother congratulated him: "Never stop trying, Chris." Katriona also stopped by to congratulate him; she took his hand in hers and kissed him on the forehead. Christy thought he was in heaven. However, painting had become something that he liked to do; it was no longer something that he loved to do. Christy's new interest was writing. His early themes were the American Wild West, boy-meets-girl stories, and detective stories.

One day, the inevitable happened; Katriona was wearing an engagement ring when she visited. She showed the diamond ring to Mrs. Brown and to Christy. She told Christy: "Don't make a sour face. I'll still come to see you after I'm married." Mrs. Brown took Christy to the wedding in his wheelchair. He was introduced to Katriona's husband, Mr. Maguire. Christy thought that he looked like a kind man, but he was jealous.

On one of her visits, Katriona asked Christy if he had ever considered visiting Lourdes. He said that he had, but he didn't know how he would pay for the trip. The Lourdes Committee, the organizers of the pilgrimage, contributed £10, and an elderly aunt contributed £5 toward the £34 cost of the trip. Katriona invited her friends to play bridge for money, and they made up the difference.

The flight to Lourdes was the first time that Christy had gone anywhere without a member of his family. As he noted in *My Left Foot*:

> As I saw all those people each with his or her own suffering, a new light began to dawn on me. I was rather bewildered; I had not imagined there could be so much suffering in the world. I had been rather like a snail shut away in his own narrow shell and that was only now beginning to see the great crowded world that lay beyond.
>
> Not only were those people afflicted, but their handicaps were actually worse than my own! Up to then, I had not thought I was seeing with my eyes and really feeling with my heart the plight of others whose burdens were so great as to make mine seem nothing in comparison.

As their van pulled into the town of Lourdes, Christy saw the beautiful Basilica and Rosary Square. He was impressed by the long, thin spire topped by a gold cross. He could hear a choir singing a hymn in the chapel. The square was crowded with people. The next morning they were taken to the healing baths, where

Christy was stripped of his clothing by two Frenchmen and lowered into the water. After he went under a second time, the men lifted him out, recited prayers in French, and gave him a small cross to kiss. He felt reborn.

In the afternoon, Christy was taken to the Grotto. The road to the Shrine was crowded with people of virtually every nationality. A marble statue of Mary in a blue robe looked down on them from a niche carved out of the rock. He prayed fervently that he might be cured. That night, Christy participated in a torch-light procession through Lourdes from the Basilica to the Shrine. Thousands of pilgrims gathered in Rosary Square. The facade of the Basilica was illuminated. Thousands of candles were lit, and everyone sang "Ave Maria." He was moved. He considered it "the most beautiful moment of my life."

Christy had been depressed about his condition before he went to Lourdes, and within a short time after he arrived back in Ireland, his depression returned. He tried to be patient and resigned to suffering like the pilgrims at Lourdes, knowing the reward that awaited them in heaven. However, Christy concluded that he was too human and not meek enough to be like them. He was optimistic that he could be productive. He wanted to accomplish more in this world before he thought about the next.

Christy summarized his visit to Lourdes in his autobiography:

> Lourdes had left a lasting impression on my mind. I saw that far from being alone and isolated as I thought myself to be, I was merely one of a brotherhood of suffering that stretched over the whole globe. I remember the courage and perseverance that shone in the faces of the afflicted people who came from all parts of the world to hope and to pray at the feet of the Virgin in the Grotto.

> There I had seen the story of my own life reflected in the eyes of those I had prayed with; those men and women who spoke different tongues and who live according to different ideals, but who were now made all brothers and sisters, all part of one family by right of a common heritage of pain. No

one thought of anyone else as a "foreigner" in that holy little village; all the barriers that separate single persons and whole nations from one another were broken down and burned away by that common need for understanding and communication which we all felt and which suffering alone could have inspired.

Back home in Dublin, Christy received a visit from Dr. Robert Collis, who ran a clinic in Dublin for the treatment of cerebral palsy. He wanted to ask Christy if he would be willing to undergo a new treatment for his ailment. When Dr. Collis looked at him, Christy felt that the doctor's penetrating eyes were looking into him. He said, "Christy, there is a new treatment for cerebral palsy— the thing that is wrong with you. I believe you can be cured—but only if you are willing to try hard enough with us. I can't help you if you don't try to help yourself. You must want to get better before anything can be done for you. Will you try if I help?"

Christy couldn't talk, but Dr. Collis read the answer in his eyes and said, "Good. We'll start tomorrow." The next day, Dr. Louis Warnants came to the Browns' house to examine Christy. He was a young man with a military bearing who radiated confidence. He planned a preliminary set of physical exercises for Christy.

In January 1949, Dr. Collis told Christy that he wanted him to be examined in London by his sister-in-law, Eirene Collis, a highly regarded specialist in cerebral palsy. Dr. Warnants met Christy and Mrs. Brown and took them to Middlesex Hospital. Mrs. Collis's examination at the hospital would determine how comprehensive a rehabilitation program should be planned.

Mrs. Collis, who put Christy at ease with her casualness, examined him. She told him: "You can be cured if you are prepared to do lots of really hard work over the next few years. But first you must make a big sacrifice. Nothing good is ever obtained without one, and yours is—you must resolve never to use your left foot again."

Christy was very apprehensive, but he agreed. Mrs. Collis's reasoning was that although using his left foot gave Christy's mind a way to express itself, it placed considerable strain on the rest of his body; the condition of his crippled muscles was worsening. The treatment would be done at Dr. Collis's clinic in Dublin, and Christy would be provided with transportation between his home and the clinic.

Christy's first visit to the clinic was terrifying. All of the other patients were young children, three years old and younger. At seventeen, he was by far the oldest one there for treatment. At Lourdes, he had seen many older people with disabilities and a few children. Seeing large numbers of severely handicapped children overwhelmed him. Christy's experiences at the clinic helped him to take a larger view of things and to stop feeling sorry for himself. One of the staff members, Sheila, was particularly helpful to him. She suggested that he begin to do productive things that he liked doing, such as writing, and never to be in a position of wondering "what might have been."

At home one day, Christy saw his twelve-year-old brother, Eamonn, struggling with a composition assignment. Christy saw an opportunity; he offered to help Eamonn with his compositions if he would help him write his life story. Christy had not read widely. Charles Dickens's novels had been his principal reading experience. His first attempts at writing produced a labored text loaded with multisyllabic words.

Christy asked Dr. Collis to read the manuscript and to give him suggestions for improvement. He told Christy that his writing was awful, mainly because its style was fifty years out of date. Dr. Collis looked up while reading the manuscript and exclaimed, "Good. You have written one sentence here that stands out like a rose among a lot of weeds, one shining little gem thrown in amongst the stones. It shows me that you could write if you knew how. That's what I wanted to find out." Dr. Collis gave him two books by Sean O'Faolain and a book of L. A. G. Strong's short stories and suggested that he work to improve his writing style. He suggested that Christy begin again on his autobiography.

Dr. Collis's advice to Christy was:

> There are two first principles attached to writing any sort of story. First you must have a story to tell and, secondly, you must tell it in such a way that the person reading it can live in it himself. Now let me give you some concrete points: Whenever you

can, use a short word rather than a long one. You have painted pictures with a brush, try and do the same thing with a pen. Practice it. Describe the room here: your queer chair, the picture on the smudged wall here, the broken mirror, the books — the colored photograph.

At the clinic, Christy was taught how to relax his muscles. Staff personnel also helped him to improve his ability to speak, beginning with learning how to breathe properly. He began to grunt less and to speak more, enunciating more clearly. Christy understood the importance of self-confidence and of being less self-conscious in learning to speak well. He respected the staff members at the clinic and had a high regard for the treatment they provided. He realized that their care was based on a feeling of pride, not pity.

Christy began writing the second version of his life story, using his thirteen-year-old brother, Francis, as scribe. Francis was not merely a scribe; he offered suggestions for improvement to Christy. Version two was clearer and more orderly than his first attempt; however, Dr. Collis thought that it was still too "literary." His writing was still too pretentious and overly dramatic. Also, he was using too many clichés.

Dr. Collis suggested that he continue his education before he wrote version three. He suggested a tutor. Katriona Maguire helped Dr. Collis to find Mr. Guthrie, a master in a large National school in the area. Twice a week, Christy learned about the philosophy of Bertrand Russell, the poetry of Yeats, mathematics, geometry, Latin, history, Shakespeare, and Shaw.

One day, Christy was attempting to dictate to Francis, but the words just wouldn't come. He told Francis to leave and ripped the sock off of his left foot and began to write. His frustration level dropped, and he could write freely. The doctor from the clinic came in and saw him writing with his left foot. The doctor said that he had wondered how long Christy could hold out from using it. He understood that dictating wasn't enough and said that he wouldn't tell Eirene Collis. However, he advised Christy only to use his left foot when he had to.

Dr. Collis planned a benefit for cerebral palsy in Dublin. He had met Burl Ives at the Chest Hospital in London, where Ives gave a concert for the patients. Dr. Collis invited Ives to Dublin for the cerebral palsy benefit sponsored by the Ireland-American Society. John Huston, the movie director, was the president of the Society. The benefit was well publicized, and over 500 people attended.

Burl Ives began the benefit by singing "The Blue-tailed Fly." The entire audience joined Ives in the singing. After Ives's concert, John Huston announced that Dr. Collis would address the audience representing the Cerebral Palsy Association. Dr. Collis didn't make a speech, and he didn't make an appeal. He said that he would read the first chapter of Christy Brown's autobiography, written with his left foot, which would give them an insider's view of cerebral palsy.

When Dr. Collis began reading, the room was noisy, but it soon became absolutely quiet. Everyone was listening. Someone in the front row was crying, and Christy's mother's eyes moistened. Complete silence reigned when Dr. Collis stopped reading. When he reached down and helped Christy to his feet, the entire ballroom broke out into loud applause. Christy was happy as he listened to Burl Ives conclude the program with "She Moved Through the Fair."

In the late 1970s, Mary Carr took care of Christy. They fell in love and were married. They lived together until Christy died in 1981. He never lost his optimism. In 1988, the movie, *My Left Foot,* based on Christy's life story, was produced in Dublin. Daniel Day Lewis starred as Christy.

CARL BRASHEAR (1931-2006) *U.S. Navy Master Diver* and Amputee

"The Navy diver is not a fighting man.
He is a salvage expert.
If it's lost underwater, he finds it.
If it's sunk, he brings it up.
If it's in the way, he moves it.
If he's lucky, he dies two hundred feet beneath the waves,
Because that's the closest he will ever come to being a hero.
No one in their right mind would ever want the job.
Or so they say."

The Diver's Creed

Carl Brashear set a goal for himself at a young age and had the motivation to achieve that goal despite having to overcome racial discrimination as well as a major physical injury. Paul Stillwell of the U.S. Naval Institute summarized Brashear's achievements:

> To become the first black master diver in the Navy, Carl Brashear used a rare combination of grit, determination, and persistence, because the obstacles in his path were formidable. His race was a handicap, as were his origin on a sharecropper's farm in rural Kentucky and the modest education he received there. But these were not his greatest challenges. He was held back by an even greater factor: in 1966, his left leg was amputated just below the knee because he was badly injured on a salvage operation.

> After the amputation, the Navy sought to retire Brashear from active duty, but he refused to submit to the decision. Instead, he secretly returned to diving and produced evidence that he could excel, despite his injury. Then, in 1974, he qualified as a Master Diver, a difficult feat under any circumstances and something no black man had accomplished before. By the time of his retirement, he

had achieved the highest rate for Navy enlisted personnel, master chief petty officer. In addition, he had become a celebrity through his response to manifold challenges and thereby had become a real inspiration to others.

Carl Brashear was born on a farm in Tonieville, Kentucky, in January 1931, the sixth of nine children of McDonald and Gonzella Brashear. McDonald Brashear was a hard working sharecropper with a third-grade education. Young Carl helped his father work the farm and attended a one-room, segregated school through the eighth grade. His mother, who had completed nine years of school, augmented his education with home schooling.

At the age of fourteen, Brashear decided that he wanted to be a military man, possibly a soldier. He was influenced by a brother-in-law in the Army. When he was seventeen, he went to the U.S. Army recruiting office to enlist. However, everyone yelled at him, making him so nervous that he failed the entrance examination. He was supposed to return to retake the exam, but he went to the U.S. Navy recruiting office instead. The Navy chief petty officer treated him well, so he enlisted in the Navy.

In February 1948, Brashear reported to the Great Lakes Naval Training Center for basic training and was assigned to an integrated company. He encountered no racial prejudice in boot camp; however, upon completion of his training, steward was the only assignment available to him. He was assigned as steward to an air squadron in Key West, Florida. The Naval Base in Key West was segregated at the time; opportunities for African-American personnel were limited.

At Key West, Brashear met Chief Boatswain's Mate Guy Johnson, who steered him toward a major turning point in his career. Chief Johnson arranged for Brashear to leave the steward assignment and work for him as a beachmaster, beaching seaplanes from the Gulf of Mexico. Brashear strongly preferred his new assignment over his old one. His duties as a beachmaster required him to get along with people, to respect others, and to work with little supervision. Chief Johnson taught him basic seamanship, gave him guidance on being a good sailor, and introduced him to the qualities of leadership.

While stationed at Key West, Brashear decided that he wanted to be a diver. One day, a buoy needed repair, and a self-propelled seaplane wrecking derrick, a YSD, was brought out to repair it. A diver with a face mask and shallow-water diving apparatus went down to make the necessary repairs.

Brashear watched the diver work and realized that diving was what he wanted to do. Brashear requested diving duty on his first two shipboard assignments, on the escort aircraft carriers *USS Palau* (CVE-122) and *USS Tripoli* (CVE-64). He was assigned to the sail locker, with boatswain's mate's duties such as splicing wire and sewing canvas. He learned about fueling rigs and anchoring and mooring methods.

While Brashear was stationed on the *Tripoli,* a TBM Avenger torpedo bomber rolled off the jettison ramp, and a deep-sea diver went down to attach wires to pull the plane out of the water. Brashear watched the diver go down and come up and observed, "Now, this is the best thing since sliced bread. I've got to be a deep-sea diver." He requested diving school routinely until he was admitted in 1954.

Brashear joined the boxing team on the *Tripoli* and won many bouts. He met Sugar Ray Robinson, who taught him how to throw jabs and to keep his hands up. Sugar Ray showed him how to be a better defensive boxer. Brashear fought in the light-heavyweight championship of the East Coast, but he lost that fight.

Brashear made boatswain's mate third class on the *Tripoli* and gained experience with paravane gear used for minesweeping and with the operations of a tank landing ship (LST). He was responsible for a division of men and learned about leadership and supervision. He had done well, but he realized that further education would increase his opportunities for advancement.

In 1953, Brashear made boatswain's mate second class. While at that rate, he won "sailor-of-the-year" honors and was called "Mr. Navy." He enrolled in United States Armed Forces Institute (USAFI) courses and passed his general educational development (GED) examination, the high-school equivalency test, in 1960. A high school diploma wasn't required for the first phase of diving school, but it was for later phases, such as mixed-gas diving.

Brashear's next assignment was in Bayonne, New Jersey, at diving school, which involved hard work and psychological stress.

When he reported for duty, the training officer thought he was reporting in as a cook or steward. When he found out that Brashear was there as a student, he told him, "Well, I don't know how the rest of the students are going to accept you. As a matter of fact, I don't even think you will make it through the school. We haven't had a colored guy come through here before."

When classes started, Brashear found notes on his bunk: "We're going to drown you today, nigger! We don't want any nigger divers." Brashear was ready to quit, but boatswain's mate first class Rutherford, on the staff of the diving school, talked him out of it. Over a beer at the Dungaree Bar, Rutherford said, "I hear you're going to quit." Brashear admitted that he planned to leave the school. Rutherford told him, "I can't whip you, but I'll fight you every day if you quit. Those notes aren't hurting you. No one is doing a thing to you. Show them you're a better man than they are." Rutherford's pep talk was the only encouragement Brashear received. One person's upbeat advice was enough to keep him on his chosen career path.

The first week of diving school was orientation; physics courses were given in the second week. Diving medicine and diving physics were followed by four weeks of pure diving, which included introduction to hydraulics and underwater tools as well as underwater welding and cutting. The course included two weeks of demolition and several weeks of salvage operations, which involved becoming familiar with beach gear and learning how to make splices.

Brashear worked hard in the sixteen-week-long diving school and didn't fail any exams. The school was stressful; the instructors continually challenged the students. Teamwork was emphasized. When working underwater, divers rely on their teammates working alongside them and rely heavily on support personnel topside. Brashear was one of seventeen out of thirty-two that started with the class who graduated.

In March 1955, Brashear was assigned to a salvage ship, *USS Opportune* (ARS-41), which had eighteen divers out of a crew of over 100. The *Opportune* was involved in many salvage jobs, including raising a gas barge in Charleston, South Carolina, recovering an antisubmarine plane that had sunk in the Virginia Capes, and pulling a cargo ship off the beach in Argentia, Newfoundland.

His experiences on the *Opportune* increased his understanding of teamwork and the importance of knowing other team members' capabilities in diving. He was promoted to boatswain's mate first class while in Argentia, Newfoundland.

Brashear's next duty station was Quonset Point (Rhode Island) Naval Air Station, where, as leading petty officer, he was in charge of the boat house. One of his assignments was retrieving aircraft that had crashed in Narragansett Bay. A collateral duty was to escort President Eisenhower's boat, the *Barbara Ann*, with a 104-foot crash boat with a crew of thirteen and two 20-millimeter guns mounted on the wings of the bridge, from Delaware to Newport, where Ike played golf. Brashear also escorted the *Barbara Ann* on pleasure cruises.

One of Brashear's next assignments was the *USS Nereus*, homeported in San Diego, California, where he made chief petty officer and was assigned to first-class diver school in Washington, D.C. First-class diver school was demanding, with courses in medicine, decompression, physics, treatments, mathematics, and mixing gases to the proper ratio. Brashear flunked out. Most salvage divers who failed first-class school left as a second-class diver.

Brashear was astounded to hear that he was leaving as a nondiver. After seven years of diving experience, he had reached the low point in his career. He wrangled a set of orders to the fleet training center in Hawaii, which he knew had a second-class diver school. Lieutenant j.g. Billie Delanoy, whom Brashear knew from a previous assignment, was in charge of that school. Delanoy knew that his old shipmate should be a diver and enrolled him in the school, which was not difficult for Brashear. He passed it easily and returned to a level he had mastered previously.

While in Hawaii, Brashear dove to inspect the hull of the *USS Arizona* (BB-39) before she could be converted into a memorial. The amount of list had to be determined before they could proceed with the work to build the memorial. Using plumb lines, they determined that the *Arizona* had two degrees of list. It gave him an eerie feeling diving around a hull containing the 1,100 shipmates who died in the Japanese attack on Pearl Harbor.

While assigned to the fleet training center in Hawaii, Brashear received temporary additional duty (TAD) to report to Joint Task Force Eight as a diver supporting nuclear testing during Operation

Dominic in 1962. Thor intermediate-range ballistic missiles (IRBMs) with 20 or 30 megaton warheads were tested on Johnston Island. Brashear was skipper of a large self-propelled harbor tug (YTB-262) and was also a diver.

After studying math for two years, in 1963 Brashear got a second opportunity to attend first-class diving school in Washington, D.C. He thought that he would go through fourteen weeks of training with the class of thirty salvage divers, learning about diving medicine, diving physics, mixing gases, and emergency procedures. However, the training officer made him go through twenty-six weeks of class as though he had never been a salvage diver. He graduated third out of seventeen who completed the course.

After serving a year on the fleet ocean tug USS Shakori (ATF-162), Brashear was assigned to the salvage ship USS Hoist (ARS-40), where he could train to become a master diver. The Hoist participated in the search for a nuclear bomb that was dropped into the sea off Palomares, Spain, when a B-52 bomber and a refueling plane collided in midair. The bomb was found by the deep-diving research vessel Alvin six miles off the coast in 2,600 feet of water after a search of two and a half months. Brashear rigged a spider, a three-legged contraption with grapnel hooks, to the bomb to bring it to the surface.

A mechanized landing craft (LCM-8) was moored alongside the Hoist to receive the bomb. Brashear was bringing the bomb up with the capstan to place it in a crate in the landing craft when a line parted, causing the boat to break loose. He saw what had happened and ran to push one of his men out of the way of the line. A pipe tied to the mooring came loose, sailed across the deck, and struck Brashear's left leg just below the knee, virtually severing it. The bomb fell back into 2,600 feet of water.

The Hoist had no doctor and no morphine and was six and a half miles from the cruiser USS Albany, the location of the nearest doctor. Corpsmen placed two tourniquets on his leg, but, because Brashear's leg was so muscular, the bleeding couldn't be stopped. He was placed on board a helicopter to be transported to the hospital at Torrejon Air Force Base in Spain.

Brashear had lost so much blood that he went into shock. By the time he reached Torrejon, he had hardly any heartbeat or pulse. The doctor thought that Brashear was going to die. He came to after they had given him eighteen pints of blood. He was told that they would try to save his leg, but that it would be three inches shorter than his right leg. However, his leg became infected, and gangrene set in. Brashear was air-lifted to the Portsmouth, Virginia, Naval Hospital where he was told that his rehabilitation would take three years.

Brashear decided that he couldn't wait that long to get on with his life, so he told the doctor to amputate. The doctor responded, "Geez, Chief! Anybody could amputate. It takes a good doctor to fix it." Brashear told them that he planned to go back to diving; they thought that he shouldn't even consider it. In July 1966, another inch and a half of his leg had to be amputated.

Brashear had read about an air force pilot with no legs who flew fighter aircraft. That was Douglas Bader, a Royal Air Force ace in World War II. He also read that a prosthesis could be designed to support any amount of weight.

Brashear was sent to a prosthesis center in Philadelphia to be fitted. He refused to have people wait on him. Brashear told the doctor, "Once I get a leg, I'm going to give you back this crutch, and I'll never use it again." They told him that he couldn't do it. In December, he was fitted with an artificial leg; he never used crutches again.

Brashear returned to the Portsmouth Naval Hospital and visited Chief Warrant Officer Clair Axtell, who was in charge of the nearby diving school. He told Axtell, whom he knew from salvage diving school, "Ax, I've got to dive. I've got to get some pictures. I've got to prove to people that I'm going to be a diver." Axtell reminded Brashear that if anything happened to him, his own career would be over; nevertheless, he obtained a photographer and gave him a chance. Brashear dove in a deep-sea rig, in shallow-water equipment, and with scuba gear while the photographer documented his activities. He returned for a second set of dives and another set of pictures.

Brashear's medical board was convened at the naval hospital, where Rear Admiral Joseph Yon from the Bureau of Medicine and Surgery (BuMed) talked with him about returning to diving. Brashear took the initiative to endorse his own orders, "FFT (for further transfer) to the second-class diving school," and reported to the school. A lieutenant commander from BuMed called Brashear at the diving school and asked how he got into the diving school. Brashear replied, "Orders, sir," which caused some confusion.

Brashear had ignored the first physical evaluation board; now they told him to report to a second one. He had sent all of his diving photographs along with the findings of the medical board to BuMed. They said, "Well, if he did that down there [in Virginia], he can do it up here, " and invited him to spend a week with a captain and a commander at the deep-sea diving school in Washington, D.C. BuMed sent observers to evaluate his performance.

At the end of the week, Captain Jacks, policy control, called Brashear in and told him: "Most of the people in your position want to get a medical disability, get out of the Navy, and do the least they can and draw as much pay as they can. And then you're asking for full duty. I don't know to handle it. Suppose you would be diving and tear your leg off." Brashear said, "Well, Captain, it wouldn't bleed." Captain Jacks jokingly told him to get out of his office.

Brashear reported back to diving school in Virginia. Brashear dove every day for a year, including weekends. He led calisthenics every morning and ran every day. Occasionally, he would return from a run and find a puddle of blood from his stump in the artificial leg. Instead of going to sick bay, he soaked his stump in a bucket of warm salt water. At the end of the year, Brashear received a very favorable report, and returned to duty with full diving assignments—the first time in naval history for an amputee.

Brashear received orders to the boat house at the Norfolk Naval Air Station, where he was a division officer in charge of the divers. Their principal duties were search and rescue and recovery of downed aircraft. They picked up helicopters and jet aircraft that had crashed and assisted civilian divers at the Norfolk Naval Shipyard.

Brashear considered becoming a warrant officer or a limited duty officer, an officer who came up from the enlisted rates. However, a Master Diver must be a chief petty officer, a senior petty officer, or a master chief petty officer, and Brashear's goal was still to be the first African-American Master Diver in the Navy.

In 1970, Brashear went from the Norfolk Naval Air Station boat house to saturation diving school at the Experimental Diving Unit in Washington, D.C. Saturation diving involves going to extreme depths and staying down for long periods of time. Upon graduation from saturation diving school, he attended master diving school. A Master Diver is proficient in all phases of diving, submarine rescue, and salvage; it is the highest position in diving.

Evaluation is done by Master Divers, ex-Master Divers, and the commanding officer and the executive officer of the Master Diving school. Emphasis is placed on emergency procedures. Considerable pressure is placed on participants, and many attempts are made to rattle them. At times, participants are given an incorrect order; they are expected to know better than to obey it. Self-confidence is a requirement. Master Divers have to know how to treat all types of diving accidents. Four out of six in the class made Master Diver, including Brashear. The commanding officer of the Master Diving school called Brashear into his office and told him, "If there was a mark that we'd give, you made the highest mark of any man that ever came through this school to be evaluated for Master. You did not make a mistake. We vote you Master."

Brashear was assigned to the submarine tender *USS Hunley* (AS-31) in Charleston, South Carolina. He was a division officer on the *Hunley*, which was a tender for nuclear submarines, both fast attack submarines and "boomers" with missiles. Divers, who were required to dive when nuclear reactors were critical, used film badges to check their radiation exposure levels. They had to make security checks, looking for foreign objects attached to the hull.

Brashear's next duty was on the salvage ship *USS Recovery* (ARS-43). He preferred salvage work to duty on a tender because salvage jobs were less repetitive. *Recovery* divers evaluated the feasibility of raising a ship that had sunk off Newport News in 1918 and salvaged a helicopter off the coast of Florida. They also dove in a flooded engine room on the *USS Saratoga* (CVA-60).

Recovery was a happy ship; Brashear contributed to this environment by being fair, leading by example, and following a policy of admitting an error when one was made. Men respected him.

Brashear's next assignment was the Naval Safety Center in Norfolk. He represented the Safety Center in investigating diving accidents, determining the cause, and making recommendations to prevent future accidents. He also conducted safety presentations and wrote "safety grams." While at the Safety Center, he was mentioned in newspapers and magazines and received television coverage. Robert Manning of the Office of the Navy's Chief of Information suggested making a short movie about Brashear; a four-and-a-half minute movie was made for TV.

From that beginning, Manning suggested that Brashear should be a candidate for the "Come Back" program about people who have been injured or stumbled in their career and made a come-back. That year a thirty-minute documentary was made about Brashear as well as Rosemary Clooney, Neil Sadaka, Freddie Fender, and Bill Veeck.

Brashear's final tour of duty in the Navy was reassignment to the *USS Recovery*. The commanding officer of the *Recovery* had requested him. Breashear considered it a feather in his cap to finish his Navy career on the *Recovery*.

Brashear retired in April 1979. His retirement ceremony was planned for the *USS Hoist*, the ship on which he had lost his leg. However, the *Hoist* was too small to accommodate everyone, so his retirement ceremony was moved to the gymnasium at the Little Creek Amphibious Base. It was announced in the newspapers three days in advance, and posters were put up all around the Amphibious Base. The gymnasium was filled; two television sta-tions covered the event.

Brashear had the resilience to reach his goal in the Navy and enjoyed an exciting, rewarding career. As with many successful people, Brashear always displayed the "can do" spirit. His life is an inspiration to us.

DOUGLAS BADER (1910-1982) *Legless WWII R.A.F. Ace*

"The nerve that never relaxes, the eye that never blanches, the thought that never wanders—these are the masters of victory."

Edmund Burke

On Monday morning, December 14, 1931, Royal Air Force pilot Douglas Bader was flying near Kenley, England, when he saw two fellow pilots take off from the airfield. He recalled that the pilots, Phillips and Richardson, were flying to Woodley airfield near Reading to visit Phillips's brother, who was stationed there. Bader joined them on their flight.

While visiting Woodley, one of the pilots questioned Bader about the aerobatics he had performed at the air show at Hendon and asked if he would do some aerobatics for them. Bader declined the request. He vividly recalled a reprimand from his commanding officer, Harry Day, for showing off in the air and taking too many chances. Also, the Gloster Gamecock they flew at Hendon had been replaced with the more modern and faster Bulldog. However, the Bulldog was heavier than the Gamecock and wasn't as maneuverable; furthermore, it had the tendency to drop out of a roll.

When the pilots prepared to return to Kenley, Bader was again asked to perform some aerobatics. This time, he took it as a dare. As he climbed, Bader banked and turned back to the airfield to make a low pass at the clubhouse. He rolled to the right and felt the Bulldog begin to drop. He was attempting to come out of the roll when the left wingtip hit the ground. His plane crashed, and the engine was separated from the fuselage.

Bader was pinned in the aircraft by his straps. He heard the loud noise of the crash, but didn't feel much pain; however, he noticed that his legs were in unusual positions. His left leg was buckled under the seat, and he could see a bone sticking out of the right knee of his coveralls and a spreading stain of blood. His first thought was that he wouldn't be able to play rugby on Saturday.

A steward came over from the clubhouse with a glass of brandy and offered it to him. Without thinking, Bader said, "No, thanks very much. I don't drink." The steward leaned over, saw all of the blood in the cockpit, became very pale, and drank the brandy himself. The plane had to be cut away with a hacksaw before Bader could be lifted from the wreckage. He was taken to the Royal Berkshire Hospital, where both legs were amputated.

Bader was fitted for artificial legs by the Dessouter brothers at Roehampton Hospital. Robert Dessouter fitted him for the artificial legs and told him that he would never walk without a cane. Bader told him that he would never walk *with* a cane.

After many tries on the first day with the new legs, Bader hobbled a few steps, unaided, over to the parallel bars. Dessouter had never seen an individual with one artificial leg do that on the first day; it was an incredible achievement for someone with two artificial legs. While Bader practiced using his new legs, Dessouter admitted that he had never seen anyone with his tenacity and resolve.

Bader asked the garage at Kenley where he had stored his MG sports car to switch the positions of the brake and clutch pedals so he could take advantage of his stronger leg and to make it easier for him to drive. When the MG was ready, a mechanic drove it to the hospital at Uxbridge where Bader was recuperating.

When Bader asked the mechanic if he had any trouble driving the car over from Kenley, the mechanic said that trouble wasn't the word for it. He kept depressing the brake pedal to shift gears and putting his foot on the clutch to stop, which was even more disconcerting. Finally, he had to drive with his legs crossed, or he would never have made it.

Bader learned how to drive his MG. He participated in dances and played squash and golf. By the summer of 1932, he was able to fly an airplane again. He applied for flight status in the Royal Air Force.

Bader reported to the Central Medical Establishment at Kingsway for a physical examination. He passed but was given an A2H rating, which meant restricted flying; he wasn't allowed to fly solo. He was assigned to the Central Flying School at Wittering for their evaluation of his abilities.

Bader's training went well at Wittering; he was confident that he would be reinstated as a pilot. He reported back to the Central Medical Establishment at Kingsway to see the Wing Commander, who acknowledged that the Central Flying School had given him a favorable report; however, he said, "Unfortunately, we cannot pass you for flying because there is nothing in the King's Regulations which covers your case."

After Hitler's invasion of Poland, Bader again asked to return to flight status. In early October 1939, he received a telegram requesting him to report to a selection board at Kingsway. Air Vice Marshal Halahan, his old commandant from the Royal Air Force College at Cranwell, was in charge of the board. Halahan was interviewing applicants for ground jobs only.

Bader wanted to fly; he requested General Duties (flying) and a A1B rating—full flying category. Air Vice Marshal Halahan forwarded a note to the Wing Commander responsible for making the decision: "I have known this officer since he was a officer at Cranwell under my command. He's the type we want. If he is fit, apart from his legs, I suggest you give him A1B category and leave it to the Central Flying School to assess his flying capabilities." The Wing Commander agreed, and he was in.

In November 1939, Bader returned to flying duties. Within three months, he was assigned to a squadron that flew Spitfires, which were much more advanced aircraft than the Gamecocks and Bulldogs he had flown in the early 1930s.

Initially, he was assigned as Squadron Leader to No. 12 Air Group at Duxford, Cambridgeshire, whose mission was to protect the industrial Midlands. He missed the first three weeks of the Battle of Britain because, in August 1940, most cross-Channel fighter sorties were flown from No. 11 Air Group fields in Kent, Sussex, and Essex. On August 30, Bader's squadron received orders to support No. 11 Air Group in the Battle of Britain.

By the end of 1940, Bader had been awarded the Distinguished Service Order (DSO), a decoration given for leadership, as well as the Distinguished Flying Cross (DFC), for individual initiative in action. Ultimately, he received the bar for each medal; he was only the third person to receive them. By August 1941, he had shot down over twenty-two enemy aircraft.

On August 9, 1941, Bader was returning from a mission over Bethune, France, when a Messerschmitt collided with his plane's tail. His right artificial leg caught on the cockpit as he jumped from the aircraft. Eventually, his leg harness broke, allowing him to open his parachute. If it had been his real right leg, he would probably have been pulled down with the aircraft. He landed in St. Omer,

France, where he was captured by the Germans and taken to a hospital. The Germans found his right artificial leg and repaired it for him. Later, a spare leg was parachuted into St. Omer by the R.A.F.

As soon as he could walk, Bader formed a rope out of knotted bedsheets and escaped from the hospital with the aid of one of the nurses. Unfortunately, another nurse informed on the one who had helped him, and he was recaptured. He was moved to a prison camp where he made another escape attempt; eventually, after trying to escape a third and fourth time, he was transferred to the maximum security prison at Colditz. After three and a half years as prisoner of war, he was liberated. When he returned home, he was promoted to Group Captain.

In September 1945, Bader was asked to plan and lead the first Battle of Britain fly-past over London to celebrate the peace and to commemorate the fifth anniversary of the Battle of Britain. In 1956, the Queen awarded him a Commander of the British Empire (CBE) in recognition of his services. In 1976, he was knighted by the Queen. Douglas Bader rebounded from his injuries to achieve his goals and use his talents to defend his country.

STEPHEN HAWKING (1942-) *Researcher / Cosmologist With ALS*

"It is the most persistent and greatest adventure in human history, this search to understand the universe, how it works and where it came from. It is difficult to imagine that a handful of residents of a small planet circling an insignificant star in a small galaxy have as their aim a complete understanding of the entire universe, a small speck of creation truly believing it is capable of understanding the whole."

Murray Gell-Mann

As an undergraduate, Stephen Hawking was an undistinguished student. He was not highly motivated; he studied an average of one hour a day. In 1963, at the age of twenty-one, Hawking was told that he had amyotrophic lateral sclerosis (ALS), which is known as motor neuron disease in Britain and Lou Gehrig's Disease in the United States. ALS attacks the nerves of the spinal cord and the portion of the brain that controls voluntary motor functions of the muscles. The nerve cells degenerate, causing muscles to atrophy throughout the body, resulting in paralysis. Memory and the ability to think are not affected.

ALS, which worsens in stages, forces the patient to deal with a series of progressively limiting plateaus. Hawking has made incredible contributions to science by ignoring his ailment, to the extent of his ability. He has probably done more than any scientist to expand our understanding of the origin and nature of the universe, and his theoretical work on "black holes" was innovative. He is especially well known for his book, *A Brief History of Time*, a best seller.

Stephen Hawking was born in Oxford, England, on January 8, 1942, the three-hundredth anniversary of the death of the Italian scientist Galileo. Both of Hawking's parents, Frank and Isobel Hawking, had attended Oxford University. Stephen Hawking wanted to major in either physics or mathematics in college, but his father insisted that his son take chemistry so that he could follow him in a medical career.

Hawking won a scholarship to University College, Oxford

University. When he completed his undergraduate studies at Oxford, he took the final examinations upon which admission to graduate school were based. Hawking achieved the first-class honors degree he needed to be admitted to graduate school at Cambridge University to study cosmology with Dr. Fred Hoyle, the foremost British astronomer of his time. In October 1962, Hawking began his graduate studies at Cambridge. He could choose between two areas of research, elementary particles, the study of small particles, or cosmology—the study of large objects. Cosmology is the study of the universe's origin, evolution, and destiny.

In Hawking's words, "I thought that elementary particles were less attractive, because, although they were finding lots of new particles, there was no proper theory of elementary particles. All they could do was arrange the particles in families, like in botany. In cosmology, on the other hand, there was a well-defined theory— Einstein's general theory of relativity."

Instead of studying with Fred Hoyle, Hawking was assigned to Dennis Sciama, an unknown to him. He was discouraged by this until he realized that Hoyle, who traveled abroad frequently, would not have been as good a mentor as Sciama, a respected scientist who conscientiously guided him in his research.

Hawking also had a personal problem with which to contend. He began to have difficulty tying his shoelaces, he bumped into walls and furniture, and, on a few occasions, he fell. Also, he experienced slurred speech without having a drink to blame it on. When he arrived home for Christmas vacation in 1962, his parents, who hadn't seen him for several months, knew immediately that something was wrong. His father thought that he might have contracted a disease in the Middle East during a trip with him over the summer. His parents referred him to a specialist.

At several parties over the holidays, Hawking met and talked with Jane Wilde, the friend of a friend, who attended the local high school. Jane planned to read modern languages at Westfield College in London in the fall. She was attracted to this intellectual and somewhat eccentric character. Their relationship blossomed from their first meeting.

In January, Hawking underwent a battery of tests; the diagnosis was ALS. He faced decreasing mobility, gradual paralysis, and ultimately death as respiratory muscles lost their functionality or he contracted pneumonia. Many ALS patients do not live two years beyond the diagnosis. He went into a deep depression, locked himself in his room, and listened to music. If Hawking had decided to study experimental physics instead of theoretical physics, his career would have been over.

Hawking questioned continuing with his research, because he might not be around long enough to get his Ph.D. Literally, he felt that he had nothing to live for. He was not a deeply religious person; nevertheless, he had an experience that helped to put things into perspective: "While I was in hospital, I had seen a boy I vaguely knew die of leukemia in the bed opposite me. It had not been a pretty sight. Clearly there were people who were worse off than me. At least my condition didn't make me feel sick. Whenever I feel inclined to feel sorry for myself, I remember that boy."

Jane visited Stephen early in his stay in the hospital and was surprised to find that he had lost the will to live. Their relationship strengthened; she was a major factor in Hawking's turning his life around. His interest in his research was revived.

During his first two years at Cambridge, Hawking's physical condition worsened. He had to use a cane, and, occasionally, he fell. He rejected offers of help in getting around. His speech grew increasingly difficult to understand. He and Jane became engaged. She said, "I wanted to find some purpose to my existence, and I suppose I found it in the idea of looking after him. But we were in love." For Hawking, their engagement gave new direction to his life and gave him something to live for.

Hawking met applied mathematician Roger Penrose at a scientific meeting at Kings College in London. Penrose explained his concept of a singularity—a mass with zero size and infinite density—occurring at the center of a black hole, a region in space where gravity is so strong that not even light can escape. He showed that the collapse of a star could lead to the formation of a singularity. One night on the train back to Cambridge from London, Hawking turned to Dennis Sciama and speculated what would happen if Penrose's singularity theory were applied to the entire universe.

Penrose had showed that the collapse of a star could cause the formation of a singularity. Hawking conjectured that an important event had begun with the singularity. The event was the reverse of Penrose's collapse, an outward explosion named by Fred Hoyle the "big bang," the origin of the universe. The "big bang" refers to the tremendous explosion that began the expansion of the universe fifteen billion years ago.

When Hawking applied Penrose's ideas to the entire universe, he really began to devote himself to his work: "I started working hard for the first time in my life. To my surprise, I found I liked it. Maybe it is not really fair to call it work. Someone once said, 'Scientists get paid for doing what they enjoy.'" This effort became the final chapter of Hawking's dissertation, "Properties of the Expanding Universe," the work for which he was awarded a Ph.D by Cambridge University. Hawking looked for a post with a salary so he and Jane could get married. He applied for a theoretical physics fellowship at Caius College, Cambridge University. He was awarded the fellowship, and he and Jane were married in July 1965.

Hawking's condition continued to decline. He now needed crutches to walk, and his ability to speak worsened. He had a difficult time getting around their house, but he refused offers of help. His strong-willed nature presented a challenge for Jane. She said, "Some would call his attitude determination, some obstinacy. I've called it both at one time or another. I suppose that's what keeps him going." When asked whether he ever became depressed over his condition, Hawking replied, "Not normally. I have managed to do what I wanted to do despite it, and that gives a feeling of achievement." He maintained a positive outlook, and he was generally cheerful. He didn't waste time worrying about his health.

In the late 1960s, Jane and their friends convinced Hawking that he should be in a wheelchair. He didn't let this change bother him; in fact, he admitted that it enabled him to get around better. His approach to life didn't change. Jane said, "Stephen doesn't make any concessions to his illness, and I don't make any concessions to him."

Hawking recalls when his first black hole breakthrough occurred. In November 1970, he was thinking about black holes while getting ready for bed. As he remembers it: "My disability makes this a rather slow process, so I had plenty of time. Suddenly, I realized that many of the techniques that Penrose and I had developed to prove singularities could be applied to black holes."

Over a six-year period, Hawking co-authored *The Large Scale*

Structure of Space Time with George Ellis. In March 1974, Hawking became a Fellow of the Royal Society at the age of thirty-two. He continued to collect prizes, six major awards in two years: the Eddington Medal from the Royal Astronomical Society, the Pius XI Medal awarded by the Pontifical Academy of Science in the Vatican, the Hopkins Prize, the Dannie Heineman Prize, the Maxwell Prize, and the Hughes Medal of the Royal Society, which cited "his remarkable results in his work on black holes."

In 1978, Hawking was awarded the Albert Einstein Award by the Lewis and Rose Strauss Memorial Fund. During the following year, Hawking co-authored *General Relativity: An Einstein Centenary Survey* with Werner Israel. Hawking was appointed Lucasian Professor at Cambridge University in 1979, 310 years after Isaac Newton was given the same honor. At about this time, an interviewer asked Hawking again about his disability. He responded: "I think I'm happier now than I was before I started. Before the illness set in, I was very bored with life. It really was a rather pointless existence."

Cambridge University Press hoped that Hawking's latest book, *The Very Early Universe,* would sell better than his previous one, *Superspace and Supergravity,* which even scientists had difficulty understanding. The University Press suggested to Hawking that he write a popular book about cosmology. The Press had success previously publishing popular science books by Arthur Eddington and Fred Hoyle.

Hawking was a tough negotiator, and the University Press didn't think that they could afford the generous advance that he demanded. The initial sample of a section of the book that Hawking provided was much too technical. In particular, it contained too many equations. The Press told him that every equation would reduce sales significantly.

Prior to signing with Cambridge University Press, Hawking heard that Bantam Books was interested in his popular book about cosmology. Bantam offered an advance for the United States and Canada. He accepted their offer. Bantam's editors also suggested that the technical content of the manuscript should be reduced.

By Christmas 1984, the first draft of the manuscript was finished. Bantam began to promote the book: "Hawking is on the cutting edge of what we know about the cosmos. This whole business of the unified field theory, the conjunction of relativity with quantum mechanics, is comparable to the search for the Holy Grail."

In 1985, Hawking spent the summer in Geneva, Switzerland, at CERN, the European Center for Nuclear Research, where he continued his research and made corrections to the manuscript of his book. One night in early August, Hawking suffered a blockage in his windpipe and later contracted pneumonia. He was placed on a life-support machine but was not in critical condition. Because he was unable to breathe through his mouth or nose, doctors recommended a tracheostomy. A cut would be made in his windpipe and a breathing device would be implanted. However, Hawking would never be able to speak again.

A California computer technologist, Walt Woltosz, gave Hawking a program called Equalizer that provided a menu of 3,000 words from which to construct sentences. The sentences were sent to a voice-synthesizer that spoke for him with an American accent. Hawking's life was transformed by this technology.

In early spring of 1988, Hawking's popular book about cosmology, *A Brief History of Time: From the Big Bang to Black Holes,* was released. Within a few weeks, this book about equating relativity theory with quantum mechanics was at the top of the bestseller list, where it stayed for many months. Stephen Hawking fan clubs were formed. Sales of the book exceeded everyone's estimates, particularly Bantam's.

More than any previous accomplishment, *A Brief History of Time* made Stephen Hawking a household name. A documentary, "Master of the Universe" won a Royal Television Society award, and ABC presented a profile of Hawking on its *20 / 20* program. Earlier, Commander of the British Empire (CBE) honors had been conferred upon Hawking, and, in 1989, he was made a Companion of Honor by Queen Elizabeth.

Hawking's list of achievements is impressive, particularly when his handicap is considered. However, he has suggested that his accomplishments might not have been as great if he hadn't been diagnosed with ALS at the age of twenty-one. Hawking, a strong-willed individual who was highly motivated, always maintained his sense of humor; his upbeat outlook on life contributed significantly to his success. He observed, "One has to be grown up enough to realize that life is not fair. You have to do the best you can in the situation you are in."

Hawking gives us all something to think about in the conclusion of his book, *A Brief History of Time*:

> However, if we do discover a complete theory, it should be in time understandable in broad principle by everyone, not just a few scientists. Then we shall all, philosophers, scientists, and just ordinary people, be able to take part in the discussion of the question of why it is that we and the universe exist. If we find an answer to that, it would be the ultimate triumph of human reason—for then we would know the mind of God.

WHAT CONSTITUTES SUCCESS

"He has achieved success who has lived well, laughed often, and loved much; who has gained the respect of intelligent men and the love of little children; who has filled his niche and accomplished his task; who has left the world better than he found it, whether by an improved poppy, a perfect poem, or a rescued soul; who has never lacked appreciation of earth's beauty or failed to express it; who has looked for the best in others and given the best he had; whose life was an inspiration; whose memory is a benediction."

Mrs. A. J. "Bessie" Stanley

BIBLIOGRAPHY

CHAPTER 1

STEVE JOBS

Aaseng, Nathan. "Steve Jobs." *Business Builders in Computers*
Minneapolis: Oliver, 2000.

Butcher, Lee. *Accidental Millionaire: The Rise and Fall of
Steve Jobs at Apple*. New York: Paragon House, 1988.

Deutschman, Alan. *The Second Coming of Steve Jobs*.
New York: Broadway Books, 2000.

Smith, Douglas K., and Robert C. Alexander. *Fumbling the Future*.
New York: William Morrow, 1988.

BILL GATES

Boyd, Aaron. *Smart Money: The Story of Bill Gates*. New York:
Morgan Reynolds, 1995.

Ichbiah, Daniel, and Susan L. Knepper. *The Making of Microsoft*.
Rocklin, California: Prima, 1991.

Manes, Stephen, and Paul Andrews. *Gates*. New York:
Doubleday, 1993.

Marshall, David. *Bill Gates and Microsoft*. New York: Exley, 1994.

Wallace, James, and Jim Erickson. *Hard Drive: Bill Gates and the
Making of the Microsoft Empire*. New York: Harper, 1992.

JEFF BEZOS

Brant, Richard. *One Click*. New York: Penguin, 2011.

Byrne, John A. *World Changers*. New York: Penguin, 2011.

Spector, Robert. *Amazon.com: Get Big Fast*. New York:
Penguin Business, 2000.

LARRY PAGE & SERGEY BRIN

Battelle, John. *The Search*. New York: Penguin, 2005.

Brandt, Richard A. *Inside Larry and Sergey's Brain*. New York:
Penguin, 2009.

Byrne, John A. *World Changers*. New York: Penguin, 2011.

MARK ZUCKERBERG

Byrne, John A. *World Changers*. New York: Penguin, 2011.

Losse, Kargweine.*The Boy Kings*. New York :Free Press, 2012.

Mezrich, Ben. *The Accidental Billionaires*. New York:
Doubleday, 2009..

CHAPTER 2

LILLIAN & FRANK GILBRETH
Gilbreth, Frank, Jr., and Ernestine Gilbreth Carey.
Cheaper by the Dozen. New York:
Thomas Y. Crowell, 1948.

Gilbreth, Frank B. *Motion Study, A Method for Increasing
the Efficiency of the Workman.* New York:
D. Van Nostrand, 1911.

Gilbreth, Frank B. *Applied Motion Study.* New York:
Sturgis & Walton, 1917.

Yost, Edna. *Frank and Lillian Gilbreth: Partners for Life.*
New Brunswick: Rutgers University Press, 1949.

EMMELINE & CHRISTABEL PANKHURST
Barker, Dudley. "Mrs. Emmeline Pankhurst." *Prominent Edwardians.*
New York: Antheneum, 1969.

Castle, Barbara. *Sylvia and Christabel Pankhurst.* New York:
Penguin, 1987.

Mitchell, David. *The Fighting Pankhursts: A Study In Tenacity*
New York: Macmillan, 1967.

Pankhurst, E. Sylvia. *The Life of Emmeline Pankhurst: The Suffragette
Struggle for Women's Citizenship.* Boston: Houghton Mifflin, 1936.

BETTY COMDEN & ADOLPH GREEN
Comden, Betty. *Off Stage.* New York: Simon & Schuster, 1995.

Comden, Betty, and Adolph Green. *Singin' in the Rain:
Story and Screenplay.* London: Lorrimer, 1986.

Robinson, Alice M. *Betty Comden and Adolph Green:
A Bio-Bibliography.* Westport, Connecticut: Greenwood, 1994.

PALO ALTO RESEARCH CENTER
Butcher, Lee. *Accidental Millionaire: The Rise and Fall of Steve Jobs
at Apple.* New York: Paragon House, 1988.

Smith, Douglas K., and Robert C. Alexander. *Fumbling the Future:
How Xerox Invented, Then Ignored the First Personal Computer.*
New York: William Morrow, 1988.

SIR JONATHAN IVE
Arlidge, John. "Jonathan Ive Designs Tomorrow." *Time,* Time, Inc.,
17 March 2014.

Elmer-Dewitt, Philip. "Jonathan Ive on Steve Jobs and the
  Fragility of Ideas." New York: Fortune.com. 24 October 2011.
Kahney, Leander. *Jony Ive: The Genius Behind Apple's Greatest
  Products*. New York: Portfolio / Penguin, 2013.

CHAPTER 3

FREDERICK DOUGLASS
Douglass, Frederick. *Life and Times of Frederick Douglass*.
  New York: Thomas Y. Crowell, 1966.
Holland, Frederic. *The Colored Orator*. New York: Funk & Wagnalls,
  1895.
Huggins, Nathan Irvin. *Slave and Citizen: The Life of Frederick
  Douglass*. Boston: Little, Brown, 1980.
Miller, Douglas T. *Frederick Douglass and the Fight for Freedom*.
  New York: Facts on File, 1988.

FLORENCE NIGHTINGALE
Boyd, Nancy. "Florence Nightingale." *Three Victorian Women Who
  Changed the World*. New York: Oxford University Press, 1982.
Strachey, Lytton. "Florence Nightingale." *Eminent Victorians*.
  New York: Harcourt Brace Jovanovich, 1918.
Woodham-Smith, Cecil. *Florence Nightingale: (1820-1910)*.
  New York: McGraw-Hill, 1951.

MOHANDAS GANDHI
Brown, Judith M. *Gandhi: Prisoner of Hope*. New Haven:
  Yale University Press, 1989.
Cheney, Glenn Alan. *Mohandas Gandhi*. New York: Franklin Watts,
  1983.
Faber, Doris and Harold. *Mahatma Gandhi*. New York: Messner, 1986.
Fischer, Louis. *Gandhi: His Life and Message for the World*. New York:
  New American Library, 1954.
Nicholson, Michael. *Mahatma Gandhi: The Man Who Freed India and
  Led the World in Nonviolent Change*. Milwaukee: Gareth Stevens,
  1988.

NELSON MANDELA
Hoobler, Dorothy and Thomas. *Nelson and Winnie Mandela*.
  New York: Franklin Watts, 1987.
Mandela, Nelson. *Long Walk To Freedom*. Boston: Little, Brown, 1994.
Vail, John. *Nelson and Winnie Mandela*. New York: Chelsea House, 1989.

MARTIN LUTHER KING, JR.

Darby, Jean. *Martin Luther King, Jr.* Minneapolis: Lerner, 1990.

Haskins, James. *The Life and Death of Martin Luther King, Jr.* New York: Lothrop, Lee & Shepard, 1977.

Jakoubek, Robert. *Martin Luther King, Jr.* New York: Chelsea House, 1989.

Oates, Stephen B. *Let the Trumpets Sound: The Life of Martin Luther King, Jr.* New York: New American Library, 1982.

Shuker, Nancy. *Martin Luther King.* New York: Chelsea House, 1985.

CHAPTER 4

COLE PORTER

Gill, Brendan. *Cole: A Biographical Essay.* New York: Holt, Rinehart & Winston, n.d.

McBrien, William. *Cole Porter, A Biography.* New York: Alfred A. Knopf, 1998.

GEORGE GERSHWIN

Reef, Catherine. *George Gershwin: American Composer.* Greensboro, North Carolina: Morgan Reynolds, 2000.

Rimler, Walter. *George Gershwin: An Intimate Portrait.* Urbana: University of Illinois Press, 2009.

HOAGY CARMICHAEL

Carmichael, Hoagy, and Stephen Longstreet. *The Stardust Road & Sometimes I Wonder: The Autobiography of Hoagy Carmichael.* Cambridge, Massachusetts: Da Gali Press, 1999.

Sudhalter, Richard M. *Stardust Melody.* New York: Oxford University Press, 2002.

Wilder, Alec. *American Popular Song: The Great Innovators 1900-1950.* New York: Oxford University Press, 1990.

RICHARD RODGERS

Ewen, David. *Richard Rodgers.* New York: Henry Holt and Company, 1957.

Hyland, William G. *Richard Rodgers.* New Haven: Yale University Press, 1998.

Secrest, Meryle. *Somewhere for Me: A Biography of Richard Rodgers.* New York: Alfred A. Knopf, 2001.

Taylor, Deems. *Some Enchanted Evenings: The Story of Rodgers and Hammerstein.* New York: Harper and Brothers, 1953.

ALEC WILDER
Balliet, Whitney. *Alec Wilder and His Friends*. Boston:
    Houghton Mifflin, 1974.
Stone, Desmond. *Alec Wilder in Spite of Himself: A Life of
    the Composer*. New York: Oxford University Press, 1996.
Zeltsman, Nancy, Ed. *Alec Wilder (1907-1980)*. Newton Centre,
    Massachusetts, 1991.

CHAPTER 5

HERMAN MELVILLE
Allen, Gay Wilson. *Melville and His World*. New York: Macmillan, 1982.
Mumford, Lewis. *Herman Melville*. New York: Harcourt, Brace, 1929.
Untermeyer, Louis. *Makers of the Modern World*. New York:
    Simon & Schuster,1955.

EMILY DICKINSON
Dickinson, Donna. *Emily Dickinson*. Dover, New Hampshire: Berg,
    1985.
Ferlazzo, Paul J. *Emily Dickinson*. Boston: Twayne, 1975.
Lingsworth, Polly. *Emily Dickinson: Her Letter to the World*. New York:
    Thomas Y. Crowell, 1965.
Olsen, Victoria. *Emily Dickinson*. New York: Chelsea House, 1990.

CHARLES IVES
Cowell, Henry and Sidney. *Charles Ives and His Music*. London: Oxford
    University Press, 1955.
Ewen, David. *The World of Twentieth-Century Music*. Englewood Cliffs:
    Prentice-Hall, 1968.
Machlis, Joseph. *American Composers of Our Time*. New York: Crowell,
    1963.
Posell, Elsa Z. *American Composers*. Boston: Houghton Mifflin, 1963.
Sive, Helen R. *Music's Connecticut Yankee, An Introduction to the Life
    and Music of Charles Ives*. New York: Atheneum, 1977.

ROBERT GODDARD
Coil, Suzanne M. *Robert Hutchings Goddard: Pioneer of Rocketry
    and Space Flight*. New York: Facts on File, 1992.
Dewey, Anne Perkins. *Robert Goddard: Space Pioneer*. Boston:
    Little, Brown, 1962.
Goddard, Robert H. *Rocket Development*. New York: Prentice-Hall,
    1948.

Lehman, Milton. *This High Man: The Life of Robert H. Goddard*. New York: Farrar, Straus, 1963.

JOHN ATANASOFF

Burks, Alice R., and Arthur W. Burks. *The First Electronic Computer: The Atanasoff Story*. Ann Arbor: University of Michigan Press, 1989.

Mollenkoff, Clark R. *Atanasoff: Forgotten Father of the Computer*. Ames, Iowa: Iowa State University Press, 1988.

Smiley, Jane. *The Man Who Invented the Computer*. New York: Doubleday, 2010.

CHAPTER 6

PAUL WITTGENSTEIN

Barchilon, John. *The Crown Prince*. New York: Norton, 1984.

Flindell, E. Fred. "Paul Wittgenstein (1897-1961): Patron and Pianist." *The Music Review*. xxxii (1971), 107-124.

CHRISTY BROWN

Brown, Christy. *My Left Foot*. New York: Simon & Schuster, 1955.

Connayghton, Shane, and Jim Sheridan. *My Left Foot* (Screenplay). London: Faber & Faber, 1989.

My Left Foot. Videocassette. Miramax Film, 1989.

CARL BRASHEAR

Robbins, David. *Men of Honor*. New York: Onyx, 2000.

Stillwell, Paul. *The Reminiscences of Master Chief Carl M. Brashear, U.S. Navy (Retired)*. Annapolis: U.S. Naval Institute, 1998.

DOUGLAS BADER

Brickhill, Paul. *Reach for the Sky: The Story of Douglas Bader, Legless Ace of the Battle of Britain*. New York: Norton, 1954.

Collier, Richard. *Eagle Day: The Battle of Britain, August 6 — September 15, 1940*. New York: Dutton, 1966.

Hough, Richard. *The Battle of Britain: The Triumph of R.A.F. Fighter Pilots*. New York: Macmillan, 1971.

Markel, Julia. *Turning Points of World War II: The Battle of Britain*. New York: Franklin Watts, 1984.

Townsend, Peter. *Duel of Eagles*. New York: Simon & Schuster, 1970.

STEPHEN HAWKING

Ferguson, Kitty. *Stephen Hawking: Quest for a Theory of the Universe*. New York: Franklin Watts, 1991.

White, Michael and John Gribben. *Stephen Hawking: A Life in Science*.
Minneapolis: Dutton, 1992.

GENERAL

Carter-Scott, Cherie. *If Success Is a Game, These Are the Rules:
Ten Rules For a Fulfilling Life*. New York: Broadway Books, 2000.
Collins, Susan Ford. *The Joy of Success*. New York:
William Morrow, 2003.
Daintith, John, Ed. *Bloomsbury Treasury of Quotations*.
London: Bloomsbury Publishing, 1998.
Portas, Jerry, and Stewart Emery and Mark Thompson. *Success Built To
Last: Creating a Life That Matters*. Philadelphia:
Wharton School Publishing, 2007.
Stevenson, Burton, Ed. *The Home Book of Quotations*.
New York: Dodd, Mead & Company, Tenth edition, 1969.
Untermeyer, Louis. *Makers of the Modern World*. New York:
Simon & Schuster, 1955.
Ziglar, Zig. *Success For Dummies*. Chicago: IDG Books, 1998.